AL STEVENS

EXTENDING TURBO C PROFESSIONAL

ADVANCED COMPUTER BOOKS

MIS: PRESS

MANAGEMENT INFORMATION SOURCE, INC.

COPYRIGHT

P.O. Box 5277
Portland, Oregon 97208-5277
(503) 282-5215

First Printing

ISBN 1-55828-013-8

Library of Congress Catalog Card Number: 89-30806

DEDICATION

For Alan, Sharon, and Wendy

ACKNOWLEDGMENTS

Thanks to those who helped while I wrote this book:

- Pete Becker for making me think.
- Borland International for my copy of Turbo C Professional.
- Jerry Cozzi for the correct changes.
- Kyle McDonald for inspiring Chapter 11.
- Chip Rabinowitz for always having a ready answer.

TABLE OF CONTENTS

DISK ORDER FORM
ON LAST PAGE
OF BOOK

PREFACE

This is a book of tricks. More specifically, this is a book about the Turbo C professional software development environment and how you can extend its capabilities and in so doing extend your software development skills. Turbo C Professional is a combination of Turbo C, the Turbo Assembler, and the Turbo Debugger. It represents one of the most powerful development tools a programmer can use. But, because of its power and sophistication and because of the complexity and uniqueness of the IBM PC and MS-DOS architectures, many programmers—veteran and novice alike—will not know how to achieve the full potential of this rich software development resource. This, then, is the Turbo C Professional programmer's survival manual—a guide to extending the reach of the compiler and the computer and thus building and maintaining your position as a productive and creative software developer.

C is often said to be "extensible," a feature claimed for the architecture of many computer languages. Some languages—Forth, for example—are based on extensibility. Others such as COBOL and BASIC are rigidly nonextensible. To be extensible, a language must have the property that allows the programmer to extend the language itself, not so much in the formats of applications data structures as in the properties of the language itself. Most languages allow you to define record formats; C allows you to define data types. Most languages give you a built-in input/output system; C has no intrinsic I/O, deferring such definitions to function libraries and thus allowing you to extend the I/O system.

If C is extensible, Turbo C Professional is more so. Designed to support the special operational platform called the IBM PC, Turbo C has within its capabilities the potential to host the development of some very special programs. This book realizes that potential and leads you in your exploration of the unique qualities of Turbo C and the PC.

In this book, I bypass introductions to the C language and restatements of what you can read in the Turbo C reference and user's guides and in countless other books on C and Turbo C. What I concentrate on here is the advanced application of some of the unique properties of Turbo C and MS-DOS in the development of sophisticated software systems. In some cases, I bring together different parts of Turbo C that you might find described in scattered places throughout the product documentation. By building these advanced software techniques from the various existing parts and pieces of Turbo C, you can essentially extend its range and usefulness.

C is a marvelous programming language, and Turbo C has some equally marvelous extensions that exploit many of the characteristics of DOS and the PC hardware. You will not get a treatise on portable programs here. You will, instead, get into the innards of your computer by using the unique features of Turbo C. Your C programs will not be portable to other platforms, but your PC programs will be significantly enhanced by the tricks and techniques described here. The discipline of portable C programming is an admirable endeavor, one that has been studied and taught, defended and championed. But it can be stodgy and boring, too, and not nearly as much fun as wringing the last bit of performance out of the complex architecture known as the PC under MS-DOS. That is the objective here.

This is not a book on graphics. Turbo C has an extensive graphics function library, and you are encouraged to explore it to the fullest. But the subject of graphics is a heavy one, beyond the scope of this book, and certainly not within the expertise of this author. The bibliography identifies reference material that can shed bright lights on Turbo C graphics.

Even though Turbo C Professional comes with a full macro assembler, this book contains little about assembly language. The assembler, TASM, is best considered a tool for extending Turbo C. That is how the developers of Turbo C Professional have used it and that is how you will use it in this book. Many of the functions in the run-time library are written with in-line assembly language. With such low-level facilities available in Turbo C, it is doubtful that you will ever want or need to write another assembly language program. But you will want to have TASM nonetheless because you too will occasionally want to get into in-line assembly code in your C programs, and the assembler is necessary for that.

Turbo C has a built-in debugger in its Integrated Development Environment. Its features are adequate for debugging most of your programs, but Turbo Debugger, the stand-alone source code debugger, is there for those tricky bugs. This book will discuss how TD can bail you out of the tight debugging spots. You will also learn how to use TD for the toughest of debugging chores, testing a Terminate-and-Stay-Resident program.

WHO ARE YOU?

To get the most out of this book, you are a C programmer who has acquired and generally understands Turbo C. You have made your way through the user's and reference guides, and you are ready to begin programming. To use the concepts offered in this book, you will need a sound understanding of DOS from the programmer's perspective. A grasp of the purpose and use of the PC's ROM/BIOS functions will help you understand parts of this book.

Where the book delves into those subjects that are not widely known, such as the DOS Memory Control Block or the way interrupts work, some time will be taken to discuss these matters. You will not find a list of DOS or BIOS functions and their parameters in this book. If you do not already have such knowledge, see the bibliography.

I have assumed that you have purchased and installed Turbo C Professional as it comes out of the yellow box. All the programs in this book will compile and execute with the default options of the Turbo C and Turbo Assembler installations. At the end of the book is a **makefile** that builds all of the code by using the tcc command-line compiler. The file assumes that the Turbo C programs can be found on the default drive in the subdirectories recommended by the Install programs.

A companion diskette is available that contains all the code from this book. I encourage you to get the diskette if you want to run the software. A quick call to 1-800-MANUALS and a credit card number will get the disk to you a lot faster than you can type the programs in. I have published tens of thousands of lines of source code and have heard from many readers who key in the code and then have problems. Those problems are nearly always because of hidden keying errors. C is a terse language with enormous ramifications from minute character differences.

WHAT IS TO FOLLOW?

Chapter 1 starts you off by identifying those aspects of Turbo C as a language that set it apart from other C compilers and that make it possible for you to extend your C software development environment for PC programs. You will learn about register pseudovariables, intrinsic functions, in-line assembly language, interrupt functions, and more.

Chapter 2 is about interrupts. Interrupts are often misunderstood and often intimidate the programmer who has not been initiated. Yet the interrupt is one of the most powerful tools available to a programmer and can, when properly understood and used, enhance your software significantly. Interrupts are not in the exclusive domain of device drivers and resident programs. Many of your standard transient programs can be enhanced through the use of interrupt functions. Chapter 3 shows you how interrupt functions work and how Turbo C can be used to tame them.

Chapter 3 shows you how the unique features of Turbo C can be used to build programs with overlays. Usually, you need a linker that builds overlay modules and an overlay manager that works with the linker. Chapter 3 shows how you can use TLINK to build an architecture of root and overlay program modules that are managed by a simple overlay manager.

Chapter 4 is a small video window library. Some of my earlier works have included complex, comprehensive screen window management packages. Almost all of my PC software depends on some kind of window display technique. Rather than send you scurrying off to the bookstore to buy another book, I have included this minimum window package here in Chapter 4 to support the rest of the software in this book.

Chapter 5 is where you can have fun with the special ways that the PC operates and the little software gizmos that can wring that extra drop of performance out of a program. There are tricks for the keyboard such as how to speed it up, how to make it automatically type without anyone pressing the keys, how to read keystrokes that BIOS doesn't know about, and other keyboard magic. There are cursor tricks, DOS error captures, environment variable tricks, secrets of the DOS Memory Control Block, how to make funny sounds with the speaker, and much more.

Chapter 6 uses the window manager functions from Chapter 4 to build a simple menu manager.

Chapter 7 uses the window manager functions and some of the programming tricks from Chapters 4 and 5 to build a window-oriented data entry template manager.

Chapter 8 describes your serial port and modem and how to use them in a communications program. This is a widely misunderstood facet of the PC, and there are several books that address it. Rather than drilling you with the details of communications theory, Chapter 8 shows you how to get the hardware working in your programs and explains enough so that you will understand what you are doing.

Chapter 9 is about memory-resident programs. Some of my earlier work addressed this weighty subject, and I've learned more about it since then. Turbo C has added some features that make memory-resident program development much easier than with other languages and with other C compilers.

Chapter 10 describes the Lotus-Intel-Microsoft Expanded Memory Specification (EMS) as you would implement it with Turbo C. EMS is a powerful feature that is overlooked by many programmers. As a result, many computers are slowly churning MS-DOS programs while several megabytes of extra memory sit idly by waiting for OS/2 to be installed or, perhaps, serving as a dull RAM disk. In Chapter 10, you will learn how to use EMS to extend the performance of the programs you write.

Chapter 11 uses the concepts introduced in Chapters 9 and 10 to build a program called TSRPLUS. This program is a memory-resident executive program that manages the loading and execution of the TSR programs you write. With TSRPLUS, your memory-resident programs are stored in virtual files either in Expanded Memory if it exists or on disk files. When a program needs to pop up, the memory it would use is swapped out to a virtual file, and the TSR is loaded. When the TSR is done, the interrupted program is swapped back in. With TSRPLUS, only the memory required for TSRPLUS itself is permanently resident.

Chapter 12 addresses advanced uses of the Turbo Debugger. The Turbo Debugger is one of the most powerful tools in Turbo C Professional, and it has potential not described in its documentation, particularly with respect to debugging memory-resident programs. Chapter 12 describes these uses of the Turbo Debugger.

Appendix A is a reference guide to all the functions that can be called from your programs as described in this book. Each function's calling parameters, operation, and return value are described. Chapter number and listing/line number references for each function are included.

Appendix B contains the Turbo C command line **makefile** for all the example programs in the book.

Appendix C is a brief description of each of the example programs that are built from the **makefile** in Appendix B. The description includes the command-line execution parameters for each program.

The software that you will find in this book generally follows a pattern where each chapter builds from the previous one. This is not always the case, but you should never need to look ahead to find functions that are being used or discussed in the chapter you are reading. If you jump around, perhaps because you already understand a subject being explained, you might find that you need to retreat to an earlier bypassed chapter to pick up a function or two. This will be more bothersome if you are typing in the source code yourself. If you are using the companion diskette, the functions will all be there. The book's index will tell you where a particular function is described.

CHAPTER 1

TURBO C: THE UNIQUE FEATURES

This chapter begins your extensions to the potential of Turbo C Professional. The chapters that follow contain software techniques, tricks, and methods that use the unique features of Turbo C to extend your programming efforts beyond those of the plain, vanilla C language environment. This chapter lays the foundation by describing those parts of Turbo C that are unique and that make these extensions possible.

What you need to understand:

- Something of the 8088/86/286 machine architecture
- DOS function calls
- ROM/BIOS function calls

New subjects discussed:

- Register pseudovariables
- Intrinsic functions
- In-line assembly language
- The interrupt function
- Text display functions

TURBO C

Turbo C is unique. In addition to being an ANSI-conforming C compiler, Turbo C contains many significant enhancements that allow you to extend the performance potential of your MS-DOS programs.

The C language, as described first by Kernighan and Ritchie (*The C Programming Language*, Englewood Cliffs, New Jersey: Prentice-Hall, 1978) and later in the ANSI standard definition, is generally unaware of the hardware on which programs will be run. Even though the large majority of programs developed today in C are written for an interactive keyboard and screen configuration, the language itself and its standard function library are indifferent to the user environment. The standard input/output functions for the console are related more to the origins of C than the ways in which it is being used. As a result, the standard library functions support a typewriter-like console device and little more. This was appropriate when C was conceived; not much else was available in the way of console devices. Things are different now, and software is written to be run in the company of sophisticated work stations and desktop computers. The user interface should not be neglected, but it is. Whether or not this is the best way to define a language is subject for debate in other quarters. Because the C language as defined treats the hardware as a stepchild (or unclaimed illegitimate offspring), it is up to its users—you and me—to extend it into a realm where it can be adequately applied to the tasks at hand. Turbo C extends C a certain distance; you extend those extensions. The stepchild can realize its birthright. In this book, you learn how to make that happen.

There are facets of the PC hardware, the BIOS firmware, and the DOS software that can be used to enhance the performance and user interface of a program. Most of these can be accessed with Turbo C's extensions. In fact, almost anything you can do with assembly language, you can do with Turbo C, even if that means dropping into in-line assembly language every now and then to solve some tricky timing problem. Following are the unique features of Turbo C that bring you a little closer to the hardware on which your programs will run.

Register Pseudovariables

The so-called Central Processing Unit (CPU) of a computer operates with ports, memory, and registers. High-level programs are usually insulated from such low-level devices. Sometimes, however, the program needs to "get down" into the silicon and diddle with the registers the same way that assembly language programmers do. The Turbo C register pseudovariable feature helps you do this.

Some of the code in this book uses the register pseudovariable feature because it needs to. With this feature, a program can directly read and write the CPU's machine registers. The registers are addressed with the format _AX, _AH, _AL, _DS, _FLAGS, etc. You can assign the contents of registers to other variables, and you can assign expressions to the registers themselves.

Understanding how and why you would use this feature requires an understanding not only of the CPU's register architecture, but also of Turbo C's use of registers within a compiled program. It is easy to defeat your purpose and make an assignment that doesn't work. For example, you might assign the contents of a register to a location when the computation of the location's address uses the same register in the compiled code. It is also possible to trash a register that the compiled code is using for something else. The Turbo C compiler does not attempt to be smart about recognizing your intentions where register pseudovariables are concerned. It expects you to know what you are doing.

Listing 1.1 is pseudo.c, a program that demonstrates the use of register pseudovariables. To understand the program, you need to know that functions compiled with Turbo C return integers in the ax register and long integers in the dx, ax register pair. The **main** function in pseudo.c calls **int_function** expecting an integer return and **long_function** expecting a long return. Those functions assign values to _AX and _DX rather than using the **return** statement. There is no point in returning values this way other than to demonstrate how register pseudovariables work. The compiler will complain that the functions do not return anything because it does not see the return statements it expects to see, but you may ignore these warnings for this example.

If you plan to use register pseudo-variables, you will want to know how the compiled code makes use of the CPU register set. The register and stack conventions for passing and returning parameters between functions are well documented in the *Turbo C Users's Guide*. But once inside a function, the compiled code will use registers in several different ways. These techniques will change depending on the kind of optimizations you select and may vary in the different versions of the compiler. One way to see how Turbo C uses registers is to use the -S option of the tcc command line compiler to get an assembly language source file of the compiled code.

Listing 1.1: pseudo.c

```
/* -------- pseudo.c --------- */

/*
 * demonstrates the use of register pseudo-variables
 */

#include <stdio.h>

int int_function(void);
long long_function(void);

void main(void)
{
        int i;
        long j;

        i = int_function();
        j = long_function();
        printf("\nthe int is: %d", i);
        printf("\nthe long is %ld", j);
}

int int_function(void)
{
        _AX = 1234;
}

long long_function(void)
```

continued...

...from previous page

```
{
        long lint = 654321L;

        _DX = (unsigned) (lint >> 16);
        _AX = (unsigned) (lint & 0xffff);
}
```

Intrinsic Functions

Turbo C has several functions that, when called, generate in-line code much the same way a macro does. The advantage of these functions is that they do not involve the overhead of a function call and, as a result, are especially handy when stack operations are involved. They look like functions in your C source code, and most other compilers do not have functions equivalent to the Turbo C intrinsic functions, so do not expect programs that use them to be portable to other C compilers.

The intrinsic functions are as follows:

- **geninterrupt**
- **enable**
- **disable**
- **inport**
- **outport**
- **inportb**
- **outportb**
- **peek**
- **poke**
- **peekb**
- **pokeb**

These functions are used for low-level interrupt, input/output, and direct memory access operations. Chapter 2 is devoted to interrupt processing, but the topic will be touched on here to illustrate the use of the intrinsic functions.

The **geninterrupt** function takes an integer interrupt vector as its parameter. If, for example, you code this statement,

```
geninterrupt(0x21);
```

the compiler inserts the machine instruction

```
INT 21H
```

into the program, and interrupt 0x21 (the DOS interrupt) is executed. You can begin to see as well the application of the register pseudovariables discussed earlier when you consider this code, which calls BIOS to read the next keystroke from the keyboard.

```
_AH = 0;
geninterrupt(0x16);
kbchar = _AL;
```

The **enable** and **disable** intrinsic functions insert the machine instructions STI and CLI to set and clear the Interrupt Flag in the flags register. These operations enable and disable external interrupts such as the timer and keyboard interrupts. It is a good idea to use these operations if you are messing with the _SS or _SP stack segment and pointer pseudovariables. An interrupt that occurs while you are changing the stack could have unpredictable results. In Chapter 3, the discussion of overlays includes stack context switching when an overlay module calls a function in a root module.

The **inport** and **outport** intrinsic functions (and their cousins, **inportb** and **outportb**) insert INP and OUT machine instructions into the program. The **poke** and **peek** (and **pokeb** and **peekb**) generate direct memory reads and writes in the program. There are real (as opposed to intrinsic) functions in the library for the port and peek/poke function calls. If you do not include dos.h in your program, or if you #undef the macros before you call them, the function counterparts are called.

In-Line Assembly Language

In-line assembly language allows the programmer to embed assembly language statements into a C program. With Turbo C, the format is as follows:

```
asm <assembly language statement>;
```

When you use this construct, the Turbo C compiler inserts whatever you code into the compiled assembly language and completes the compilation by calling the TASM Turbo Assembler. Without in-line assembly language in the source file, the compiler does not need to call TASM because it compiles directly to relocatable machine language. But because it sees that you are using in-line assembly language code and because the compiler does not know how to translate assembly language, it passes the job on to TASM. Since Turbo C does know how to compile to assembly language source code, it shifts gears into that mode and sticks your assembly language statements in with its own. Be aware that if you make mistakes with the **asm** statements, TASM will catch them, and the reported line numbers might not make any sense to you because they are the line numbers of a compiled assembly language file.

By the way, you cannot use the Turbo C Integrated Development Environment to compile programs that contain in-line assembly code. The IDE does not know how to generate assembly language source code or how to call TASM. You must use the tcc command line compiler for such programs. If you want to include the .OBJ output from such a compilation into an IDE project, you can name the .OBJ file in the project make file, and the code will be included in the link.

Turbo C is not the first C compiler to implement in-line assembly language. The origins of C are as a low-level language with a high-level structure. Its founders recognized the need to depart from the language and get into the depths of the machine, and many (but not all) C compilers include in-line assembly language. The first compilers compiled to assembly language that you assembled as a subsequent step, thus making the use of in-line assembly code easy to implement. But the construct has never been standardized because the C language is supposed to be hardware-independent, and the framers of our standards do not bother themselves with such frivolities as implementation-dependent issues.

The Interrupt Function

Chapter 2 discusses interrupts: what they are and how they are used. An integral component in a system with interrupts is the interrupt service routine, the function that executes when an interrupt occurs. Interrupt service routines have special requirements. Inasmuch as they execute by interrupting the orderly sequence of another—perhaps unrelated—function, they must be able to save and restore the machine state of the interrupted process. This involves pushing the registers on the stack on entry and popping them on exit. When an interrupt occurs, the machine flags register is pushed on the stack, and the processor makes the equivalent of a far call to the address stored in the corresponding interrupt vector. Besides popping the registers on exit, the interrupt service routine must use the IRET return instruction to pop the code segment, instruction pointer, and flags register and return to the interrupted program.

If all this is new and foreign to you, don't worry. Chapter 2 explains it all. The purpose for addressing it here is to identify the special needs of the interrupt service routine.

Traditionally, interrupt service routines are written in assembly language, or at least by using the in-line assembly language feature of a C compiler. Turbo C includes an extension called the **interrupt** function type. A function defined with the **interrupt** type executes differently from other functions. When it first executes, it pushes all the registers on the stack, sets the BP register to the then-current value of the SP register, and sets the DS register to the data segment for the interrupt service routine. All this sets the function up for correct execution no matter where the interrupted program was when it was interrupted. When the **interrupt** function exits, it pops all the registers and executes the IRET instruction.

Once again, when the interrupt service routine enters, it pushes all registers on the stack; when it exits, it pops the registers from the stack. An interrupt service routine that is called by a program gets its parameters in registers and passes its results in registers. Because the registers are pushed on the stack when the function begins, they are in the stack frame in the same manner as the parameters received by any other C function. Those parameters can be named and read by the interrupt function. If the interrupt function changes any of them, the changes will be popped into the registers when the function returns. Understanding this is critical to using the **interrupt** function type, not only for original interrupt processing but to intercept and chain system interrupts as well.

To get at the pushed (and to-be popped) registers, you must name them as parameters in the definition of the interrupt function. You can name them individually as in this example,

```
void interrupt
newisr(bp,di,si,ds,es,dx,cx,bx,ax,ip,cs,flgs)
```

or you can define them in a structure and name the structure as the input. This approach exploits the Turbo C convention for passing structure parameters on the stack. Chapter 2 includes software that uses the structure approach with a structure defined thus:

```
typedef struct {
        int bp,di,si,ds,es,dx,cx,bx,ax,ip,cs,fl;
} IREGS;
```

In the declaration of the interrupt function, the IREGS structure is specified as in this example:

```
void interrupt newisr(IREGS ir)
```

Statements in the function can use the values of the registers by referencing them as **ir.ax**, **ir.bx**, etc. To modify the values that are returned in registers from the interrupt function, you can assign the new values to the registers as described in the IREGS structure as shown here:

```
ir.ax = 123;
```

When the interrupt function returns, the values in the IREGS structure are popped into the registers; therefore, the values you assign to the structure's copies of the registers will be popped into the real machine registers. Normally, an interrupt service routine saves and restores registers and does not modify them. But when the routine is intercepting and chaining a system call, perhaps a DOS or BIOS interrupt function, the returns from those calls must override the pushed registers. The interrupt functions in Chapter 2 illustrate this technique.

Text Display Functions

Turbo C includes the standard input/output functions in the manner specified by the ANSI X3J11 committee. As explained earlier, these standards ignore the video screen. Turbo C is used to develop programs for the universal PC hardware platform, and that includes a defined set of video screen adaptor devices. Granted, there are more of them than we would like to deal with, but the number is small and the devices are well-defined. Their evolution has followed a trail that sees advances in display technology implemented under a philosophy that keeps a measure of compatibility with the older gear. If your program will run with the text display features of the Color Graphics Adaptor that came with the first PC in 1981, then it will run without modification on the latest VGA device, and that is a good way to improve hardware.

Turbo C includes a library of text display functions that supports the visual display techniques that are used with the PC. These functions are oriented to the video window and respond to programmed window boundaries and text colors. They essentially improve on the C standard library of console functions by wrapping themselves in a virtual viewport system. To conform to the ANSI standard, Turbo C does not improve the standard functions in this manner, but instead introduces a few new ones that you will immediately want to use in place of the standards.

You will want to read about these functions in the *Turbo C Reference Guide*; they figure significantly in the programs that are in this book. Chapter 1 in the *Reference Guide* includes tables of functions by category. See the category named "Text Window Display Routines." Others are given in the "Input/Output Routines" category because they are defined by ANSI as functions with a degree of implementation dependence or because they are available on UNIX. These functions are as follows:

- **cprintf**
- **cputs**
- **cscanf**
- **getche**
- **putch**
- **getpass**

Although **cgets** is included in this category, it is neither UNIX nor ANSI and does not use the window boundaries or color settings. It would be a useful function if it worked with the rest, so this book includes a rewrite of **cgets**, one that works the way it should. Chapter 5 contains the details.

SUMMARY

Now you have the foundation for your extensions to Turbo C Professional. In the next chapter you will dive into one of the most intimidating of software subjects, the dreaded interrupt.

CHAPTER 2

INTERRUPTS

This chapter is about interrupts and interrupt service routines in Turbo C. It includes example programs that show you how to build programs that use interrupt service routines. There is a brief explanation of the theory of interrupts and the interrupt structure of the PC and its family, but for more comprehensive coverage of this subject, you should read the referenced works in the bibliography.

If you have never worked at this level of programming, this is a good place to get your feet wet. Do not be afraid of this subject. Once the trick is explained, the magician loses his mystique. Once you have a comprehensive understanding of interrupts, you have reached a new plateau in your programming skills.

What you need to understand:

- The interrupt function type
- Register pseudovariables
- Intrinsic functions

New subjects discussed:

- Interrupt vector hooks and chains
- Simple memory-resident programs

THE INTERRUPT

An interrupt is the immediate interruption of the orderly progress of a program. In most cases, the interrupted program never knows that the interrupt has occurred as the consequence of an external event. Here is how it happens: Your program is proceeding through its execution. An interrupt occurs. The processor is now executing code somewhere else in memory. When that code is done, your program continues from the point of the interruption as if the interrupt never happened. This event is typical of the hardware interrupt. In other cases, the interrupt is initiated by your program when it needs the services of DOS, BIOS, or a device handler or memory-resident program that communicates through an interrupt. This type of interrupt is the software interrupt.

Interrupts provide a means for a program to execute code in another program, one that is physically and logically separate from the calling program in the view of the operating system. Interrupts also provide a way for a program to monitor external events without polling them. In a polled system, the program tests frequently to see if the device event needs attention. In an interrupt-driven system the event interrupts the program, and its occurrence is processed. Some programs use a combination of the two approaches where the interrupting event is queued in a buffer that is polled by the main program. This technique supports environments where the event is time-critical and the main program might not get around to polling the device fast enough.

Sometimes, the interrupt provides services that are either unrelated or only remotely related to your program, and the interrupt has no apparent effect on what your program is doing. An example of this is the system timer interrupt. The system clock interrupts 18.2 times every second, and the code executed by the clock interrupt updates the system's time of day and date. Your program might not be affected by this process. If you never use the clock, the interrupt has no influence on your program. On the other hand, the clock could have a side effect on your process. If you create a file, for example, DOS will record the time and date of its creation in its directory entry, and the time and date are calculated values based on the ticks of the system clock.

At other times, the effects of the interrupt are directly related to your program. For example, if you are computing the elapsed time of an event by using the start and stop times reported by the system, then the clock interrupt is an integral part of your program. In another example, if you are managing the reception of data from the serial port, the serial input interrupt is closely related to your program.

Because an interrupt disturbs the orderly sequence of the code it interrupts, the interrupt service routine must preserve the machine state when the interrupt occurs and restore the machine state when the interrupt service routine is done. The interrupt itself, by virtue of its occurrence and because of how interrupts work, preserves the interrupted address and the CPU's flags register on the stack. The interrupt service routine must push all registers it will use, perform its function, and then pop the registers before returning. The interrupt service routine must then use the CPU's IRET instruction, which restores the flags register and returns to the interrupted location.

Remember the two varieties of interrupt: the hardware interrupt and the software interrupt. The clock interrupt just discussed is an example of a hardware interrupt. When the clock ticks, the interrupt occurs and the interrupt service routine that is attached to the clock's interrupt is executed. Another hardware interrupt occurs when you press a key on the keyboard. Each of these hardware interrupts causes the interruption of whatever is being executed and the overriding execution of the interrupt service routine, which is code dedicated to processing the interrupt. The system needs a way to know what code to execute for each of these hardware interrupts, and that is determined by the interrupt controller and the interrupt vector table, both discussed shortly.

A software interrupt is different. The so-called interrupted program initiates them by executing the CPU's INT instruction, so it isn't really an interrupt at all. But it looks to the system just like one, and it is processed through the same interrupt vector table logic as a hardware interrupt. All software calls to the BIOS and DOS functions are achieved with software interrupts.

Software interrupts differ from hardware interrupts in two ways. First, they are executed by the program that is running rather than occurring in spite of it. Second, they do not always need to completely restore the machine state when they return. The interrupt service routine often returns the results of its process in one or more of the machine registers. For this reason, it would not be appropriate for the interrupt service routine to restore all of the registers when it is finished running as would a hardware interrupt.

Other than for the two differences mentioned above, hardware and software interrupts are identical. The interrupt service routines cannot tell whether they are running as the result of hardware or software interrupts. You could use a software interrupt to execute a hardware interrupt, and the code would not know it.

INTERRUPT VECTORS

The first 1024 bytes of the PC's memory are dedicated to the 256 interrupt vectors. Each vector is a four-byte far pointer to the interrupt service routine for the particular interrupt. Many interrupt vectors are dedicated to system software functions such as the BIOS and DOS function calls. Others are dedicated to hardware interrupts such as the timer, keyboard, and serial port interrupts. Others are available for applications programs to use.

Hardware interrupts occur when a hardware device asserts one of the IRQ lines on the system bus. The 8259 interrupt controller (the PC has one 8259, the AT has two) reacts to the IRQ assertion by generating an interrupt to the vector associated with the IRQ.

Software interrupts occur when a program executes the CPU's INT instruction. The eight-bit operand of the instruction determines which of the 256 interrupt vectors is involved.

As the result of either kind of interrupt, the CPU's flags, code segment, and instruction pointer registers are pushed onto the stack, and the far pointer in the interrupt vector is loaded into the code segment and instruction pointer register. This sequence causes the interrupt service routine pointed to by the vector to be executed.

You should exercise caution when you decide to select an interrupt vector for your private use. The designers of the PC's interrupt architecture assumed a single-user, single-tasking environment. They set aside some vectors, assuming that any program that used the vectors would have full use of the machine for the duration of its process. They did not anticipate the plethora of resident programs and device drivers that stretch the PC far beyond its original intent. It is not uncommon to find conflicting uses of interrupt vectors among the developers of hardware and software. If, as a general rule, you restrict your use of interrupts to orderly and well-behaved use of the standard interrupt vectors, you can avoid such conflicts. If you must have a private one, be prepared to deal with the conflicts.

HOW TO USE INTERRUPTS

Unless you are writing a device driver for a new hardware device, your use of interrupts will usually be confined to intercepting and chaining the existing interrupts in the PC's architecture. Suppose, for example, you want to examine every keystroke that is returned from BIOS before it gets to the program that is reading the keyboard. You want to do this to trap a general-purpose help function key, for example, and you do not want to modify every C function that might be reading the keyboard. One technique would be to intercept the BIOS keyboard service, which is attached to interrupt number 0x16. That service is called by most programs, including DOS, to read the keyboard, and use of the service is the accepted well-behaved method for keyboard input. When the programs want the next keystroke, they call INT 0x16. The code pointed to by the 0x16 interrupt vector is then executed. Usually, that code is in BIOS, but when a program attaches to the vector, the vector will point to the program rather than BIOS. The code that a vector points to is an interrupt service routine (ISR) and must obey the rules of ISRs to prevent system crashes and other unpredictable behavior.

THE INTERRUPT SERVICE ROUTINE

Turbo C includes the **interrupt** function type described in Chapter 1. Your ISR functions will be this type. As a result, when the interrupt you are intercepting is called, your ISR is running with the data segment register pointing to its data segment and with all registers pushed on the stack of the caller. When your ISR completes, the registers are restored, and the calling program resumes operation.

ATTACHING INTERRUPT VECTORS

To get an ISR attached to an interrupt vector, you must write the address of the ISR into the vector. Each vector is a far pointer, so the address that is written into the vector will consist of the code segment address and code segment offset of the ISR. The Turbo C function named **setvect** writes its far pointer argument to the interrupt vector named as its first parameter. Suppose, for example, you declared an ISR to be an interrupt function as shown here:

```
void interrupt mykeyboard(IREGS iregs)
```

You could attach that ISR to the keyboard interrupt vector with the following statement:

```
setvect(0x16, mykeyboard);
```

The next call to INT 0x16 by a program will result in execution of the **mykeyboard** interrupt service routine.

CHAINING INTERRUPT VECTORS

If you attach to an interrupt vector that supports a system function, you must either completely replace that system function or chain to the ISR that had the vector before you got it. Obviously you do not want to recode the entire BIOS keyboard handler just for something as simple as watching for a help function key, so you need a way to chain to the original interrupt service routine. If, before you attach to the vector, you read and save its original contents, you can use that value to chain the ISRs. The Turbo C **getvect** function reads the value of a specified interrupt vector in this manner:

```
void interrupt (*oldkeyboard)(void);

oldkeyboard = getvect(0x16);
```

With this code, you save the original value of the BIOS keyboard interrupt vector into the far pointer named **oldkeyboard**. When the interrupt occurs, you can chain to the earlier ISR by calling it through the far pointer.

A TIMEOUT UTILITY

Listings 2.1 and 2.2 are timer.h and timer.c, respectively. These files provide the functions to let you set and test for timeout conditions in your programs. Suppose, for example, you prompt the user for an input and want to modify your process if the user hesitates for 30 seconds. You can set a 30-second timeout and test to see if it has expired while you wait for the keystrokes. These functions support this timeout capability.

Before you begin your timeout test, you must call **intercept_timer**. This function attaches the timer interrupt vector to the interrupt service routine named **newtimer** that will process the time-out. You can, optionally, specify the address of a function that will be executed when the timer times out. Use a NULL for the parameter if you are specifying no such function. If you use this option, remember that the function will execute asynchronously to the execution of the other code in your program. The function must have a clear and separate purpose, and it must achieve that purpose without altering any data variable that the main program might be using. After calling **intercept_timer**, you use the **set_timer** macro defined in timer.h to start a countdown for the number of seconds in your macro call. The timer is set by multiplying the number of seconds by roughly 18.2 and storing the result in a variable named **ticker**. While you are watching whatever might time out, you can test the timer with the **timed_out** macro, also defined in timer.h, or you can let the interrupt service routine call your function when the timeout has occurred. When the programmed time has elapsed, the **timed_out** macro will return a true value. During the timeout test you can restart the timer by calling **set_timer** again, perhaps each time the user presses a key. You can also respecify the function to be called by another call to **intercept_timer** without disturbing the countdown.

When you are done looking at the timer, call the **restore_timer** function to unhook the timer interrupt from the interrupt service routine. Be sure to call this function before the program terminates. If you terminate a program that has interrupt vectors attached, the vectors will still point to the memory that had been occupied by the interrupt service routines. When any of the interrupts occurs, the system will jump to whatever happens to be in that memory space, and a system crash is almost certain.

This timeout capability figures prominently in communications programs that are exchanging packets with remote processors. Sometimes a timeout is the only way to tell that the remote processor has gone out of service in the middle of a transmission. This subject is addressed in more detail in Chapter 8.

Listing 2.1: timer.h

```
/* ---------- timer.h --------------- */
extern unsigned ticker;

/* -------- timer prototypes --------- */
void intercept_timer(void (*)(void));
void restore_timer(void);

/* ------------ timer macros -------------- */
#define timed_out() (ticker==0)
#define set_timer(secs) ticker=(secs)*182/10+1
```

Listing 2.2: timer.c

```
/* ---------- timer.c --------------- */
#include <stdio.h>
#include <dos.h>
#include "timer.h"
#include "interupt.h"

unsigned ticker;

static void (interrupt far *oldtimer)(void);
static void interrupt far newtimer(void);
static void (*timeout_function)(void);

/* ---- intercept the timer interrupt vector ----- */
void intercept_timer(void (*fn)(void))
{
    if (oldtimer == NULL)    {
        oldtimer = getvect(TIMER);
        setvect(TIMER, newtimer);
    }
    timeout_function = fn;
}

/* ---- restore timer interrupt vector ------- */
void restore_timer()
{
    if (oldtimer != NULL)
```

continued...

...from previous page

```
            setvect(TIMER, oldtimer);
        timeout_function = NULL;
    }

    /* ------ ISR to count timer ticks ------- */
    static void interrupt far newtimer()
    {
        (*oldtimer)();
        if (ticker > 0)
            if (--ticker == 0 && timeout_function != NULL)
                (*timeout_function)();
    }
```

AN EXAMPLE: THE SCREEN SAVER

Listing 2.3 is scrnsave.c, a memory-resident program that blanks the screen if no key has been pressed within a specified number of seconds and then restores the screen when a key is pressed. When you run it, include the delay count in seconds on the command line. If you do not give a count, the program assumes that the delay is for one minute.

By calling a BIOS EGA-specific function, the scrnsave program tests to see if the EGA is being used. The video BIOS function 0x12, subfunction 0x10 is used to read EGA configuration information. If the function does not change the value of the **bl** register, the EGA is not installed. If an EGA is not installed, the program tests for the MDA by calling BIOS for the video mode. Mode 7 belongs to the MDA and is the only mode the MDA supports, so if mode 7 is returned, the MDA is installed. The CGA and MDA are blanked by writing a zero into the video enable bit of the Mode Select Register. The only difference is that the CGA addresses the register at port address 0x4b8, and the MDA uses 0x3b8. The EGA does not respond to the video enable bit, so it is necessary to use BIOS to turn off all the colors in the palette register to blank the screen.

The program begins by calling **intercept_timer** and attaching and chaining the BIOS keyboard service interrupt. Next, the program sets a timer for the specified number of seconds and uses the Turbo C **keep** function to terminate and stay resident. For every tick of the clock, the **newtimer** interrupt function in timer.c is executed. First, the function chains to the earlier ISR by calling through the **oldtimer** function pointer. Then, if the ticker variable is greater than zero, the **newtimer** function decrements the ticker variable and returns. When the ticker reaches zero, **newtimer** calls the **time_out** function in scrnsave.c. If the screen is not already blanked, the program blanks it by writing a value to the video system's mode select register.

When a program asks for a keystroke from BIOS by calling interrupt 0x16, the interrupt service routine named **newkb** is executed. The **newkb** function saves the value of the ax register because the BIOS function number is in there. The **newkb** function is interested in reads to the keyboard only. Next, **newkb** chains to the old keyboard service routine by calling through the **oldkb** function pointer. For a keyboard read service request, BIOS does not return until the user presses a key. For other keyboard services, BIOS returns immediately. If upon return from BIOS the caller's requested function was a read, the **newkb** function resets the ticker variable. If the screen has been blanked, the **newkb** function enables video output by writing to the video system's mode select register. The program also watches the value at 0:0x417. This is where BIOS records the setting of the Ctrl, Alt, and Shift keys. If any of these keys is pressed, the **newkb** function treats it as another key press.

The **newkb** function could have been attached to interrupt vector 9, the keyboard hardware interrupt. The statements related to _AX and _FLAGS and the test for the value at 0:0x417 could be omitted because the keyboard hardware interrupt 9 occurs for all key presses. The scrnsave example uses the 0x16 BIOS interrupt to show that a software interrupt is attached and chained in the same way as a hardware interrupt.

Listing 2.3: scrnsave.c

```
/* ----------- scrnsave.c -------------- */

/*
 * A program to blank the screen after a programmed timeout
 * with no keystrokes at the keyboard. If the screen is blanked,
 * the next key press will cause it to be redisplayed.
 * This program illustrates attaching and chaining hardware
 * and software interrupt vectors.
 */

#include <dos.h>
#include <stdlib.h>
#include "interupt.h"
#include "timer.h"

#define VIDEO_ENABLE 8    /* video enable signal               */
#define CURRMODE 0x29     /* the normal text, 25x80 setting    */

/* ------ interrupt vector chain ------ */
static void interrupt (*oldkb)(void);

/* ------ interrupt service routine ------- */
static void interrupt newkb(IREGS);

/* ------- timeout function ------------- */
static void time_out(void);

int MODESELECT = 0x3d8; /* address of CGA mode select port   */
static int blanked;     /*true if the screen has been blanked*/
static int kbfunc;      /*holds the INT 0x16 function        */
static int timeout = 60;/*number of seconds to time out      */
static int ega;         /*true if the video system is an EGA */

/* ---- begin execution of memory-resident screen saver ---- */
void main(int argc, char *argv[])
{
    if (argc > 1)
        timeout = (atoi(argv[1]));
```

continued...

...from previous page

```
    /* -------- test for EGA ------------- */
    _AH = 0x12;
    _BL = 0x10;
    geninterrupt(0x10);
    ega = (_BL != 0x10);
    if (!ega)   {
        /* ------ test for MDA -------- */
        _AH = 0x0f;
        geninterrupt(0x10);
        if (_AL == 7)
            MODESELECT = 0x3b8;
    }
    /* --------- intercept the timer -------- */
    intercept_timer(time_out);
    /* ----- get original interrupt vector ----- */
    oldkb = getvect(KEYBOARD);
    /* ----- attach vector to resident program ----- */
    setvect(KEYBOARD, newkb);
    /* ----- terminate and stay resident ------- */
    set_timer(timeout);
    keep(0, 200);
}
/* ------ timeout function ------- */
static void time_out(void)
{
    if (!blanked)   {
        blanked = 1;
        if (ega)    {
            _AX = 0x1000;
            _BX = 0x0012;
            geninterrupt(0x10);
        }
        else
            outportb(MODESELECT, CURRMODE & ~VIDEO_ENABLE);
    }
}
/* ----- keyboard interrupt service routine ------ */
static void interrupt newkb(IREGS iregs)
{
```

continued...

...from previous page

```
    kbfunc = _AX;
    (*oldkb)();
    iregs.ax = _AX;
    iregs.fl = _FLAGS;
    if (kbfunc == 0 || (peekb(0,0x417) & 0xf))  {
        set_timer(timeout);
        if (blanked)    {
            if (ega)    {
                _AX = 0x1000;
                _BX = 0x0f12;
                    geninterrupt(0x10);
            }
            else
                outportb(MODESELECT, CURRMODE);
        }
        blanked = 0;
    }
}
```

SUMMARY

Now you know a lot about interrupts and how to use them in your programs. Later chapters will use this capability to its maximum potential, so you haven't heard the last of it. The next chapter will apply a bit of imagination and creative trickery to make Turbo C do something that everyone agrees it cannot do: support overlays.

CHAPTER 3

OVERLAYS

This chapter is about program overlays in Turbo C. It includes the library functions and example programs to allow you to build a program that has overlays. The technique described in this chapter is called the Poor Man's Overlay Manager. Why so? Well, for a full-blown Turbo C overlay system, you need a linker from a third-party vendor and an overlay manager. These items are not a part of Turbo C. So, rather than shell out your hard-earned money for more software, why not figure out how to make overlays with the tools at hand? You will learn how to do just that in this chapter.

What you need to understand:

- The interrupt function type
- Variable argument lists
- Register pseudovariables

New subjects discussed:

- The spawn... functions
- In-line macros

THE OVERLAY

An overlay is a piece of a program. When a program becomes too big to fit into available memory or too big to allow other programs to share memory, then you must do something to reduce the size of the program. One approach is to break the program into smaller pieces and load the pieces into memory as they are needed. This way, the entire program is never resident at one time. Only the pieces that are needed at a given time are resident. When a nonresident piece is needed, it is read in on top of – or it overlays – a resident piece that is not currently needed, thus the name "overlay." Although Turbo C Professional has no defined support for programs with overlays, this chapter describes how you can build such programs by using the features of Turbo C alone. This is a significant addition to your bag of tricks. Programmers have been asking Borland to add the overlay feature ever since Turbo C 1.0 was introduced. Little did they know the capability was always there. All it takes is some imagination and creative and unconventional use of the unique Turbo C implementation of the C language.

ROOT AND OVERLAY PROGRAM MODULES

A typical overlaid program has the following structure: There is a root module and a number of overlay modules. Modules consist of data space and executable code. The root module is loaded and executed when the program is first run and remains resident as long as the program is running. The root module usually contains the overlay manager software, global data that is to be shared among the root modules and the overlay modules, and the common software functions or subroutines that overlay modules might call. The overlay modules contain transient software functions and data. Normally, overlays do not communicate laterally between themselves, but in some implementations of overlays, an overlay module can be a root module for other subordinate overlays, thus forming a tree-structured hierarchy of program modules. The approach in this chapter will include this feature.

To support overlays, the language development environment must allow you to segment a program into one root and multiple overlays. Then you must be able to specify shared data and functions between the root and its overlays. Usually, the architecture of the root-to-overlay tree is described to and built by the linker program. The loading of and communication with overlay modules is done by an overlay manager software function in the root.

AN EXAMPLE PROGRAM WITH OVERLAYS

Consider this example: You are building an integrated document processing program with lots of shared data and common functions. It is an on-line interactive program, and you do not want to divide it into discrete programs that the user must execute from the command line. The volume of shared data is significant, and you do not want the software modules to use disk files to share data. This program is a candidate for overlays. You build a root module that manages the top-level menus and options. The root module might contain the data base manager and user interface functions. The overlay modules contain the software to manage the various selections from the top-level menu. When the user makes a selection, the overlay manager in the root module loads the proper overlay into memory and executes its function. The software in the overlays can read and change the data values in the common area of the root module, or it can work with its own copies. The overlay functions can execute subroutine functions that are resident in the root module. With this approach, you have built your modular application into the smallest possible memory space.

The design and maintenance of a program that has overlays requires more discipline than that required of conventional program architecture. You must be careful in your definition of the relationship between the root and the overlays. Your maintenance of the files that contain the software must be rigorous. Trying to run root and overlay modules that were built for different versions of the program can have peculiar results.

OVERLAYS AND C

In some programming languages, overlays are an integral part of the language design. In others, such as C, overlays are not a language feature but are left to be optionally implemented by the compiler. The ANSI C standard does not specify that overlays are required, and Turbo C does not support them. There are third-party linkers that will allow you to build Turbo C programs with overlays, but your Turbo C Professional package does not document any such capability. The features of the C language and the extensions of Turbo C will support overlays, but the technique described in this chapter has not been addressed before now. Perhaps no one ever thought of it.

OVERLAYS, DOS, AND TURBO C

MS-DOS has a built-in way for program systems to be segmented. Function 0x4b of the DOS interrupt 0x21 allows one program to load and execute another. The first program, called the "parent," waits for the second program, called the "child," to finish execution before the parent resumes its own execution. The parent passes to DOS the address of a string of commands. The child program processes the string as if the program had been executed from the command line with the string typed on the command line. This string is called a "command tail." The child program inherits the parent program's environment block and file handles. When the parent program regains control, it can read the child program's return code. With this capability, a parent program can function as a rudimentary root module, and child programs can function as rudimentary overlay modules.

Turbo C gives you several variations on the use of DOS function 0x4b. At its simplest level, the TC **system** function lets you execute any command that a user can execute from the command line. The **system** function uses DOS 0x4b to load a second (or third, etc.) copy of the DOS command processor, COMMAND.COM. The disadvantages to this approach are that you pay the memory and execution overhead for an extra copy of COMMAND.COM, and the parent program cannot read the return code from the child because COMMAND.COM does not pass it through. The advantage to the **system** command is that it allows you to execute batch files and intrinsic DOS commands, such as **chdir** and **type**, as well as executable programs.

The more advanced and flexible Turbo C program execution functions are the **exec...** and **spawn...** processes. These functions execute child programs without using COMMAND.COM. The **exec...** functions execute a child program by replacing the parent program with the copy of the child. When the child program exits, the parent is not resumed, so the **exec...** functions are not appropriate for use in a root and overlay structure. The **spawn...** functions execute the child program in memory space above the parent and return to the parent when the child program exits. This is more appropriate for the root/overlay architecture.

There are eight varieties of the **spawn...** function. These varieties are as follows:

- **spawnl**
- **spawnle**
- **spawnlp**
- **spawnlpe**
- **spawnv**
- **spawnve**
- **spawnvp**
- **spawnvpe**

The suffixes to the function names specify how the child program is executed. The functions suffixed with **l** mean there are a fixed number of parameters in the command tail for this particular call to the **spawnl...** function, and each parameter is named in the call.

For **spawnv...** the parameters are represented by a NULL-terminated array of character pointers. The **p** suffix tells the function to search the path specified in the PATH environment variable for the child program. Otherwise only the current directory is searched. The **p** suffix is more appropriate for an overlay manager because applications programs can change the current directory without notifying the overlay manager and because the root program can be executed while the user is logged into a different directory. The overlay manager cannot count on the current directory to tell it where the overlays are, so using the DOS path is the best bet. The **e** suffix lets the parent program specify an environment variable block other than its own for the child program to use.

If the command line parameters, environment block, file contents, and return code can suffice for communication between the root and its overlays, then the **spawn...** function set is all you need to support an overlay manager. Often, however, this is not the case.

In the traditional root/overlay architecture, the program processes large data blocks in memory that the root software and the overlay software must share. The program as a whole has common software functions that all modules must use. These functions are typically kept in the root module. A properly designed program with multiple levels of overlays will keep the functions used by overlay modules in their common root module. If you use the **spawn...** functions without any enhancements, you cannot build such an overlaid program. What follows is the technique that uses the unique properties of Turbo C to provide most of the capabilities of a traditional overlay manager.

THE POOR MAN'S OVERLAY MANAGER (PMOM)

PMOM is a technique for building a set of programs where a root module executes overlay modules in the manner described previously in this chapter. The overlay module can process data space in the root and can execute functions in the root. The root executes the overlay by using the Turbo C **spawnvp** function. The root uses the command line parameter mechanism to pass ASCII representations of far pointers to data items and functions in the root. The overlay program translates those ASCII far pointers into true far pointers and can then read and write arrays, structures, strings, integers, and any other data items that the root tells the overlay about. The overlay translates the ASCII function pointers into true function pointers and can thus call functions in the root.

To use the PMOM technique, you must follow some rules for writing root and overlay programs. The following paragraphs and programs explain by example each of these rules and their underlying principles.

The PMOM Source Files

Listing 3.1 is pmom.h, the first of two source files that constitute the Poor Man's Overlay Manager. You will include this file in your root modules where overlay modules are loaded and where global functions are declared. You will also include pmom.h in the overlay modules where the data and function arguments are interpreted and where root functions are called.

Listing 3.1: pmom.h

```
/* -------------- pmom.h ---------------- */

/*
 *  Include this header file in the source files for
 *  the root and overlay modules of an overlay program
 */

#define MAXARGS 10

/* --------- the program and DOS context -------- */
typedef struct {
    unsigned ss;                /* stack segment          */
```

continued...

...from previous page

```
    unsigned sp;             /* stack pointer          */
    unsigned psp;            /* program segment prefix */
    char far *dta;           /* disk transfer address  */
} CONTEXT;

extern CONTEXT rctx;    /* context of the root module    */
extern CONTEXT octx;    /* context of the overlay module */

#define  ROOTREGS IREGS rtregs
#define  ROOTFUNCTION far interrupt

/* ------ enter a root function from an overlay call ------- */
#define ENTER                 \
{                             \
    disable();                \
    octx.ss=_SS;              \
    octx.sp=_SP;              \
    _SS=rctx.ss;              \
    _SP=rctx.sp;              \
    _BP=_SP;                  \
    enable();                 \
    octx.dta=getdta();        \
    setdta(rctx.dta);         \
    _AH = 0x51;               \
    geninterrupt(0x21);       \
    octx.psp = _BX;           \
    _BX = _psp;               \
    _AH = 0x50;               \
    geninterrupt(0x21);       \
}

/* ------- exit from a root function ------- */
#define EXIT                                  \
{                                             \
    _BX = octx.psp;                           \
    _AH = 0x50;                               \
    geninterrupt(0x21);                       \
    setdta(octx.dta);                         \
    disable();                                \
    _SS=octx.ss;                              \
```

continued...

...from previous page

```
        _SP=octx.sp;                            \
        _BP=_SP;                                \
        enable();                               \
}

/* ----- return a value from a root function ------- */
#define RETURN(r)                               \
{                                               \
        rtregs.ax=(unsigned)((r) & 0xffff); \
        rtregs.dx=(unsigned)((r) >> 16);    \
}

/* -------- overlay function prototypes ---------- */
int load_overlay(char *, ...);
void far *getarg(int);
```

The first item of interest in pmom.h is the global symbol **MAXARGS**. As shown here, it is defined to be the value 10, and it is the maximum number of function and data pointers that a root module can share with an overlay module. You can increase this value if 10 is not enough.

Context Switching

The structure named CONTEXT is used by PMOM to record and swap the stack and DOS contexts of the root and overlay modules. Its use is transparent to your application's root and overlay programs, but it is a critical part of PMOM's ability to let an overlay module call functions in a root module.

When an overlay module calls a function in a root module through a far pointer, what you have is one discrete program executing code in another. This is the equivalent of a program calling an interrupt service routine that is not a part of the calling program. DOS has an internal record of the currently running program, and Turbo C makes several assumptions about where segment registers point. These conditions are known as the "context" of a program. If you called a root function without changing from your context to its context, any calls it made to DOS would be relative to your DOS context, and any references it made to its own data segment would be relative to your data segment. Obviously, this will not work.

Chapters 1 and 2 discuss the Turbo C **interrupt** function type. Its purpose is to support interrupt service routines, but PMOM will use it to support the global common functions of the root module. When you execute an **interrupt** function, it pushes the registers on the stack and changes the data segment register to the data segment of the program where the function resides. When the function returns, it pops the registers off the stack and thus restores the data segment register to the data segment of the calling program.

Interrupt functions are usually called by a software or hardware interrupt. Nothing, however, prevents a program from simply calling the interrupt function as if it were any other function. Turbo C accommodates this capability by seeing that the called function is defined with the interrupt type and emulating an interrupt to it by pushing the flags register on the stack ahead of the call. This method maintains the stack's integrity when the interrupt function returns with its IRET machine instruction.

By defining the root's global common functions with the interrupt function type, PMOM effectively supports the swapping of the data segment context between overlays and the root.

There are four other items of context that must be swapped when a root global common function is executed and returns. These items are saved in the CONTEXT structures named **rctx** (root context) and **octx** (overlay context).

The first two context items saved in the CONTEXT structures are the program's stack segment and stack pointer. If this were an assembly language system, the stack would not necessarily be switched here. Turbo C, however, has a feature where each function can check the validity of the stack pointer when the function is called. This is an optional feature that facilitates debugging and is usually turned off after a program is checked out. You do not know, however, that all the library functions you call were compiled with the option turned off; therefore, it is better to ensure that the stack pointer points to an acceptable address within the context of the program module being executed.

The next item of context to be saved in the CONTEXT structures is the current Program Segment Prefix (PSP) address. The PSP is a memory block that precedes the program and describes it to DOS whenever the program calls DOS. DOS, being a single-tasking operating system, keeps a record of the PSP of only the currently running task. If, through programming trickery, the computer is executing code in a program other than the one that DOS knows about, DOS will try to perform its functions in the name of the program it knows about. Therefore, you must change what DOS thinks is the current PSP when you switch contexts between the root and the overlay.

DOS has a holdover from its earlier versions called the Disk Transfer Area (DTA). Certain DOS functions – typically disk directory functions – use this area to read disk sectors. Programs can change the DTA address, and each program has its own current DTA that DOS knows about. If you jump into another program without telling DOS to change the DTA, the DOS functions that use the DTA will work unpredictably. The CONTEXT structures contain holders for the DTAs of the root and overlay modules.

Running in the Root

Listing 3.2 is root.c. This program is an example of a root module and will serve to guide you through the PMOM operation. It also serves as a model for root modules that you will develop for your own overlaid applications.

This discussion will jump from source file to source file as the different aspects of PMOM are addressed.

Begin by looking at the external data items in root.c. These will provide examples of how an overlay module can read and modify data items in the root. There is a character array named **line**, a structure named **P2**, and an integer named **lineno**. Farther down is a function named **global_function** that the overlay module will execute. That function will be described in turn.

The **main** function of root.c displays some information on the screen and calls the **load_overlay** function. The **load_overlay** function will load and execute the overlay module. The first parameter is the file name with the extension of the overlay module, in this case, "overlay.exe." The next three parameters are far pointers to the data items that the overlay will see. Note the use of the Turbo C MK_FP macro and the _DS pseudovariable. This construct uses these features to form far pointers to the data items. If the program was built with the compact or large data models, the MK_FP would not be needed; only the addresses of the data items would be required. The last parameter in the call to **load_overlay** is the address of the **global_function** function.

Listing 3.2: root.c

```
/* --------- root.c ---------------- */

/*
 * This program is an example of the root module of
 * an overlaid program.
 */

#include <stdio.h>
#include <conio.h>
#include <dos.h>
#include "interupt.h"
#include "pmom.h"

void ROOTFUNCTION global_function(ROOTREGS, int op);

/* --------------------------------------------------------
   These are arrays and structures in the root module
   that are accessible to the overlay module.
   -------------------------------------------------------- */

/* --- a character array used to display the dashed line --- */
static char line[] =
    "\r\n============================================";

/* ---- a structure. The overlay can read and modify it ---- */
static struct pp {
    char p1[25];
    char p2[25];
} P2 = {"--original data--", "--CRISPY DATA--"};

/* -- an integer variable that the overlay module can use -- */
static int lineno = 1;

/* --------------------------------------------------------
   Begin the program at the main function of the root module
   -------------------------------------------------------- */
void main(void)
{
    int rtn;
```

continued...

...from previous page

```
        cprintf(line);
        cprintf("\r\n[%d] Begin processing in the root", lineno++);
        cprintf("\r\n    Load and execute Overlay");
        rtn = load_overlay("overlay.exe",
                          MK_FP(_DS, &lineno),
                          MK_FP(_DS, line),
                          MK_FP(_DS, &P2),
                          global_function,
                          NULL);
        cprintf(line);
        cprintf("\r\n[%d] Continue in the root",rtn);
        cprintf("\r\n    Overlay changed P2 to: %s", P2.p2);
        cprintf("\r\n    Exit from the root");
        cprintf(line);
    }

    /* --------------------------------------------------------------
       A global function in the root module that the overlay
       module can call. The overlay module can pass parameters
       and the root function can return an int, long, or pointer.
       -------------------------------------------------------------- */
    void ROOTFUNCTION global_function(ROOTREGS, int ovp)
    {
        static int pp;              /* holder for parameter */
        pp = ovp;
        ENTER;
        {
            int inside = 4444;      /* a local variable */
            cprintf(line);
            cprintf("\r\n[%d]     Root global function running",pp);
            cprintf("\r\n        inside = %d", inside);
            cprintf("\r\n        Overlay passed %d to root",pp);
            cprintf("\r\n        Root function returns %d",pp+1);
        }
        EXIT;
        RETURN(pp+1);
    }
```

Loading the Overlay

Listing 3.3 is pmom.c, the core of PMOM. It contains two functions, the first of which is **load_overlay** and the second to be discussed later. The pmom.c program contains the two CONTEXT structures, **rctx** and **octx**, described previously.

The **load_overlay** function is defined as one with a variable argument list. This definition uses the ANSI-standard **va...** function declaration conventions.

First **load_overlay** saves the context of the root module by storing the stack segment and pointer registers in the **rctx** structure. This operation uses the register pseudovariable feature that is unique to Turbo C. Note that the saved value of the stack pointer is decremented by 256. This makes some space for the **load_overlay** function to use more stack before the overlay calls any global functions in the root. Next, the **getdta** function is called to save the root module's DTA address.

The **load_overlay** function now builds the overlay's command line arguments. Because the **spawnvp** function is to be used, the command line arguments will be represented by one pointer to an array of string pointers. First, the strings must be built. Each string will be an ASCII representation of the far pointer that is to be passed to the overlay. If the hexadecimal value of the pointer is, for example, 0x072e for the segment and 0x5d3e for the offset, then the command line argument will be "072e:5d3e" as the string that the overlay program reads. To make this conversion, the **sprintf** function is used with the "%Fp" formatting string. Each far pointer in the parameter list to **load_overlay** is thus converted and saved in the **args** array of character arrays. Each entry in the **args** array has its address as an entry in the **arglist** array.

The overlay file is loaded and executed by a call to the **spawnvp** function with the constant P_WAIT parameter, the name of the overlay file, and the address of the **arglist** array.

Listing 3.3: pmom.c

```
/* ----------- pmom.c ------------ */

/*
 * The Poor Man's Overlay Manager (PMOM)
 * Link the .obj version of this file with the
 * root and overlay modules of an overlay program.
 */

#include <stdio.h>
#include <process.h>
#include <stdarg.h>
#include <dos.h>
#include "interupt.h"
#include "pmom.h"

CONTEXT rctx;    /* context of the root module    */
CONTEXT octx;    /* context of the overlay module */

/* -------- load and execute an overlay module ------------
                 Called from the root module.
                 The variable parameters are:
         [1] far pointers to data items in the root module
                          and/or
         [2] far pointers to functions in the root module
   ---------------------------------------------------------- */
int load_overlay(char *overlayname, ...)
{
    va_list ap;
    void far *param;
    char *arglist[MAXARGS + 1];
    char args[MAXARGS] [10];
    int rtn, argctr = 0;

    /* ------ save the context of the root module -------- */
    rctx.ss = _SS;
    rctx.sp = _SP;
    rctx.sp -= 256;
    rctx.dta = getdta();
    /* ---- build the *argv[] command line parameters ---- */
```

continued...

...from previous page

```
    va_start(ap, overlayname);
    arglist[argctr++] = overlayname;
    while (argctr < MAXARGS &&
            (param = va_arg(ap, void far *)) != NULL)    {
        sprintf(args[argctr], "%Fp", param);
        arglist[argctr] = args[argctr];
        argctr++;
    }
    arglist[argctr++] = NULL;
    /* ------ load and execute the overlay -------- */
    rtn = spawnvp(P_WAIT, overlayname, arglist);
    return rtn;
}

/* ------- convert command line arg to far pointer --------
      Overlay modules call this function to translate the
      command line version of far pointers into real far
      pointers. For example:
                char far *fp = getarg(2);
      This translates the second comand line argument into
      a far character pointer.
   -------------------------------------------------------- */
void far *getarg(int n)
{
    void far *fp;
    sscanf(_argv[n], "%Lp", &fp);
    return fp;
}
```

Running the Overlay

Listing 3.4 is overlay.c. This file is an example of an overlay module. The first item of interest is the definition of the **pp** structure. This defines for the overlay the format of the data structure in the root module. In a real application, you would record such a definition in an application-dependent header file that both programs include. The **fp2** pointer and **pstruct** structure will be used to show how an overlay can access global data in the root by reference (using a pointer) or by value (using a local copy). Although the program expects command line parameters, there are no **argc**, **argv** parameters in the main function declaration. The parameters will be parsed by using the Turbo C **_argv** variable instead.

Listing 3.4: overlay.c

```
/* ------- overlay.c ---------- */

/*
 * This program is an example of an overlay module of
 * an overlaid program.
 */

#include <stdio.h>
#include <conio.h>
#include <dos.h>
#include <string.h>
#include "pmom.h"

/* -----------------------------------------------------------
   A definition of the structure in the root module that the
   overlay can view and change. Such definitions will usually
   be in application-dependent header files.
   ----------------------------------------------------------- */
struct pp {
    char p1[25];
    char p2[25];
};

/* -----------------------------------------------------------
   The overlay can use a far pointer to deal with the global
   data or it can use a local copy of the data.
   ----------------------------------------------------------- */
struct pp far *fp2;     /* far pointer to the root structure */
struct pp pstruct;      /* local copy of the root structure  */

void drawline(void);

/* -----------------------------------------------------------
   Execution of the overlay begins with its main function.
   The overlay returns to the root when the main function
   returns or when the overlay calls the C exit() function.
   ----------------------------------------------------------- */
int main(void)
{
```

continued...

...from previous page

```
    int ROOTFUNCTION (*fnp)(int);
    int lineno;

    /* --- get a local copy of the global integer ----- */
    lineno = *(int far *)getarg(1);
    drawline();
    cprintf("\r\n[%d]   Overlay is executing", lineno++);

    cprintf("\r\n      The structure data argument contains: ");
    /* ---- get a pointer to the global structure ----- */
    fp2 = getarg(3);
    /* ---- make a local copy of the global structure ---- */
    pstruct = *fp2;

    /* ------ access the global structure ---------- */
    cprintf("\r\n          %s", pstruct.p1);
    cprintf("\r\n          %s", pstruct.p2);

    /* ------- change the global structure ----------- */
    strcpy(pstruct.p2, "--Changed Data--");
    *fp2 = pstruct;

    /* ---- call the global function --------- */
    cprintf("\r\n      Overlay calls Root function with %d",
        lineno);
    fnp = getarg(4);
    lineno = (*fnp)(lineno);

    drawline();
    cprintf("\r\n[%d]   Root returns to Overlay",lineno);

    /* ------- return to the root module ---------- */
    cprintf("\r\n      Overlay is exiting with return code %d",
        ++lineno);
    return lineno;
}
/* ----- use global char array to draw the dashed line ----- */
void drawline(void)
{
```

continued...

...from previous page

```
    char far *fp1 = getarg(2);
    while (*fp1)
        putch(*fp1++);
}
```

The first PMOM interface you see is when the overlay calls **getarg** to get a far pointer to the first parameter. The **getarg** function is in pmom.c. You need to keep this distinction straight.

Both the root and the overlay are linked with pmom.c. These are two separately linked programs, so when the overlay module is in a function defined in pmom.c, that is not the same code as the code for the same function in the root module.

The **getarg** function uses the Turbo C function **sscanf** to translate the command line ASCII far pointer to a real far pointer. The format string "%Lp" makes the translation, and **getarg** returns the translated pointer. The first example of this is where the overlay gets the address of the first parameter, an integer in the root module. This integer is put into the **lineno** variable in overlay.c.

The **main** function in overlay.c calls the **drawline** function also in overlay.c. This function displays a line of equal signs on the screen. It gets the line to display from the root module by using **getarg** to get a pointer to the array in the root module that contains the string.

The assignment to the **fp2** far structure pointer shows how the overlay can get a pointer to a structure in the root. This pointer is used to make a local copy of the structure. This technique is preferred for most parameters. Your root and overlay modules will usually be in the small data model, and all the Turbo C library functions that take pointers as their parameters expect near pointers. The far pointers that **getarg** returns cannot be passed to the library functions and cannot be coerced into near pointers because the data values themselves are in a remote data segment in the root module.

The overlay modifies its copy of the root's structure and moves the structure back into the root with an assignment that has the far pointer on the left.

Calling a Global Common Function in the Root

The overlay uses **getarg** to compute the far pointer to the root's global common function and calls that function through the computed pointer. Note that the call includes a parameter passed to the root function and a value returned from the root function.

Change now to root.c again and look at the function named **global_function**. This function is an example of one that is in a root module and that can be called from an overlay module. The definition and structure of such functions must adhere to a strict format. First you will see that the function is declared **void** in this file and declared **int** in overlay.c. Because of the contextual nature of these functions, they do not use normal return conventions. But, because the overlay expects a return, you must tell the compiler in overlay.c that the function returns something. Because the function does not return a value in the traditional C manner, you must tell the compiler in root.c that the function does not return anything.

You will use the ROOTFUNCTION type to declare all such global common functions. This symbol is defined in pmom.h to use the **far interrupt** function type. You must include the ROOTREGS symbol as the first parameter in the functions parameter list. This sets up the register parameters that Turbo C pushes on the stack when an interrupt function is executed. The parameters that follow the ROOTREGS parameter can be anything else that you pass to the function from the overlay module that called it.

ROOTFUNCTION functions may not have local **auto** variables that are accessed inside the function. The stack context is going to be changed before the function begins to execute, and all parameters and initial local **auto** variables are kept on the stack by Turbo C. Therefore, each parameter must be moved into a static or external variable before the function switches context. The static integer named **pp** in **global_function** is an example of this construct.

The next statement is the ENTER macro and is required before the function continues. The ENTER macro is defined in pmom.h and switches the context from the overlay module to the root module. As defined, the ENTER macro is an example of using the C **#define** statement to generate in-line C code. Because the procedure fiddles with the stack, a function is not appropriate. The act of calling the function would change the stack and muddle up the process. The ENTER macro collects the current stack segment and pointer registers into the **octx** CONTEXT structure and then assigns to those registers the corresponding values from the **rctx** CONTEXT structure. ENTER saves the overlay's DTA and sets the root's DTA. ENTER then calls DOS to get and save the overlay's PSP and sets the PSP to the value in the Turbo C global variable named **_psp**, which is the PSP of the root module.

After the ENTER macro has switched contexts, **global_function** executes a brace-surrounded block of code. By using braces, the function can have its own local **auto** variables as illustrated by the **inside** integer. The function can access any of those local variables or any of the external or static variables in the root module. If the function is to prepare a return value, it should write the value into a static or external variable. These functions can return integers, longs, and far pointers. When the global common function is done, it executes the EXIT macro, which is defined in pmom.h. This macro switches the context from the root module to the overlay module. If the function is to return a value to the overlay module, it must use the RETURN macro, also defined in pmom.h. The ROOTREGS parameter is a structure of integers that represent the registers pushed on the stack when the function was executed. When the function returns, those registers will be popped off the stack. By changing their values on the stack, the global function can change what is in the registers when the overlay module resumes following its call to the global function. Turbo C returns 16-bit values in the ax register and 32-bit values in the DX:AX register pair. The RETURN macro puts its parameter in these two registers.

Back to the Root Module

When the overlay module is ready to return to the root module, it can return from its **main** function or use the Turbo C **exit** function. Either way, it can return a value with the DOS return value mechanism. You will see that the call to **load_overlay** in root.c returns a value. This will be the overlay module's exit return value.

Building the Software

The makefile in the appendix to this book will build the example root.c and overlay.c programs that are described in this chapter. It uses the Turbo C tcc command-line compiler and the tlink command-line linker to build both programs. You can execute the example program by typing this command:

```
c>root
```

You will see the screen display shown in Figure 3.1.

```
C>root

=============================================
[1] Begin processing in the root
    Load and execute Overlay
=============================================
[2]   Overlay is executing
      The structure data argument contains:
        --original data--
        --CRISPY DATA--
      Overlay calls Root function with 3
=============================================
[3]     Root global function running
        inside = 4444
        Overlay passed 3 to root
        Root function returns 4
=============================================
[4]   Root returns to Overlay
      Overlay is exiting with return code 5
=============================================
[5] Continue in the root
    Overlay changed P2 to: --Changed Data--
    Exit from the root
=============================================
C>
```

Figure 3.1 Screen display for example root.c and overlay.c programs

SUMMARY

The software in this chapter provides a capability that many programmers have been asking for: an overlay manager for Turbo C. By carefully following the rules outlined here, and by including the Poor Man's Overlay Manager software functions with your code, you can build programs with the full features of a root/overlay architecture.

CHAPTER 4

VIDEO WINDOWS

This chapter is about video windows with Turbo C. Several of the programs that come later in the book use video windows and need a window manager. The package presented here will serve that purpose and, at the same time, give you examples of how the Turbo C text window functions can be used to support a window management library. To extend the usefulness of the window package, later chapters will add a pop-down menu manager and a general-purpose data entry template manager.

What you need to understand:

- The Turbo C text display routines

New subjects discussed:

- Pop-up windows

POP-UP WINDOWS

As you operate the Turbo C Integrated Development Environment and most other popular PC programs, you use a dialogue with the computer that is based on pop-up windows. The window is a rectangular subset of the screen. The pop-up window appears on top of other screen displays, remains as long as it is used, and when it goes away, restores the earlier display. Turbo C's pull-down menus use windows. So do the data entry boxes where you set compiler options and other variable information.

The requirements of this book for window management are small. The software that follows in later chapters uses a system of windows where the most recent window is current, and all earlier windows are visible or partially visible under the most recent one. This author's earlier work, *Turbo C: Memory-Resident Utilities, Screen I/O, and Programming Techniques* (MIS:Press, 1987) contains a comprehensive window management package that includes menus, data entry windows, context-sensitive help windows, and a window text editor. The programs in this book do not require the full functionality of that earlier library. You can refer to the first book if your needs demand a complete window library. Many programs can get by with the simpler window functions in this chapter.

THE TURBO C TEXT WINDOW DISPLAY ROUTINES

Certain functions in Turbo C are oriented to the video architecture of the PC. Unlike the standard output device, which is more Teletype-like, the Turbo C text window display routines are oriented to the concept of a video window. Once a window is declared with the **window** function, the display and cursor routines deal with that space as a virtual screen. Screen clearing, cursor position, and color controls are relative to the window rather than the entire screen. This window-oriented console output is an extension to the standard C library, which treats the screen as a glass typewriter, has no standard way to clear the screen, and knows nothing of cursor position. The standard C language, including the ANSI standard, ignores the fact that most contemporary C programs are written in an interactive environment with a screen and keyboard. The extent of support for that environment varies from compiler to compiler, and no common approach is taken. Turbo C has text window display functions superior to most, but they do not represent a window management system. Rather, they are a set of functions that allow you to define and write to a single window at a time.

The Turbo C text window display functions are generally faster than standard output, and they deal with the video hardware in ways that used to be the concerns of the programmers. Your program no longer needs to care about the address of the video memory segment or whether to wait for video retrace blanking cycles to avoid the video interference called "snow."

What the text window display functions do not provide is a hierarchy of open windows. If you use the **window** function to open a window, the software forgets what the previous window was. The **gettext** and **puttext** functions can save and restore what was under a new window, but opening and closing windows does not cause that to happen automatically. In fact, there is no provision for closing a window with the Turbo C text window display library other than by opening another window.

THE WINDOW LIBRARY EXTENSIONS

The functions in this chapter extend the Turbo C library functions by maintaining a record of open windows, automatically saving what a window covers when you open the window, and restoring the previous display when you close the window. Most of window management involves these few steps, so a window library to perform those steps is a helpful addition to your Turbo C extensions.

Listings 4.1 and 4.2 are window.h and window.c. These source files contain the window library that extends the functionality of the Turbo C text functions to support a stack of windows.

You can open as many windows as you have specified in the MAX_WINDOWS global symbol in window.h. When you open a window, you specify its location, size, color, and whether or not it has a frame. You open a window by calling the **open_window** function in window.c as shown here:

```
open_window(left,top,right,bottom,foreg,backg,frame,shadow);
```

The window corner coordinates are relative to the entire screen, beginning with 1,1 in the upper left corner and ending with 80,25 in the lower right corner. The foreground and background colors are the global symbols that are defined by Turbo C in the conio.h header file. The **frame** variable is zero if the window has no frame or one or two to specify single- or double-line frame characters. Frame characters are taken from the PC's ASCII graphics character set. The **shadow** variable is zero if you want no shadow, one if you want a transparent shadow, and two if you want an opaque shadow.

The last window you open is the one that is current. When you open a window, it is drawn on the screen and cleared to all blanks. Subsequent calls to **gotoxy**, **cprintf**, **putch**, and **cputs** from the Turbo C text window display and console I/O functions will be relative to this most recent window. When you close a window, the one opened before it is now current. This is the feature missing in the Turbo C library—the ability to maintain a stack of windows.

To close the current window, you call the **close_window** function with no parameters. You can close only the current window, and when you do, it will be erased, and what was under it will be visible again.

You can give the appearance of promoting an existing window to the top of the stack by opening a duplicate of it and writing the same data values into it. This, of course, is a duplicate and not the same window as the one you are promoting, so, when you close the promoted window, you are effectively demoting it to its former place in the stack. If you close all the windows at once, you must remember the earlier copy.

The **open_window** function uses **malloc** to allocate a window save buffer and **gettext** to save the video memory into the save buffer. It describes the window with the **window**, **textbackground**, and **textforeground** functions and uses **gettextinfo** to get a copy of the Turbo C **text_info** structure. The frame attribute and save buffer pointer are not a part of the **text_info** structure, so window.c maintains an array called **dressing** to keep these parts of the window's description.

Window Frames

When a window has a frame, the displays and cursor positions should be inside the frame rather than including it. The window described to **open_window** includes space for the frame, and if left that way, subsequent calls to **cprintf** and other functions would overwrite the frame characters. This problem is solved by the **clear_window** function, which writes the first blank copy of the window on the screen. If the window has no frame, the blank copy is drawn with the **clrscr** function. Otherwise, the **clear_window** function writes the frame characters into the window. The bottom coordinate is redefined to be one plus the value specified from the window because the Turbo C console functions scroll the window up one line if you write a character into the lower right character position. That position is precisely where the lower right border character must be written. After the frame is drawn, the window is redefined with corner positions inside the frame. This lets the console output functions write to the window without overwriting the frame characters. The array of **text_info** structures remembers the original definition, however, to accommodate restoring the video save buffer.

Window Shadows

Giving a window a shadow gives visual emphasis to the window. The shadow is a dark border to the right and bottom of the window that gives the illusion of a shadow of the window cast by a light from above and to the left of the user. Shadows can be transparent or opaque. A transparent shadow allows the characters under the shadow to be seen. This effect is achieved by displaying the shadow area with light gray characters on a black background. If the window pops up over text that has color in the foreground or background, the shadow is apparent. An opaque shadow is made of black spaces; the characters do not show through. You can use the two shadow formats to add different levels of emphasis to your displays.

Notices and Error Messages

The **error_message** function in window.c is there because you will need to send error notices to the user from time to time. The process is so universal that it warrants its own dedicated function. Associated with it is the **notice** function. The two functions use different colors, and the **error_message** function includes sounding the audible alarm, but the functions are otherwise the same. They both call the **post_message** function, which computes the window's size and center position on the screen, based on the length of the one-line message passed to it. Then it displays the message in the window along with a prompt to the user to press any key. When the user presses a key, the function closes the window and returns.

Listing 4.1: window.h

```
/* ---------- window.h ----------- */

void open_window(int,int,int,int,int,int,int,int);
void close_window(void);
void error_message(char *);
void notice(char *);
int yesno(char *);

#define MAX_WINDOWS 10          /* maximum windows open at once */
#define TRUE 1
#define FALSE 0
```

Listing 4.2: window.c

```
/* ----------------------- window.c --------------------- */
#include <stdlib.h>
#include <conio.h>
#include <string.h>
#include <bios.h>
#include <ctype.h>
#include "window.h"
#include "keys.h"

```

continued...

...from previous page

```
/* --------- window definition structures ----------- */
struct text_info windows [MAX_WINDOWS];
struct text_info wkw;   /* working window */
/* ----------------- window dressing ---------------------- */
struct {
    int frame;   /* true if the window has a frame             */
    int shadow;  /* 0 if the window has no shadow              */
                 /* 1 if the window has a transparent shadow */
                 /* 2 if the window has an opaque shadow     */
    char *wsave; /* points to the video memory save buffer   */
} dressing [MAX_WINDOWS];
int curr_wnd = 1;       /* current window */
static void clear_window(void);
static int post_message(char *, int, int, int);

/* ----------- open a new window -------------- */
void open_window(left,top,right,bottom,foreg,backg,frame,shadow)
{
    int bfsize;
    int sinc = 0;

    if (shadow && right < 80 && bottom < 25)
        sinc = 1;
    bfsize = (bottom-top+1+sinc) * (right-left+1+sinc) * 2;
    if (curr_wnd < MAX_WINDOWS) {
        if (curr_wnd == 1)
            gettextinfo(windows);
        else    {
            windows[curr_wnd-1].curx = wherex();
            windows[curr_wnd-1].cury = wherey();
        }
        if ((dressing[curr_wnd].wsave=malloc(bfsize))!=NULL) {
            gettext(left, top, right+sinc, bottom+sinc,
                dressing[curr_wnd].wsave);
            window(left,top,right,bottom);
            textcolor(foreg);
            textbackground(backg);
            gettextinfo(&wkw);
            dressing[curr_wnd].frame = frame;
            dressing[curr_wnd].shadow = shadow;
            clear_window();
```

continued...

...from previous page

```
            windows[curr_wnd++] = wkw;
        }
    }
}

/* --------- window frame characters ---------------- */
#define NW   (dressing[curr_wnd].frame == 1 ? '\xda' : '\xc9')
#define NE   (dressing[curr_wnd].frame == 1 ? '\xbf' : '\xbb')
#define SE   (dressing[curr_wnd].frame == 1 ? '\xd9' : '\xbc')
#define SW   (dressing[curr_wnd].frame == 1 ? '\xc0' : '\xc8')
#define SIDE (dressing[curr_wnd].frame == 1 ? '\xb3' : '\xba')
#define LINE (dressing[curr_wnd].frame == 1 ? '\xc4' : '\xcd')

/* ------- blank the window and draw its frame -------- */
static void clear_window(void)
{
    int x, y;
    int ht = wkw.winbottom - wkw.wintop + 1;
    int wd = wkw.winright - wkw.winleft + 1;
    char line[81];

    clrscr();
    if (dressing[curr_wnd].shadow)  {
        textcolor(LIGHTGRAY);
        textbackground(BLACK);
        window(wkw.winleft,wkw.wintop,wkw.winright+1,
                    wkw.winbottom+2);
        for (y = 2; y < ht+1; y++)  {
            gotoxy(wd+1,y);
            putch(dressing[curr_wnd].shadow == 2 ? ' ' :
                *(dressing[curr_wnd].wsave+((wd+1)*y-1)*2));
        }
        gotoxy(2, ht+1);
        for (x = 0; x < wd; x++)
            putch(dressing[curr_wnd].shadow == 2 ? ' ' :
            *(dressing[curr_wnd].wsave+(((wd+1)*ht+1)+x)*2));
        window(wkw.winleft,wkw.wintop,wkw.winright,
                    wkw.winbottom);
        textattr(wkw.attribute);
    }
```

continued...

...from previous page

```
    if (dressing[curr_wnd].frame)    {
        window(wkw.winleft,wkw.wintop,wkw.winright,
                    wkw.winbottom+1);
        memset(line+1,LINE,wd-2);
        line[0] = NW;
        line[wd-1] = NE;
        line[wd] = '\0';
        cputs(line);
        for (y = 2; y < ht; y++)    {
            gotoxy(1,y);
            putch(SIDE);
            gotoxy(wd,y);
            putch(SIDE);
        }
        line[0] = SW;
        line[wd-1] = SE;
        cputs(line);
        window(wkw.winleft+1,wkw.wintop+1,wkw.winright-1,
                    wkw.winbottom-1);
        wkw.curx = wkw.cury = 1;
        gotoxy(1, 1);
    }
}

/* ------------ close a window ------------------ */
void close_window(void)
{
    int sinc = 0;

    if (dressing[curr_wnd-1].shadow)
        sinc = 1;
    if (curr_wnd > 1)    {
        puttext(wkw.winleft,wkw.wintop,
            wkw.winright+sinc,
            wkw.winbottom+sinc,
            dressing[curr_wnd-1].wsave);
        free(dressing[curr_wnd-1].wsave);
        wkw = windows[(--curr_wnd)-1];
        textattr(wkw.attribute);
        if (dressing[curr_wnd-1].frame)
```

continued...

...from previous page

```
                window(wkw.winleft+1,wkw.wintop+1,
                    wkw.winright-1,wkw.winbottom-1);
            else
                window(wkw.winleft,wkw.wintop,wkw.winright,
                    wkw.winbottom);
            gotoxy(wkw.curx, wkw.cury);
        }
}

/* ------- write an error message ------------- */
void error_message(char *ermsg)
{
    post_message(ermsg, YELLOW, RED, FALSE);
}

/* ------- write a notice ------------- */
void notice(char *note)
{
    post_message(note, WHITE, GREEN, FALSE);
}

/* --------- ask a question ----------- */
int yesno(char *ques)
{
    return post_message(ques, BLACK, WHITE, TRUE);
}

/* -------- post a message ------------ */
static int post_message(char *s,int foreg,int backg,int test)
{
    int c;
    int lf = (80-strlen(s)+2)/2;
    int rt = lf+max(strlen(s)+2,15);
    open_window(lf, 11, rt, 14, foreg, backg, 1, 2);
    cputs(s);
    if (backg == RED)
        putch(BELL);
    cputs(test ? "\r\n (Y/N) ..." : "\r\n any key ...");
    do  {
```

continued...

...from previous page

```
            c = bioskey(0) & 255;
        } while (test && tolower(c) != 'y' && tolower(c) != 'n');
        close_window();
        return (test && tolower(c) == 'y');
}
```

A WINDOW DEMONSTRATION

Listing 4.3 is demowind.c, a program that calls the window management functions to demonstrate their use.

The program has two poems coded as strings pointed to form two arrays of character pointers. There is nothing about this particular storage technique that is intrinsic to the window library; the method is merely the one chosen for this program.

The **main** function begins by opening a window that has a double-line frame. Then, it writes the first poem to that window by using the **cputs** function. Next, the program opens a second window that has no frame, a transparent shadow, and that overlaps the first window. Then, it writes the second poem into this window. Finally, it opens a window with a single-line frame and uses **cgets** to let you type some text. If you do not type anything (just press Enter), the program calls **error_message** to complain. If you type random text, **cgets** displays it. When you press Enter at the end of the text, the program clears the window and starts over again. If you type "end" as the first three characters in the window, the program closes the window and steps through a sequence of reading the keyboard and closing the first two windows. The last **cputs** shows that when no window is open, the entire screen is the destination for all console displays.

The Turbo C **cgets** function has some problems. It uses DOS to write to the screen, so the displays do not use the window's colors. If you press Ctrl-C or Ctrl-Break, **cgets** terminates your program and dumps you out to the DOS command line. If you press the Esc key, **cgets** displays a slash and puts the cursor on the next line in the first column of the screen (not the window). If your buffer is wider than the remaining space on the line in the window, **cgets** echoes the characters you type beyond the window. These problems are of little consequence in a demonstration program such as demowind.c, but they can be a major headache in production programs. Chapter 5 offers an improved **cgets** function that has none of these problems. The makefile at the end of this book links demowind with the new **cgets**.

Listing 4.3: demowind.c

```
/* ---------- demowind.c ------------ */

/*
 * A program to demonstrate the small window
 * library.
 */

#include <stdio.h>
#include <conio.h>
#include <string.h>
#include "window.h"

static char *poem1[] = {
    " TRAVELLER'S CURSE AFTER MISDIRECTION\r\n",
    "\r\n",
    "May they stumble, stage by stage\r\n",
    "On an endless pilgrimage,\r\n",
    "Dawn and dusk, mile after mile,\r\n",
    "At each and every step withal\r\n",
    "May they catch their feet and fall;\r\n",
    "At each and every fall they take\r\n",
    "May a bone within them break;\r\n",
    "And may the bone that breaks within\r\n",
    "Not be, for variation's sake,\r\n",
    "Now rib, now thigh, now arm, now shin,",
    "But always, without fail, THE NECK.\r\n",
    "\r\n",
    "                  Robert Graves",
    NULL
};

static char *poem2[] = {
    "            THE DARK HILLS\r\n",
    "\r\n",
    "Dark hills at evening in the west,\r\n",
    "Where sunset hovers like a sound\r\n",
    "Of golden horns that sang to rest\r\n",
    "Old bones of warriors under ground,\r\n",
    "Far now from all the bannered ways\r\n",
```

continued...

...from previous page

```
    "Where flash the legions of the sun,\r\n",
    "You fade--as if the last of days\r\n",
    "Were fading, and all wars were done.\r\n",
    "            Edwin Arlington Robinson",
    NULL
};

void main(void)
{
    char **cp;
    char txt[40];
    /* ------- a window with a double frame  ----------- */
    open_window(24, 3, 63, 19, CYAN, BLUE, 2, 0);
    for (cp = poem1; *cp; cp++)
        cputs(*cp);
    /* ---------- a frameless window ------------------- */
    open_window(5, 4, 40, 15, WHITE, GREEN, 0, 1);
    for (cp = poem2; *cp; cp++)
        cputs(*cp);
    /* ------- a window with a single frame  ----------- */
    open_window(20, 6, 60, 9, RED, WHITE, 1, 1);
    while (strncmp(txt+2,"end",3))  {
        cputs("Type text. Type 'end' when you are done");
        *txt = 38;
        gotoxy(1,2);
        if (*cgets(txt) == '\0')
            /* --------- an error message ------------- */
            error_message("Error: You didn't type anything");
        clrscr();
    }
    close_window();
    getch();
    close_window();
    getch();
    close_window();
    /* -------- this writes to the console screen ------ */
    cputs("Now it is done.");
}
```

SUMMARY

Now that you have interrupts and overlays under your belt and can put video windows into your programs, you are ready to take a pleasant side trip into the world of programming tricks and secrets. The next chapter is a potpourri of little twists and techniques that you can use to tame your PC and make it behave.

CHAPTER 5

PROGRAMMING TRICKS WITH TURBO C, MS-DOS, AND THE PC

In this chapter, you will explore the insides of the PC and DOS by extending Turbo C's approach to them. You can do more in software with a PC or AT than is generally understood, and Turbo C provides sufficient low-level hardware and DOS access to achieve these extensions.

What you need to understand:

- Interrupts
- BIOS functions
- File I/O

New subjects discussed:

- Keyboard tricks
- Cursor tricks
- Sound effects
- DOS memory structure
- Program Segment Prefix
- DOS handles

KEYBOARD TRICKS

You'd think a full-featured keyboard like the one on the AT would do everything a keyboard should do. But for some reason the BIOS firmware lacks the power to realize the full potential of the keyboard hardware.

For example, when you hold a key down it repeats at ten keys a second. That sounds fast, but when you are using it to move a cursor around the screen or scroll through a text file, the ten-key rate is agonizingly slow. At that rate, it takes eight seconds to move the cursor from one side of the screen to the other. That's too long, and nothing says the keyboard must be that slow. It just is. For another example, there are key combinations that you can press that will be ignored by BIOS. These are keys that you'd like to use, such as Ctrl-Up arrow, but BIOS has decided that you do not need them. There are other problems with the way the keyboard is integrated with BIOS and DOS as well as some extensions that you would like to have. This corner of this chapter's bag of tricks addresses these concerns.

The BIOS contains the code that reads keys and translates them into meaningful ASCII values for the programs to process. There isn't much similarity between what the keyboard transmits when you press a key and what the program sees as the keystroke, and not all key combinations are available from BIOS.

DOS is worse than BIOS. If you use DOS to read the keyboard, you cannot read the function keys. DOS ignores them. DOS does other untoward things with keystrokes. If you press Ctrl-C or Ctrl- Break while reading a key from DOS, your program aborts. There are ways to tell DOS not to do that, but they are generally unreliable, and even if you get DOS to not abort your program, DOS still wants to display a ^C token on the screen wherever the cursor is located. Most unfriendly.

By the way, DOS watches for that Ctrl-C or Ctrl-Break during writes to the console, too. You are best advised to completely avoid DOS for any and all console input and output. This advice means that you must not use many of the standard C functions in a program that must be protected from accidental termination. What is accidental termination? The user presses Ctrl-C when another key was intended. What programs must be protected? Programs that attach interrupt vectors, programs that perform complicated inter-file data base management, programs that manage on-line communications with other processors; the list is endless.

If you press the Esc key during a DOS console read, DOS displays a slash and jumps the cursor to the beginning of the next line. It doesn't matter that your program wants the cursor to stay in a field on a data entry template, for example; DOS just has its own way with that cursor.

When should you use DOS for console input/output? The best application of DOS console I/O is for filter programs that use input/output redirection and pipes. These are usually simple batch-like programs that operate from a command-line user interface. Other appropriate uses of DOS console routines are in test and demonstration programs. You will see some **printf** calls in this book, for example.

In the paragraphs that follow, you will see how to take control of the keyboard and get it to do your bidding. From now on, assume that under no circumstances will you use **scanf**, **gets**, **getchar**, **cgets**, **getc,** or the **stdin** file handle to read the keyboard. At the very least, you will use **getch**, **bioskey**, or the improved **cgets** from farther down. Preferably, you will always use the new **cgets** or another new function named **getkey** described later in this chapter.

The BIOS Keyboard Read-Ahead Buffer

An understanding of how BIOS deals with keystrokes is important for the discussions that follow. First you must have a passing acquaintance with the keyboard hardware. When you press a key, an interrupt is generated. The keyboard interrupt is attached to an interrupt request line on the 8259 interrupt controller so that interrupt 9 occurs. The interrupt vector for interrupt 9 is at location 0000:0024, and that vector originally contains the address of the BIOS keyboard interrupt service routine. Some versions of DOS (version 3.30, for example) attach the vector themselves. Many memory-resident programs attach the interrupt to watch for their hot key. Word processing programs often attach the vector. The programs developed in this and other chapters will do so as well. But all programs, if they are well behaved, will chain the interrupt vector to its former location, and eventually BIOS will be called when an interrupt 9 occurs.

When the keyboard hardware interrupt 9 vectors to the BIOS keyboard interrupt service routine, BIOS reads the keyboard and translates the scan code into a scan code/ASCII code pair of bytes and stores them in the BIOS keyboard read-ahead buffer. That buffer is located at memory address 0x40:0x1a and consists of two offset pointers and fifteen entries for keystrokes. The pointers and entries are each one word.

The first word of the BIOS keyboard read-ahead buffer is an offset to the next key value to be returned when a program requests a key from BIOS. This offset will be called the "next-off" value. The second word of the buffer is an offset to the next location where a key value will be stored when the user types one. This offset will be called the "next-on" value. The offsets are in the range 0x1e through 0x3c to correspond to the actual offsets of the key entries from the BIOS segment 0x40. When the offsets are equal, the buffer is empty. When the next-on value is logically one less [1] than the next-off value, the buffer is full. If you press a key in that condition, you will hear BIOS beep at you to say it has not accepted your key press.

Note: The phrase "logically one less" means that if the next-on offset has a value that is numerically two less than next-off, or if next-on is 0x3c (offset to the last entry in the buffer) and next-off is 0x1e (offset to the first entry in the buffer), next-on is logically one less than next-off.

Here is what happens: You press a key, any key. The keyboard interrupts whatever is going on, and the code that is pointed to by interrupt vector 9 is called. Eventually the BIOS keyboard interrupt service routine is executed. The keyboard is connected to an input port that the BIOS interrupt service routine reads. The value read from the port is called a scan code and is an integer that has no meaning to any application program you might write. The BIOS translates the scan codes into ASCII values and puts them into the circular read-ahead buffer of fifteen keys, logically incrementing the next-on offset value. When a program issues a BIOS interrupt 0x16, function 0 to read the next keystroke, BIOS removes the first unread key value from the buffer, logically incrementing the next-off offset value. BIOS decides what keys go into the buffer and what their values are. Although the buffer's key value is an eight-bit byte, BIOS encodes only seven-bit values. There are more key combinations on the keyboard than can be represented in seven bits, so BIOS codes the function keys and keypad keys as two-byte sequences with a zero value in the first byte and the scan code in the second. If you read a key with BIOS and it has a zero value, you must read another input character to see what function key was pressed. What's more, not all the key combinations are supported. No one seems to know why it works that way, but it does.

From time to time, you will need to put characters into the BIOS keyboard read-ahead buffer, or you might need to flush the buffer completely. Listing 5.1 is biosbuff.c, a set of functions that manages the BIOS keyboard read-ahead buffer for you. There are two functions: The first is called **stuffkey**, and you call it to insert a key into the buffer. The parameter is the word that will be stuffed. You should set the most significant byte to zero. Use the values defined in keys.h to insert function keys into the buffer.

The second function is called **clear_biosbuff**, and you call it with no parameters to clear the buffer. It works by setting the next-on and next-off offsets to the same value, the condition that exists when all the keys that BIOS has added to the buffer have been removed by BIOS keyboard reads from within programs. Many programs clear the read-ahead buffer in case the user has been pounding away at the keyboard before the reads are issued. Users know about the read-ahead feature of BIOS and will use it.

Sometimes a program will take an unexpected path to read a different data element and will not want the advance keystrokes from the user. For example, you might find yourself at a point in your program where a data error has occurred. You issue the error message "Abort? (Y/N)." You do not want any keys from the user until the user has read that message. This circumstance would be an appropriate time to call **clear_biosbuff**.

The prototypes for these functions are in keys.h, which is discussed in the next section.

Listing 5.1: biosbuff.c

```
/* ----------- biosbuff.c ------------ */

/*
 * Manage the BIOS keyboard read-ahead buffer
 */

#include <dos.h>
#include "keys.h"

static int far *nextoff = MK_FP(0x40,0x1a);
static int far *nexton  = MK_FP(0x40,0x1c);

```

continued...

...from previous page

```
/* --- stuff a key value into the BIOS read-ahead buffer --- */
void stuffkey(int k)
{
    if (k & 128)          /* a keys.h function key? */
        k = (k << 8) & 0x7f00;
    if (*nexton+2 == *nextoff ||
        (*nexton == 0x3c && *nextoff == 0x1e))
            return;
    poke(0x40, *nexton, k);
    *nexton += 2;
    if (*nexton == 0x3e)
        *nexton = 0x1e;
}

/* -------- clear the BIOS read-ahead buffer ---------- */
void clear_biosbuff(void)
{
    *nextoff = *nexton;
}
```

The Function Key Problem

When you press a function key, BIOS serves up the two-byte sequence described previously. The first byte is a zero and the second is a seven-bit value. What you want is a unique eight-bit value that defines the key that was pressed. If you add 128 to the second byte, what you get is a unique value that will identify the key. Listing 5.2 is keys.h, a header file with definitions for the function and keypad combinations with values that correspond to the BIOS key code plus 128. To get these values, you use BIOS to read the keyboard, and if the character is a zero, you read the next character and add 128 to it. That is a workable solution, but a bother to need to remember all the time. Listing 5.3 is keyboard.c, the source file that includes the function named **getkey**. This function will manage the keyboard input in the manner just described. All you need to do is include keys.h and use **getkey** for your keyboard reads, and the hard part is handled for you.

Listing 5.2: keys.h

```
/* ---------- keys.h ----------- */

#define RUBOUT     8
#define BELL       7
#define ESC       27

#define F1  187
#define F2  188
#define F3  189
#define F4  190
#define F5  191
#define F6  192
#define F7  193
#define F8  194
#define F9  195
#define F10 196

#define CTRL_F1  222
#define CTRL_F2  223
#define CTRL_F3  224
#define CTRL_F4  225
#define CTRL_F5  226
#define CTRL_F6  227
#define CTRL_F7  228
#define CTRL_F8  229
#define CTRL_F9  230
#define CTRL_F10 231

#define ALT_F1   232
#define ALT_F2   233
#define ALT_F3   234
#define ALT_F4   235
#define ALT_F5   236
#define ALT_F6   237
#define ALT_F7   238
#define ALT_F8   239
#define ALT_F9   240
#define ALT_F10  241

#define HOME    199
```

continued...

...from previous page

```
#define UP      200
#define PGUP    201
#define BS      203
#define FIVE    204     /* non-BIOS keystroke value */
#define FWD     205
#define END     207
#define DN      208
#define PGDN    209
#define INS     210
#define DEL     211

#define CTRL_HOME    247
#define CTRL_UP      141     /* non-BIOS keystroke value */
#define CTRL_PGUP    132
#define CTRL_BS      243
#define CTRL_FIVE    143
#define CTRL_FWD     244
#define CTRL_END     245
#define CTRL_DN      145     /* non-BIOS keystroke value */
#define CTRL_PGDN    246
#define CTRL_INS     146     /* non-BIOS keystroke value */
#define CTRL_DEL     147     /* non-BIOS keystroke value */

#define ALT_HOME     151     /* non-BIOS keystroke value */
#define ALT_UP       152     /* non-BIOS keystroke value */
#define ALT_PGUP     153     /* non-BIOS keystroke value */
#define ALT_BS       155     /* non-BIOS keystroke value */
#define ALT_FIVE     156     /* non-BIOS keystroke value */
#define ALT_FWD      157     /* non-BIOS keystroke value */
#define ALT_END      159     /* non-BIOS keystroke value */
#define ALT_DN       160     /* non-BIOS keystroke value */
#define ALT_PGDN     161     /* non-BIOS keystroke value */
#define ALT_INS      162     /* non-BIOS keystroke value */
#define ALT_DEL      163     /* non-BIOS keystroke value */

int getkey(void);
void autotype(char *);
void repeat_rate(int);
void stuffkey(int);
void clear_biosbuff(void);

extern int cgets_returnkey;
```

Listing 5.3: keyboard.c

```
/* ---------- keyboard.c ---------- */

#include <bios.h>
#include <dos.h>
#include "keys.h"

/*
 * Read a keystroke
 */
int getkey(void)
{
    int c;
    while (bioskey(1) == 0)
        geninterrupt(0x28);
    if (((c = bioskey(0)) & 255) == 0)
        c = (c >> 8) | 0x80;
    return c & 255;
}
```

The Case of the Missing Keys

There are key combinations on your keyboard that do not serve up a key value no matter what you do. For example, that five on the numeric keypad is dead unless the NumLock toggle is on. Other dead keys are Ctrl-Up Arrow, Ctrl-Down Arrow, and any of the keypad keys with the Alt key held down. The keys that do not work are indicated in keys.h with a comment. There is no reason why these keys have no meaning except that someone decided to leave them out when the original BIOS was written. Successors to the PC architecture have been forevermore stuck with those original arbitrary decisions in the name of compatibility. If you use Borland's SuperKey keyboard enhancer product, those keys magically take on meaning and have values. The values used in SuperKey are the same as those shown in keys.h. You will now see how that is done and how you can use a similar technique in your own programs.

In Chapter 2, you attached the screen saver program to the BIOS keyboard interrupt vector to watch for keystrokes. Here, you will take similar measures to extort the missing key values from the keyboard, except that you must intercept the keyboard's hardware interrupt instead of the BIOS interrupt. Listing 5.4 is newkeys.c, a program that illustrates how you extend the keyboard to access the key combinations that BIOS left out.

The newkeys.c program begins with a table named **kbxlat** that contains an entry for each of the phantom keys. The first element in each table entry is the key value that you want when the associated key is pressed. The second value is the shift code associated with the Ctrl, Alt, Right Shift, Left Shift, NumLock, Scroll Lock, Caps Lock, and Ins keys. The third value is the scan code transmitted by the keyboard for the missing keys. You will use this table to intercept the keys that BIOS has ignored.

The **main** function of newkeys.c represents your program. You would begin by attaching and chaining the keyboard interrupt in the manner shown. The interrupt service routine is called **newkb**. Your program would operate to completion, enjoying all the key values in the table. When the program was ready to terminate, it would unhook the interrupt vector and return.

The **newkb** interrupt function is executed whenever any key on the keyboard is pressed. You are interested in two values — the scan code from the keyboard and the shift status that BIOS maintains. BIOS is watching the keyboard, and when the shift status keys are pressed, BIOS posts their condition in a byte at memory location 0x40:0x17. You do not need to watch for these keys because BIOS does it for you. You need only test each scan code to see if it is in your table. If it is, and if the shift status matches the table entry, then the user has pressed one of the phantom keys. Now you need to get that key into the system.

As you learned earlier, when BIOS interprets a key, it puts the interpreted ASCII value into a read-ahead buffer in low memory. The buffer is a circular queue with fifteen key value entries, and you need to get your new key values into it. The **newkb** interrupt service routine calls the **stuffkey** function, and that function puts the key into the buffer.

With that action, you have extended the usefulness of your keyboard to accept more keystrokes than in the original design. If you want to have more values, you can add entries to the table. Be careful that the return values you select do not collide with any of those in keys.h.

Listing 5.4: newkeys.c

```
/* ----------- newkeys.c ---------- */
#include <stdio.h>
#include <conio.h>
#include <dos.h>
#include <ctype.h>
#include "interupt.h"
#include "keys.h"

static void interrupt (*oldkb)(void);

/* ---- table of keyboard code, shift keys, scan code ---- */
int kbxlat[] = {
    FIVE,      0, 76,
    CTRL_UP,   4, 72,
    CTRL_FIVE, 4, 76,
    CTRL_DN,   4, 80,
    CTRL_INS,  4, 82,
    CTRL_DEL,  4, 83,
    ALT_HOME,  8, 71,
    ALT_UP,    8, 72,
    ALT_PGUP,  8, 73,
    ALT_BS,    8, 75,
    ALT_FIVE,  8, 76,
    ALT_FWD,   8, 77,
    ALT_END,   8, 79,
    ALT_DN,    8, 80,
    ALT_PGDN,  8, 81,
    ALT_INS,   8, 82,
    ALT_DEL,   8, 83,
    0
};

/* ----- ISR to translate non-keys to keys ------- */
static void interrupt newkb()
{
    static int scancode, shiftkeys, *xl;

    scancode = inportb(KBDATA);
    shiftkeys = peekb(0x40, 0x17);
```

continued...

...from previous page

```
    for (xl = kbxlat; *xl; xl += 3)
        if (scancode == *(xl+2))
            if ((shiftkeys & 0x2f) == *(xl+1))
                stuffkey(*xl);
    (*oldkb)();
}

/* ------- test the keyboard driver program -------- */
void main(void)
{
    int c;
    oldkb = getvect(KYBRD);
    setvect(KYBRD, newkb);
    while ((c = getkey()) != ESC)
        cprintf("\r\ngetkey returns %d (%c)",
                    c, isprint(c) ? c : '.');
    setvect(KYBRD, oldkb);
}
```

An Improved cgets

Turbo C includes a handy function called **cgets** that reads a string of characters from the keyboard. It has the following advantages:

- First, you specify the maximum number of characters that can be read.
- Second, it tells you how many characters were typed.
- Third, it manages backspaces and rubouts.
- Fourth, it does not put the terminating newline into the buffer.

Cgets is in the conio.h family of console functions and is from neither UNIX nor ANSI. It would appear to be in the category of functions that you could use within your window applications, but it is not. Borland took the easy way out when they wrote the **cgets** function. They used the DOS function 0x0a for buffered input, which works exactly the way the **cgets** function is described in the *Turbo C Reference Manual*. The problems are as follows: the function has all the quirks discussed before about DOS console input; your colors are not in effect for the characters that are echoed; the current window boundaries are not respected.

Enter the new **cgets**. Listing 5.5 is cgets.c, an improved version of the Turbo C **cgets** function, and you should probably use the TLIB utility to replace the old one in your library files in the Turbo C library subdirectory. Normally, it is not good practice to build nonstandard system libraries, but the **cgets** function is mostly useless, and you would rarely use it anyway.

The new **cgets** uses the same parameter and return value conventions as the Turbo C **cgets** with these extensions. It writes to the screen by using **putch**, so all its output is done within the scope of the current window and color settings. It reads the keyboard by calling the **getkey** function, so the values returned can include function keys. Like the original **cgets**, however, the **cgets** in this chapter does not put function key values in the string. Instead, it allows a function key or the Esc key to terminate the string entry the same way the Enter key does. The terminating key value is recorded in the global **cgets_returnkey** variable defined in cgets.c and declared as an external integer in keys.h. A program that uses **cgets** can test the contents of **cgets_returnkey** to see which key terminated the text entry. In Chapter 7, the data entry template software uses this feature to manage the movement of the cursor from field to field and to tell when the user has finished entering data.

The demowind.c program in Chapter 4 uses **cgets**. It works with either the version in this chapter or with the Turbo C version, but with this chapter's version, it is more reliable and maintains the color scheme of the window you opened.

Listing 5.5: cgets.c

```
/* ------------ cgets.c -------------- */

/*
 * An improved cgets function, one that works within
 * the window environment.
 */

#include <conio.h>
#include <ctype.h>
#include "keys.h"

int cgets_returnkey;

char *cgets(char *s)
```

continued...

...from previous page

```
{
    char *bf = s+2;
    int c = 0;

    while ((c = getkey()) != '\r')  {
        if (c == BS)                    /* left arrow        */
            c = '\b';                   /* same as ...       */
        if (c == '\b')              {   /* Big left arrow    */
            if (bf > s+2)   {           /* do a rubout       */
                --bf;
                cputs("\b \b");
            }
        }
        else if (isprint(c) && bf < s + *s + 1) {
            putch(c);               /* echo the keyed character */
            *bf++ = c;              /* put it in the buffer     */
        }
        else if (c==ESC || c & 0x80)    /* Esc/function key */
            break;
        else
            putch(BELL);        /* Ding! */
    }
    *bf = '\0';                 /* Null terminate the buffer   */
    s[1] = bf - s - 2;          /* Put the count in the buffer */
    cgets_returnkey = c;
    return s+2;                 /* Return pointer to data      */
}
```

Typematic Rate

When the PC was originally designed, its creators decided that the keyboard would operate at a maximum rate of ten characters per second. If you hold a key down, that is how fast it repeats. When the AT came out, it had a programmable keyboard, and one of the programmable features is the repeat rate. At first, you had to know the cryptic language of the keyboard and its output port address in order to program it, but in 1985 the BIOS was improved to include a function that would reprogram what has come to be known as the "typematic" rate.

There are two values to be dealt with in relation to the typematic rate. The first is the delay rate, the time after you first press a key that the keyboard waits before it kicks in the repeat operation. There are four values that you can program for this delay: 250, 500, 750, and 1000 milliseconds. The second value is the repeat rate expressed in characters per second. There are 31 possible values with the slowest being 2 characters per second and the fastest being 30 characters per second. The intervening values are not all whole numbers.

Listing 5.6 is typematc.c, a program that reprograms the AT typematic rate according to the parameters you define in the program. Define the DELAY parameter as 0, 1, 2, or 3 with 0 being 250 milliseconds, the shortest delay. Define the REPEAT parameter as a value in the range 0 to 31 where 0 is 30 characters per second, the fastest repeat. As published, both values are zero, giving the shortest delay and the fastest repeat rate. The program works by reprogramming the AT's keyboard. Some versions of BIOS include interrupt 0x16, function 03, subfunction 05 to do this for you, but because many machines do not have this later improvement in the BIOS, you are using the C language code to reprogram the keyboard yourself.

Listing 5.6: typematc.c

```
/* ------------- typematc.c -------------- */

/*
 * A program to reprogram the AT keyboard typematic rate
 */

#include <dos.h>
#include "interupt.h"

#define DELAY  0 /* delay factor after 1st keystroke:
                    0,1,2,3 = 250,500,750,1000 milliseconds */
#define REPEAT 0 /* repeat rate for keystrokes:
                       0 to 22 = 30 cps to 4 cps (approx)   */

/* ------- local prototypes ------- */
static void waitforkb(void);
static void sendkb(int);

void main(void)
```

continued...

...from previous page

```
{
    waitforkb();
    disable();
    waitforkb();
    enable();
    outportb(KBSTATUS, 0xad);
    waitforkb();
    sendkb(0xf3);
    sendkb((DELAY << 5) | REPEAT);
    waitforkb();
    outportb(KBSTATUS, 0xae);
}

static void waitforkb(void)
{
    int ct = 0;
    while (--ct)
        if ((inportb(KBSTATUS) & 2) == 0)
            break;
}

static void sendkb(int c)
{
    int ct = 10000;
    outportb(KBDATA, c);
    while (--ct)
        ;
    outportb(KBSTATUS, 0xae);
}
```

The typematic problem is more complex on PCs and XTs. The older keyboards are not programmable, and you have to solve the problem with software that runs along with your program.

When you press a key, an interrupt occurs and the interrupt service routine reads the data port of the keyboard. Here's the interesting part: When the user releases the key, a different code is delivered when you read the port, a code that consists of the original scan code with the most significant bit set on. With this value, you can tell when the key has been released. As a consequence, you can build your own delay and repeat rates in software. The following paragraphs show you how.

Listing 5.7 is fastkeys.c, a memory-resident program that speeds up the keyboard on a PC or XT. It will work on an AT as well, but with the versatility of the AT keyboard, it hardly seems worth the trouble, unless, of course, you want the keyboard running faster than 30 keys per second. You run the program from the command line. You can specify a command-line parameter that controls the speed somewhat. The default parameter is 1, and it delivers a typematic rate of about 26 characters per second, close to the 30 cps maximum of the programmable AT keyboard. Higher parameters give faster rates. Anything higher than 3 becomes too fast to control, but you can experiment with it. The program works as follows.

When you load fastkeys, it attaches the timer, keyboard hardware, and BIOS keyboard interrupt vectors. Then it declares itself resident and terminates. When you press a key, the **newkb** interrupt service routine is executed. It reads the keyboard data port to see if the interrupt is the result of a key release by the user. If so, **newkb** clears a flag that tells the program that keys are being automatically repeated and resets the typematic delay timer variable. If the key is a key press rather than a release, the program looks to see if it is one of the eight null keys. These are keys that do not generate BIOS codes but are used along with other keys or to set keyboard modes. The null keys are Ctrl, Alt, both Shifts, Caps Lock, Num Lock, Scroll Lock, and Break. No action is taken if the key press is one of these. If the key is anything else, a flag is set to tell the program that automatic key repeats are to be generated.

When a program requests a key from BIOS, the **newkeyboard** interrupt service routine is executed. It chains to the BIOS routine and then, if the caller's request was for a keyboard read, the value returned from BIOS is remembered as the value that will be automatically repeated.

For every tick of the clock, the **newtimer** interrupt service routine checks to see if a repeat value has been picked up from BIOS and if the keyboard hardware interrupt is saying that a key is being held down. If these two conditions are true, the delay timer variable is tested. If it is not zero, it is decremented and the routine returns. If the counter is zero, the routine calls **stuffkey** to insert the remembered key value into the BIOS keyboard read-ahead buffer. The calls to **stuffkey** are repeated for as many times as was specified on the command line when fastkeys was executed.

The effect is as follows. Your keyboard repeats at 10 characters per second. If no higher repeat rate is specified on the command line, the fastkeys memory-resident program will add one more duplicate character for every tick of the clock until the key is released. Because the clock ticks at about 18 times per second, that is how many characters will be added. The theoretical character rate will then be (10 + 18 * P) where P is the command-line parameter. This rate will be influenced by other factors, such as the time it takes your program to get around to reading the keyboard.

Listing 5.7: fastkeys.c

```
/* ---------- fastkeys.c ----------- */

#include <dos.h>
#include <stdlib.h>
#include "interupt.h"
#include "keys.h"

#define TICKS 6

static int lastscan = 0;
static int stuffing = 0;
static int keyrate = 1;
static int ticker = TICKS;

static void (interrupt far *oldtimer)(void);
static void interrupt (*oldkb)(void);
static void interrupt (*oldkeyboard)(void);

static void interrupt far newtimer(void);
static void interrupt newkb(void);
static void interrupt newkeyboard(IREGS);

/* ------- timer interrupt service routine ------- */
static void interrupt newtimer(void)
{
    static int i;

    if (lastscan && stuffing)
        if (ticker)
```

continued...

...from previous page

```
            --ticker;
        else
            for (i = 0; i < keyrate; i++)
                stuffkey(lastscan);
    (*oldtimer)();
}

static void interrupt newkb(void)
{
    static int kbfunc, i;
    static int nullkeys[] = {56,58,42,54,29,69,70,84};

    if ((kbfunc = inportb(KBDATA)) & 128)
        stuffing = 0, ticker = TICKS;
    else    {
        for (i = 0; i < 8; i++)
            if (kbfunc == nullkeys[i])
                break;
        stuffing = (i == 8);
    }
    (*oldkb)();
}

static void interrupt newkeyboard(IREGS ir)
{
    static kbfunc;

    kbfunc = (ir.ax >> 8) & 255;
    _CX = ir.cx;
    _BX = ir.bx;
    _AX = ir.ax;
    (*oldkeyboard)();
    ir.ax = _AX;
    ir.fl = _FLAGS;
    if (kbfunc == 0)
        lastscan = ir.ax;
}

void main(int argc, char *argv[])
{
```

continued...

...from previous page

```
    if (argc > 1)
        keyrate = atoi(argv[1]);
    oldtimer = getvect(TIMER);
    setvect(TIMER, newtimer);
    oldkeyboard = getvect(KEYBOARD);
    setvect(KEYBOARD, newkeyboard);
    oldkb = getvect(KYBRD);
    setvect(KYBRD, newkb);
    keep(0, 200);
}
```

Automatic Typing

Automatic typing is the ability to make the computer react as if a programmed sequence of keys had been typed by the user. To do this, you must coerce the software into thinking that it has received keystrokes from the hardware. There are many applications for this feature. The best-known use of it is found in keyboard macro programs such as SuperKey and ProKey. These programs allow you to assign a sequence of keys—a macro—to a selected keystroke. When you press the selected key, the programmed macro is typed. Many word processors and text editors include built-in keyboard macro processors.

Another use for automatic typing is to drive the operation of an external program from a parent program. You might have a word processor integrated into a document processing system. The document processor executes the word processor and causes it to open and load a file and search to a predetermined phrase. You can effect this integration seamlessly with automatic typing. You tell the keyboard input routines that your string is to be handed to the next caller for keystrokes one character at a time. The string has the commands and text that the word processor would recognize. Then you spawn the word processor, and it thinks a user is typing what automatic typing is feeding it.

You can build a clever on-line tutorial program by using automatic typing. Your tutorial program executes the applications program and commands it by way of automatic typing.

There seems to be no limit to the application of this valuable tool. The following paragraphs describe how it works.

If automatic typing were always limited to 15 keys, then implementing it would be a simple matter of stuffing the values to be typed into the BIOS keyboard read-ahead buffer and letting BIOS deliver them up when a program calls for the next key. Fifteen keys is an impractical low number, however, so automatic typing must take other measures. Listing 5.8 is autotype.c, a module with the **autotype** function that you call to effect automatic typing. You pass the function a pointer to a string that contains the keys to type. You can make several successive calls to the **autotype** function, and the keys will be typed in the order in which you pass them. Your string can include the function key values found in keys.h; the automatic typing software will translate them into values that BIOS recognizes. The **autotype** function uses a 256-byte circular buffer so your strings should not exceed that length between opportunities for the caller to relieve the buffer.

Before you call **autotype**, you can call **repeat_rate**, specifying the number of milliseconds that the system will delay between automatic keystrokes. This feature allows you to slow down the automatic typing so that a user can observe its progress.

When you first call **autotype**, it attaches the **newkb** interrupt function to the BIOS keyboard interrupt vector. Then, whenever a program calls for a key from the keyboard, **newkb** intercepts and stuffs the next key from the **autotype** buffer into the BIOS keyboard readahead buffer. When **newkb** sees that the **autotype** buffer is empty, **newkb** de-attaches itself from the BIOS keyboard interrupt vector.

Listing 5.8: autotype.c

```
/* --------- autotype.c ---------- */

/*
 * Automatic typing. Stuff a string of characters into the
 * BIOS keyboard read-ahead buffer.
 */

#include <stdio.h>
#include <dos.h>
#include <string.h>
#include "interupt.h"
#include "keys.h"

static char biosbuffer[256];
```

continued...

...from previous page

```
static char *nxton  = biosbuffer;
static char *nxtoff = biosbuffer;
static int rate = 0;
static void interrupt (*oldkb)(void) = NULL;
static void interrupt newkb(IREGS);
static void insertkey(int);
static void nextbuff(void);

/* ----- autotype a string as if from the keyboard ----- */
void autotype(char *s)
{
    while (*s)
        insertkey(*s++);
    if (oldkb == NULL)  {
        oldkb = getvect(KEYBOARD);
        setvect(KEYBOARD, newkb);
    }
}

/* ----- set repeat rate in timer ticks ------------ */
void repeat_rate(int n)
{
    delay(0);
    rate = n;
}

/* ----- put a keystroke into the autotype buffer ------ */
static void insertkey(int c)
{
    if (nxton+1 == nxtoff ||
        (nxton+1 == biosbuffer+256 && nxtoff == biosbuffer))
        return;
    *nxton++ = c;
    if (nxton == biosbuffer+256)
        nxton = biosbuffer;
}

static void interrupt newkb(IREGS ir)
{
    static kbfunc;
```

continued...

...from previous page

```

    kbfunc = (ir.ax >> 8) & 255;
    if (kbfunc < 2 && nxton != nxtoff)  {
        /* --- read or status check w/ chars in buffer --- */
        if (kbfunc == 1)    {
            /* ----- status check ------ */
            if (*nxtoff == -1)  {
                /* ---- force no character ready ----- */
                ir.fl |= ZEROFLAG;
                nextbuff();
            }
            else    {
                /* --- return character, don't advance --- */
                ir.ax = (*nxtoff) & 0xff;
                ir.fl &= ~ZEROFLAG;
            }
            return;
        }
        /* ------- read keyboard -------- */
        while (*nxtoff == -1 && nxtoff != nxton)
            nextbuff();
        if (nxtoff != nxton)    {
            if (*nxtoff > 127)  {
                ir.ax = 0;
                *nxtoff &= 0x7f;
            }
            else    {
                ir.ax = (*nxtoff) & 0xff;
                nextbuff();
                enable();
                delay(rate);
                disable();
            }
            return;
        }
    }
    /* ---- not read or status or buffer is empty ---- */
    _CX = ir.cx;
    _BX = ir.bx;
    _AX = ir.ax;
```

continued...

...from previous page

```
        (*oldkb)();
        ir.ax = _AX;
        ir.fl = _FLAGS;
}

/* ------ increment next off buffer pointer ------- */
static void nextbuff(void)
{
        nxtoff++;
        if (nxtoff == biosbuffer+256)
            nxtoff = biosbuffer;
        if (nxtoff == nxton)    {
            setvect(KEYBOARD, oldkb);
            oldkb = NULL;
        }
}
```

Listing 5.9 is demoauto.c, a program to demonstrate the automatic typing feature. It lets you program a simple keyboard macro to be automatically typed whenever your selected key is pressed. Then, as you type text, whenever you press the selected key, the string you programmed is typed for you. When you press the Esc key, the program terminates.

Listing 5.9: demoauto.c

```
/* ------------ demoauto.c ------------- */

/*
 * A program to test autotyping
 */

#include <process.h>
#include <stdio.h>
#include <conio.h>
#include "keys.h"

void main(void)
{
```

continued...

...from previous page

```
    int mkey, c;
    char macro[80];

    cprintf("\r\nPress a key to use for a macro ... ");
    mkey = getkey();
    cprintf("\r\nEnter the macro string ...\r\n");
    *macro = 78;
    cgets(macro);
    cprintf("\r\nNow type some text (Esc when done) ...\r\n");
    while ((c = getkey()) != ESC)
        if (c == mkey)
            autotype(macro+2);
        else    {
            putch(c);
            if (c == '\r')
                putch('\n');
        }
}
```

Listing 5.10 is driver.c, a program that allows you to drive another program's activity with automatic typing. For this example, the **demowind** example program from Chapter 4 has been chosen as the program to drive. The driver.c program sets the repeat rate to 500 milliseconds and calls **autotype** to load some text into the **autotype** buffer. Then the driver.c program uses the Turbo C **system** function to execute the program. The program will start up and the programmed keys will be automatically typed into the program.

Listing 5.10: driver.c

```
/* -------- driver.c ------------ */

/*
 * A program to test autotyping into another program
 */

#include <process.h>
#include <stdio.h>
#include <conio.h>
```

continued...

...from previous page

```
#include "keys.h"

void main(void)
{
      repeat_rate(500);
      autotype("I will type for you\rend\r\r\r");
      system("demowind");
}
```

Some application programs flush the BIOS keyboard read-ahead buffer before they begin to read keys. The idea is that some stray keys could be in there from who knows where. This book's biosbuff.c includes the **clear_biosbuff** function to flush the buffer. The programs will either read the keyboard status with BIOS until no keys are ready or will simply reset the BIOS keyboard read-ahead buffer offsets. These maneuvers can defeat automatic typing. To deal with the first condition, you can put the value 0xff into the buffer at places where you suspect the application is flushing the keyboard. The **newkb** function will return a "not ready" status when it finds this value in your string. In the case where you suspect the application program will reset the pointers, you can insert 15 of the 0xff tokens.

CURSOR TRICKS

There are three things you'd probably like to do to the PC's cursor. From time to time you'd like to hide it. Sometimes you'd like to change its shape. Other times you'd like to stop it from blinking. Listings 5.11 and 5.12 are cursor.h and cursor.c, the code modules that have the cursor tricks in them. The discussion that follows the listings addresses how each of the tricks works.

Listing 5.11: cursor.h

```
/* ----------- cursor.h -------- */

void hidecursor(void);
void unhidecursor(void);
void block_cursor(void);
void default_cursor(void);
void savecursor(void);
void restorecursor(void);
void normalcursor(void);
```

Listing 5.12: cursor.c

```
/* ----------- cursor.c --------- */
#include <dos.h>
#include <conio.h>
#include "cursor.h"
#include "interupt.h"

static void interrupt far (*oldkb)(void);
static void interrupt far newkb(IREGS);
static void invert_block(void);

/* ----- keyboard BIOS (0x16) functions -------- */
#define READKB 0
#define KBSTAT 1

/* ------- video BIOS (0x10) functions --------- */
#define SETCURSORTYPE 1
#define SETCURSOR     2
#define READCURSOR    3
#define READATTRCHAR  8
#define WRITEATTRCHAR 9
#define HIDECURSOR 0x20

static int cursorpos;
static int cursorshape;

/*
```

continued...

...from previous page

```
 * Low-level get cursor shape and position
 */
static void getcursor(void)
{
    _AH = READCURSOR;
    _BH = 0;
    geninterrupt(VIDEO);
}

/*
 * Save the current cursor configuration
 */
void savecursor(void)
{
    getcursor();
    cursorshape = _CX;
    cursorpos = _DX;
}

/*
 * Restore the saved cursor configuration
 */
void restorecursor(void)
{
    _AH = SETCURSOR;
    _BH = 0;
    _DX = cursorpos;
    geninterrupt(VIDEO);
    _AH = SETCURSORTYPE;
    _CX = cursorshape;
    geninterrupt(VIDEO);
}

/*
 * Make a normal cursor
 */
void normalcursor(void)
{
    _AH = SETCURSORTYPE;
    _CX = 0x0607;
```

continued...

...from previous page

```
    geninterrupt(VIDEO);
}

/*
 * Hide the cursor
 */
void hidecursor(void)
{
    getcursor();
    _CH |= HIDECURSOR;
    _AH = SETCURSORTYPE;
    geninterrupt(VIDEO);
}

/*
 * Unhide the cursor
 */
void unhidecursor(void)
{
    getcursor();
    _CH &= ~HIDECURSOR;
    _AH = SETCURSORTYPE;
    geninterrupt(VIDEO);
}

/*
 * Make a block cursor
 */
void block_cursor(void)
{
    hidecursor();
    oldkb = getvect(KEYBOARD);
    setvect(KEYBOARD,newkb);
}

/*
 * Return to the default blinking cursor
 */
void default_cursor(void)
{
```

continued...

...from previous page

```
        unhidecursor();
        setvect(KEYBOARD,oldkb);
}

/*
 * Interrupt Function to display and clear the block cursor
 */
void interrupt far newkb(IREGS ir)
{
        static int cset = 0;
        static char kfunc;

        kfunc = _AH;            /* the BIOS kb function requested */
        if (kfunc == READKB || kfunc == KBSTAT) {
            if (cset == 0)  {
                cset = 1;
                invert_block();
            }
        }
        _AX = ir.ax;
        (*oldkb)();             /* chain to old int 16  */
        ir.ax = _AX;            /* int 16 returns these */
        ir.fl = _FLAGS;
        if (kfunc == READKB && cset == 1)   {
            cset = 0;
            invert_block();
        }
}

/*
 * Invert the video attribute at the current cursor position
 */
static void invert_block(void)
{
        static int c, at;

        /* --- read attribute and character at the cursor --- */
        _BH = 0;
        _AH = READATTRCHAR;
        geninterrupt(VIDEO);
```

continued...

...from previous page

```
    c = _AX;                        /* ah = attribute, al = char */
    /* ----- swap background RGB with foreground RGB ----- */
    at = (c >> 8) & 0xff;
    at = ((at >> 4) & 7) | ((at << 4) & 0x70) | (at & 0x88);
    /* --- write attribute and character at the cursor --- */
    _CX = 1;                    /* one char to write */
    _BH = 0;                    /* page zero         */
    _BL = at;                   /* new attribute     */
    _AL = c & 0xff;             /* character         */
    _AH = WRITEATTRCHAR;
    geninterrupt(VIDEO);
}
```

Changing the Cursor's Shape

This one is easy. BIOS has a function that relates to how the 6845 CRT controller chip deals with the cursor. BIOS interrupt 0x10, function 3 lets you define the shape the cursor takes in terms of the scan lines where the cursor starts and stops. You put the start scan line in the CH register and the stop scan line in the CL register. The default cursor starts on line six and stops on line seven. These lines range from zero to seven, representing the eight-pixel depth of the character box, so the default cursor is a double line at the bottom of the box, exactly what you see when you turn the computer on.

To program a full box cursor, put this code in your program:

```
#include <dos.h>

_CX = 0x0007;              /* start on 0, stop on 7   */
_AH = 3;                   /* define cursor box       */
geninterrupt(0x10);        /* call BIOS video service */
```

To return to the default, assign 0x0607 to _CX and make the same call. Many text editor programs use a box cursor to indicate insert mode and a default cursor to indicate typeover mode. When your program exits, be sure to reset the cursor to its default configuration. It retains its shape when you return to DOS, and most folks get uncomfortable if the cursor looks unnatural at the familiar DOS prompt.

Hiding the Cursor

When you use the **cputs** and **cprintf** functions to display menus and data entry screens, you will see the cursor flash across as each line of the format is drawn. You might have a text processor that updates its status line display with every keystroke. If the cursor is allowed to flash across the screen to rewrite the status line every time the user presses a key, your poor user is going to come down with a bad case of flicker vertigo. These flashing cursors are an annoyance, and you need a way to turn the cursor off.

The traditional way to turn off the cursor is to position it to a nonexistent area on the screen. This works fine until you want to display something. The **cprintf** and **cputs** functions want to display data beginning with where the cursor points. If it points into nowhere, nothing gets displayed, so that technique for hiding the cursor is not usable. Fortunately, you have an alternative. The same function that changes the cursor's shape can be used to hide the cursor altogether. If you call BIOS's interrupt 0x16, function 3 with the 0x20 bit in the cursor start line field (register ch) set to one, you hide the cursor. All cursor movements are still operational, and all displays that depend on the cursor position still work. But the cursor is not seen. To restore the cursor, make the same call with the 0x20 bit set to zero.

The hide and unhide cursor operations are so widely required that they have been included as functions in cursor.c. Call **hidecursor** to hide the cursor and **unhidecursor** to unhide it.

Stopping the Blinking Cursor from Blinking

While we are on the subject of cursors, ask yourself why the cursor has to blink? Someone decided that the PC would work better with a blinking cursor and we are stuck with it. The earlier personal computers used video terminals with nice big steady reverse video cursor blocks. You never needed to squint and search for the cursor on a busy screen.

The 6845 CRT controller chip that drives the PC's display adaptors has the ability to generate a steady cursor, but if you attempt to reprogram it, BIOS or somebody overrides your efforts, and the cursor keeps blinking. Now you can solve that problem if you'll agree with earlier advice not to use DOS for console input/output any more.

When you start up certain popular word processors, you get a solid block cursor just like the ones on the old video terminals. Other programs allow you to set a configuration option that selects such a cursor. If the BIOS refuses to let you turn the blinking off, how is it done? The answer is that the video cursor from the 6845 chip is not used at all. You hide that cursor in the manner described earlier, and you make your own. The following paragraphs describe how.

Characters in video memory are stored as two bytes: the ASCII value of the character to be displayed and an adjacent video attribute byte. Bits zero, one, and two are the foreground color, and bits four, five, and six are the background color. The three bits of each color attribute control the red, green, and blue components. When all three bits are one, the color is solid white, and when all three are zero, the color is solid black. Bit three controls foreground intensity, and bit seven controls foreground blinking. You can look at the color values defined in Turbo C's conio.h file to see the colors that result from various bit combinations.

The solid block cursor is nothing more than the character at the current cursor position with the foreground and background colors reversed. If you are looking at a screen that has white letters on a black background, the character where the cursor is located is a black character on a white background. To get this to happen, all you need to do is determine when and where to set and reset the cursor color reversal. Knowing when to turn the cursor on and off is easy. A user needs to be aware of a cursor when he or she is about to type a character; therefore, you will turn the block cursor on just before the call to the BIOS function that reads a keyboard character. After the BIOS function returns, you will turn the cursor off. Whenever you are looking at the screen and deciding which key to press, you will see the reverse-video cursor where the cursor should be. How do you know where the cursor should be? You call BIOS and ask for the current cursor position. Even though the cursor is hidden, BIOS keeps track of its position.

In Listing 5.12, cursor.c, you will find two functions, **block_cursor** and **default_cursor**, that enable the block cursor and restore the default cursor. These functions involve the interception of the BIOS keyboard interrupt 0x16 to see when a key is to be read. These functions do not work when the Turbo C program uses DOS to read the keyboard. They do, however, work just fine if you do your own calls to BIOS to read the keyboard or, better yet, if you always use the **getkey** function described above.

The **block_cursor** function hides the blinking cursor with a call to **hidecursor** and attaches the BIOS keyboard interrupt 0x16 to the **newkb** interrupt service routine. This routine is executed whenever a program calls interrupt 0x16. It looks at the function to see that the caller is reading a key or testing the keyboard status. If so, and if the cursor has not already been displayed, the function calls **invert_block** to turn the cursor on. Then the function chains the old interrupt 0x16. After BIOS returns and if the caller was reading a key, the function calls **invert_block** again to turn the cursor off.

Listing 5.13 is demoblck.c, a program that demonstrates the block cursor. It calls **block_cursor** to change to the solid, steady block cursor. Then it opens a window, displays some text, and lets you type away. When you press the Esc key, the program calls **default_cursor** to put things back the way they were and exits. It is vitally important that you call **default_cursor** before you exit so that the interrupt vectors get unattached.

Listing 5.13: demoblck.c

```
/* --------- demoblck.c ----------- */

/*
 * A program to demonstrate the steady (non-blinking) cursor
 */

#include <stdio.h>
#include <conio.h>
#include "cursor.h"
#include "window.h"
#include "keys.h"

void main(void)
{
    int c;
    block_cursor();
    open_window(20,5, 60, 22, BLACK, YELLOW, 2, 1);
    cprintf("Enter text as on a typewriter:");
    cprintf("\r\n (Esc to quit)\r\n");
    while ((c = getkey()) != ESC)   {
        if (!(c & 0x80))
            putch(c);
```

continued...

...from previous page

```
            if (c == '\r')
                putch('\n');
        }
        close_window();
        default_cursor();
}
```

SOUND EFFECTS

The PC has a sound system. It isn't much of a system, but you can use it to achieve some interesting sound effects and thereby enhance the user interface of your programs. The audio system consists of a tiny speaker with a single voice. The small size of the speaker prevents you from making any booming, resonating, wall-rattling sound effects. The single voice limits you to one tone at a time, which places more limits on the kinds of sounds you can produce. You cannot, for example, generate a sustained musical chord on the PC.

There are MIDI and voice synthesis add-in boards for the PC that will extend the sound generation capabilities of your computer, but these are not universally accepted, and the methods of programming them vary. This book will restrict itself to the built-in audio system of the standard PC.

Sound

Sound results when something moves air back and forth with enough intensity, frequency, and duration that the vibrations sensed by your eardrums register in your brain. If a tree falls in the forest, that air is moved around whether any eardrums are nearby or not. So, in theory at least, the sound occurs. When alternating current electricity is used to vibrate a magnetic coil attached to a speaker core, the core shakes back and forth and moves air to vibrate eardrums. If you can control that movement in a way that replicates intelligible sound, you are simulating the original source of that sound. If that air vibrates the same way it does when Dexter Gordon plays the saxophone, everyone is happy.

Thomas Edison did it mechanically by having the sound source vibrate a diaphragm at the apex of a big horn. The horn converged the vibrations onto the diaphragm, which then vibrated a needle that etched a pattern of vibrations into tracks on a rotating cylinder. When that same needle was dragged through those same etched tracks on the cylinder, the etchings vibrated the needle in the same pattern, the needle vibrated the diaphragm, the diaphragm vibrated the horn, which moved air, which rattled our eardrums. The first recording to be demonstrated was the poem "Mary Had a Little Lamb" spoken in Edison's voice.

To make the PC's speaker do something resembling intelligible sound, you must jiggle it in a predefined pattern of vibrations. The most basic way for a Turbo C program to get a tone out of the speaker is this way:

```
putch(7);
```

This function sends the ASCII BEL character to the BIOS screen driver. In keeping with its origins, the PC tries at all times to look like a Teletype machine. Those ancient machines had a real metal bell that would ring when the machine received the BEL character. To perpetuate that tradition, the PC's BIOS will sound a tone on the speaker when it receives the BEL character. Many programs, including some of the ones in this book, use this feature to call attention to things such as error messages.

There are two other ways to generate sound on the PC. One way is to control the speaker directly, pulsing it whenever you want it to pulse. The other way is to use the system timer to pulse the speaker at a programmed frequency.

Controlling the Speaker Directly

To control the speaker directly, you can vibrate it by toggling a bit in the speaker register port. The frequency at which you toggle the bit will determine the frequency of the sound that is generated. This technique requires the full attention of the CPU and needs a timing strategy that is independent of the CPU's clock speed. If you simply use a software loop to manage the duration and frequency of the speaker toggle, the faster CPU will generate a higher frequency for a shorter duration. The Turbo C **delay** function, which delays processing for the number of milliseconds specified in the parameter, can be used to control frequencies up to about 500 cycles per second. The code to directly drive the speaker is as follows.

```
int spkrin  = inportb(97) & 0xfc;
int spkrout = spkrin | 2;
while (duration--)      {
        outportb(97, spkrin);
        delay(frequency);
        outportb(97, spkrout);
        delay(frequency);
}
```

The duration variable represents how long the tone is to be held. The frequency variable can be as low as one millisecond or can be zero. This is an inefficient way to drive the speaker.

Some demonstration programs simulate voice synthesis by controlling the speaker directly. The sentence to be spoken is recorded and digitized by some hardware other than standard PC stuff. The resulting bit string is saved on a disk file and then passed through a tight program that uses it to pulse the speaker in the manner shown above. The effect is that of a distant bad connection through a cheap telephone or an old Rudy Vallee record. This trick requires a lot of memory and a dedicated CPU, and is just a trick with limited application because of the demands it makes on the computer's resources.

Using the Timer to Pulse the Speaker

To use the system timer to pulse the speaker, you use the Turbo C **sound** function. This function takes an unsigned integer as the frequency (cycles per second) for the tone to be generated. The **unsound** function turns the speaker off. To control the duration of a tone, you can use the Turbo C **delay** function.

Tones

When you have your piano tuned, the tuner tries to tune it "to 440." This means that the A nearest the center of the keyboard oscillates at 440 cycles per second (hertz). Each octave on a piano contains twelve tones, with each next higher tone oscillating at a frequency greater than the one before it. The adjacent tones are called "half tones." The frequency changes are derived from a multiplier that, when applied to each next half tone, doubles the frequency with each octave, so that the next A above the middle one oscillates at 880 hertz. The multiplier that delivers this result is approximately 1.0594645, and the resulting scale is called the "Equal Tempered Chromatic Scale" and has been officially sanctioned by the American Standards Association.

The piano tuner does not stick rigidly to these mathematics. It seems that when a piano is tuned perfectly with these frequencies, the human ear rejects the perfection of the higher and lower octaves, and the piano sounds out of tune. To compensate for this peculiarity in our hearing, the tuner graduates his tuning so that the highest note is approximately one quarter tone sharp and the lowest note is approximately one quarter tone flat. (A sharp tone is one that oscillates at a higher frequency than it should. A flat tone oscillates at a lower frequency. For a demonstration go to the nearest piano bar and ask the person on the next stool to sing "Some Enchanted Evening.")

This book's tone-generating software cannot stick to the Equal Tempered Chromatic Scale either—not because of our hearing deficiency, but because of the limitations of the way the PC's timer is programmed. The timer's output registers accept a 16-bit integer value that is the quotient you get by dividing the frequency of the desired tone into 1,193,180. The **sound** function takes care of all this, but accepts as its argument only the integer part of the frequency. The software can, therefore, get only close to the true frequency of a note. As it turns out, the software can get close enough for most of us. The piano tuner and concert master can probably hear the difference, but most of us cannot. Music is only one of the ways you can use the PC's audio system. You will probably use it for music less often than for interesting sound effects. Its low fidelity and single voice make for some pretty dull music. But there are some other neat tricks you can do.

A Noisemaker

Listing 5.14 is tune.c, a program that demonstrates only some of the ways you can use the **sound** function to drive the speaker. The program consists of several demonstrations, the first two of which are musical while the others are sound effects.

To begin, the program computes eight octaves worth of musical notes. Next there is a call to **delay** with a zero parameter to allow the **delay** function to synchronize with the CPU speed. Then the program plays a C7 arpeggio, which is a run up the scale, repeating the notes C, E, G, and B-flat in each octave. The arpeggio then comes down, with a rippling effect followed by a trill of the notes C and D with a sustained C to lead you into the tune you are about to play. If the program could fire up a candelabra, it would.

Next comes a tune taken from the arrays named **mary** and **m1**. The **mary** array contains integer offsets to notes to be played. The **m1** array contains an entry for each note to compute its duration. Each entry indicates the number of 250-millisecond quarter-note times to sustain its note. The song is "Mary Had a Little Lamb." You have come full circle. You can change the song by changing the arrays. Because the song is in the key of F, the C7 arpeggio from before leads into it. So much for the music.

After the concert, the program demonstrates three different sound effects. The first is a bubbly effect that comes from a random note generator. The bubbly effect is a factor of the two-octave spread starting at the sixth octave and the random 100 millisecond delay between notes. The second effect is what is known as a "Bronx Cheer" and is not found in programs said to be user friendly. It works just like the happier bubbly effect but in the bottom two octaves with a random delay of only 10 milliseconds.

The third effect is a siren. It does not use the notes in the scale but instead computes each next frequency by tracing a sine wave with a spread of 2000 points peak-to-peak and adjusting it to be between 1300 and 3300 cycles per second. This effect does not call the **playnote** function like the others do because the siren effect works best if you do not call **nosound** between calls to **sound**.

By playing with these demonstrations, you can generate many different sound effects that can enhance your programs. Developers of game programs are probably the most prolific users of the PC's little speaker. You should exercise some judgement in how and how often you assault your business users with cute noise pollution. Blow them out of their leather executive chairs, and they'll stop using your stuff.

Listing 5.14: tune.c

```
/* ------------- tune.c ---------------- */

#include <stdio.h>
#include <stdlib.h>
#include <math.h>
#include <dos.h>
#include <string.h>
#include <time.h>

float notes [8] [12];    /* six octaves of notes */

void playnote(float, int);

/* ----- Notes for Mary Had a Little Lamb in F --------- */
int mary[] =
    {9,7,5,7,9,9,9,7,7,7,9,12,12,9,7,5,7,9,9,9,9,7,7,9,7,5};

/* ----- Quarter note count for each note in Mary ------ */
int m1[] =
    {1,1,1,1,1,1,2,1,1,2,1, 1, 2,1,1,1,1,1,1,1,1,1,1,1,1,4};

/* --------- C7 chord (C, E, G, B-flat --------- */
int C7[] = {0,4,7,10};

void main(void)
{
    int oct, nt, dl, i;
    float value = 16.35;
    float x;

    /* ------ build the note values ------ */
    for (oct = 0; oct < 8; oct++)
        for (nt = 0; nt < 12; nt++) {
            notes[oct] [nt] = value;
            value *= 1.0594645;
        }
    delay(0);
    /* ---------- C7 Arpeggio ----------- */
    for (oct = 2; oct < 8; oct++)
```

continued...

...from previous page

```
        for (nt = 0; nt < 4; nt++)
            playnote(notes[oct][C7[nt]], 150);
    for (oct = 7; oct > 1; --oct)
        for (nt = 0; nt < 4; nt++)
            playnote(notes[oct][C7[nt]], 100);
    /* --------- C, D trill ------------ */
    for (i = 0; i < 7; i++) {
        playnote(notes[4][0], 100);
        playnote(notes[4][2], 100);
    }
    /* ------- hold a C for 3 beats -------- */
    playnote(notes[4][0], 750);
    /* --------- play a tune in F ---------- */
    oct = 4;
    for (i = 0; i < sizeof mary / sizeof(int); i++)
        playnote(notes[oct][mary[i]], m1[i] * 250);
    delay(500);
    /* -------- bubbly sound effects ------ */
    randomize();
    for (i = 0; i < 50; i++)    {
        oct = random(2) + 5;
        nt = random(12);
        dl = random(100);
        playnote(notes[oct][nt], dl);
    }
    delay(500);
    /* ------- raspberries -------- */
    for (i = 0; i < 200; i++)   {
        oct = random(2);
        nt = random(12);
        dl = random(10);
        playnote(notes[oct][nt], dl);
    }
    delay(500);
    /* ----------- siren --------- */
    for (x = 0; x < 20; x += 0.02)  {
        sound((unsigned)(sin(x) * 1000.0) + 2300.0);
        delay(5);
    }
    nosound();
```

continued...

...from previous page

```
}

void playnote(float nt, int dl)
{
    unsigned ctr;

    ctr = (unsigned) (nt + 0.5);
    sound(ctr);
    delay(dl);
    nosound();
}
```

TRICKS WITH DOS

DOS is a complex program with many jobs to perform. DOS provides the COMMAND.COM interface to the user to manage programs and data files. DOS provides a set of utility programs to further enhance the user's administration of the computer. DOS manages the file system with a set of functions a program can call. DOS manages the environment in which programs operate. To support these many jobs, DOS maintains a set of internal data structures and algorithms. By understanding how these structures and algorithms are formed and how they operate, you can use them to your advantage. This section addresses a number of things you can do with Turbo C programs that take advantage of this knowledge.

DOS Memory Structure

You can gain an understanding of the operating environment of Turbo C programs by looking at the environment in which all programs operate. DOS was designed to support the execution of a single task at a time. The operating system manages the loading and execution of a task and responds to requests for input and output services. It manages the placement of disk directories and files, deals with the system clock, writes to the system printer, writes to the video console, and returns characters typed at the keyboard. DOS is, in essence, a hierarchical file and unit-record device server that supports a single user running a single task. It serves that purpose well.

When DOS is first booted, and before any programs are executed, the memory space from 0 to the 640K upper limit supported by the PC (or whatever your machine contains) is allocated as shown in Figure 5.1. The lower 0x400 memory locations are reserved for interrupt vectors. Above the vectors is the DOS program. Next are device driver programs that are loaded when DOS is booted. For example, if you use a RAM disk or the ANSI.SYS console driver, those device drivers are located above DOS. Above the device drivers is the resident portion of the DOS command processor program. This program processes the DOS command line and executes programs, and it is split into a resident portion and a transient portion. The Transient Program Area (TPA) is above the resident command processor. When the user runs a program from the command line, the program is loaded into the TPA. At the top of the TPA is the transient portion of the command processor. A user's program is allowed to use the memory that the transient command processor occupies. If that memory is used, the resident command processor will reload the transient command processor when the user's program terminates.

When the command processor loads a program, the program begins execution. When the program needs DOS support, such as for a file operation, it calls DOS by invoking a software interrupt and passes function parameters in registers. DOS takes over and executes the function. The calling program remains suspended until the DOS function is completed. The results of DOS functions are returned in registers and in the setting of the carry flag.

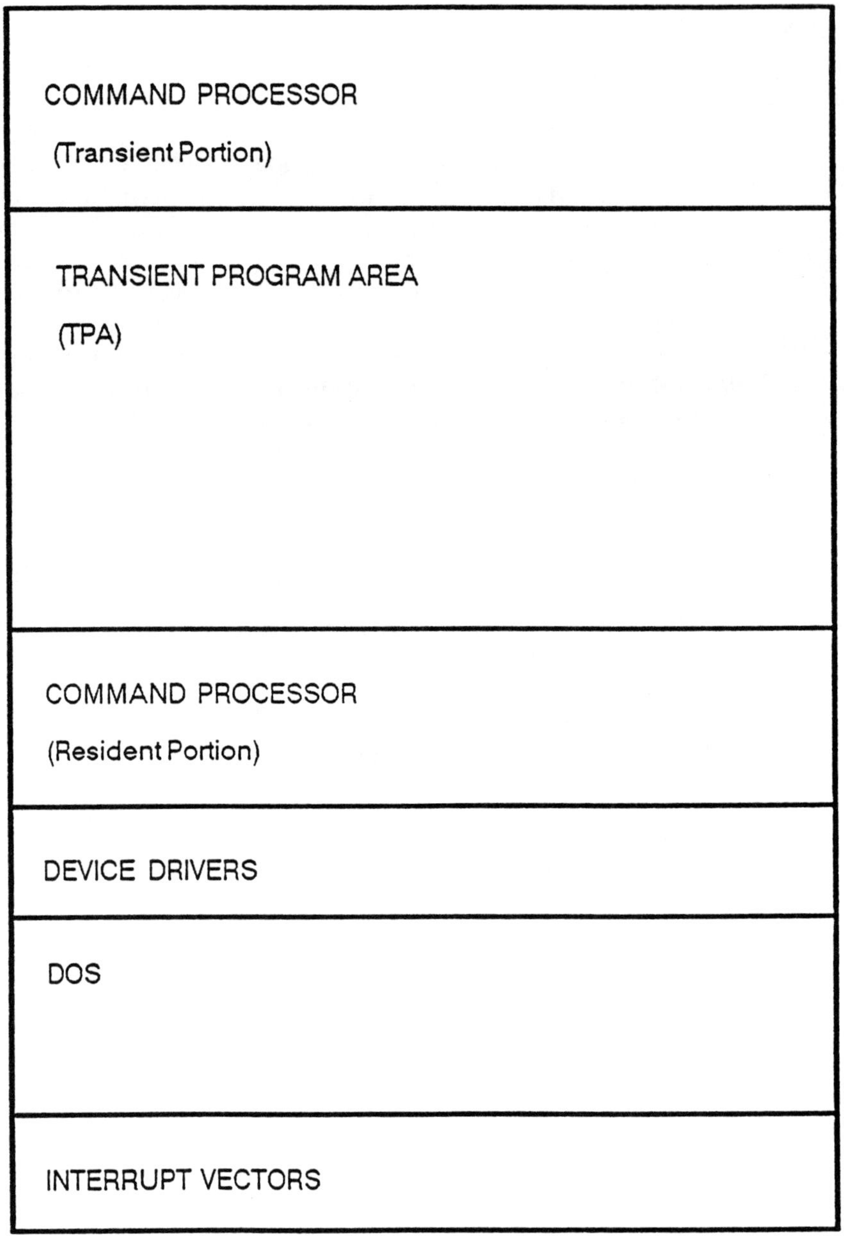

Figure 5.1 The DOS Memory Map

The DOS Memory Allocation Chain

When DOS runs a program, DOS allocates two blocks of memory, one for the program itself and one for the program's copy of the DOS environment variable space. Programs themselves can call upon DOS to allocate memory. All such allocations are made from the DOS-maintained Memory Allocation Chain. A DOS-allocated block of memory consists of a 16-byte Memory Control Block (MCB) followed by the memory block that is allocated. The Memory Allocation Chain is a set of one or more MCBs. The MCB contains the following fields:

- A one-byte token that identifies the MCB. All but the last MCB in the chain will have the value 0x4d in this token. The last MCB will have the token value 0x5a.

- The two-byte PSP address of the process that owns the memory. If a memory block is free, this field has a zero value.

- The two-byte size of the block in paragraphs. This size does not include the MCB.

The MCB is followed immediately by the memory block that it represents. MCB-memory block sets are contiguous in memory. The segment address of the next MCB can be computed from the address and contents of the current MCB. The MCB's address plus the size of the memory block plus one will equal the address of the next MCB in the chain. If you have the address of the first memory block allocated by DOS, you can trace the chain.

DOS has an undocumented function that can be used to derive the address of the first MCB in its chain. This function, number 0x52, returns a segment address in the **es** register and an offset in the **bx** register. The effective address of this segment:offset pair minus two is the address of a word that is the segment address of the first MCB in the DOS memory allocation chain. A program can begin at this address and walk through the chain. In later chapters, you will use this chain-walking technique.

Field	Offset
INT Call to DOS Process Terminator	0000
Top of Memory Segment Address	0002
0	0004
Call Instruction to DOS Function Handler	0005
Terminate Handler Address (INT 0x22)	000A
Ctrl – Break Handler Address (INT 0x23)	000E
Critical Error Handler Address (INT 0x24)	0012
Segment Address of Parent Process's PSP	0016
File Handle Array	0018
Segment Address of Environment Block	002C
Stack Address at Time of DOS Function Call	002E
Size of File Handle Array	0032
Segment:Offset Address of File Handle Array	0034
Reserved	0038
File Control Block # 1	005C
File Control Block # 2	006C
Command Tail / Disk Transfer Area	0080

Figure 5.2 The Program Segment Prefix (PSP)

The Program Segment Prefix

The PSP is a 256-byte control area at the front of every program in memory. The prefix contains fields that DOS uses to manage the processing environment of the program. Figure 5.2 shows the format of the PSP, and the following discussion addresses each of its fields. Note that many of these fields are not officially acknowledged by Microsoft or IBM. They are used in the manner described here, but their use or modification by applications programs is neither endorsed nor sanctioned by the vendors. Except where otherwise specified, these characteristics are true for the versions of DOS currently in use—versions 2.0, 2.1, 2.11, 3.0, 3.1, 3.2, 3.3, 4.0, and the DOS 3.X Box in OS/2. It is safe to use the PSP fields documented here in the manner discussed.

INT Call to Process Terminator (PSP:0)

This field contains an INT 0x20 machine instruction; its original purpose was to support programs that were converted from CP/M to DOS. Under CP/M, programs terminated themselves with a call or jump to memory location 0. Now the instruction is often used as a signature that determines if a DOS Memory Control Block points to a PSP.

Top of Memory Segment Address (PSP:2)

When a program is executed, DOS allocates a block of memory into which the program is loaded. This field contains the segment address of the top of that block of memory.

Terminate Handler Address (PSP:0xa)

When a program is executed, DOS saves the previous contents of the interrupt 0x22 vector in this field. When the program terminates, DOS restores the vector by using this saved field. The 0x22 interrupt vector usually points to the DOS program termination handler unless a parent program has it intercepted when the program associated with this PSP is executed.

Ctrl-Break Handler Address (PSP:0xe)

When a program is executed, DOS saves the previous contents of the interrupt 0x23 vector in this field. When the program terminates, DOS restores the vector by using this saved field. The 0x23 interrupt vector usually points to the DOS Ctrl-Break handler unless a parent program has it intercepted when the program associated with this PSP is executed.

Critical Error Handler Address (PSP:0x12)

When a program is executed, DOS saves the previous contents of the interrupt 0x24 vector in this field. When the program terminates, DOS restores the vector by using this saved field. The 0x24 interrupt vector usually points to the DOS critical error handler unless a parent program has it intercepted when the program associated with this PSP is executed.

Note that DOS restores the previous three vectors when a memory-resident program terminates and declares itself resident. If the program needs to intercept these interrupts, it must attach itself to them each time it is popped up.

Segment of Parent's PSP (PSP:0x16)

The program that owns this PSP was executed as the result of another program's call to DOS. The executing program is called the parent program. Usually the parent program is the DOS command processor, COMMAND.COM, although any program can be the parent of another. This field in the PSP contains the PSP segment address of the parent program.

The command processor has no parent other than DOS; therefore, this field in the command processor's PSP contains the segment address of the command processor's own PSP, which is effectively a pointer to itself.

File Handle Table (PSP:0x18)

This field is an array of twenty bytes, each of which represents a file handle. When a program opens a file, DOS returns a handle for the program to use when it calls DOS to read and write records in the file. (C programs that use the stream I/O functions do not directly address this handle— they use the FILE pointer defined in stdio; however, the standard C library functions that support stream I/O use these handles in a manner that hides them from the calling program.) These file handles are subscripts into this array. The elements of this array are subscripts into a DOS array of file control tables.

Environment Block Segment Address (PSP:0x2c)

This field is the segment address of the environment block that DOS establishes for a program when the program is executed. The environment block is an allocated block of memory that can be deallocated by a task if it has no need for the environment settings.

Stack Address during DOS Function Calls (PSP:0x2e)

When a program calls a DOS function, DOS saves the program's current stack segment and pointer registers in this field. Then DOS switches to its own stack for the execution of the function. Before returning to the program, DOS uses the saved values in this field to restore the program's stack segment and pointer registers.

Size of File Handle Table (PSP:0x32)

This field is an integer count of the number of entries in the file handle table. Normally, this count contains the value 20. This field has no value or use in versions of DOS before version 3.0.

Address of File Handle Table (PSP:0x34)

This field is a long pointer to the file handle table; its segment value is usually the same as the PSP's segment address, and its offset is usually 0x18. This field has no value or use in versions of DOS before version 3.0.

The previous two fields will allow a program to extend the maximum of 20 files that it can have concurrently open. By allocating a longer table, putting its entry count and address in these fields, and copying the 20 values from the PSP into the new program, a program can increase its maximum file open count to that specified in the FILES= statement of the CONFIG.SYS file in the boot disk's root directory.

File Control Block #1 (PSP:0x5c)

This field is a file control block built by DOS if the command line that executes a program has a file name as its first parameter.

File Control Block #2 (PSP:0x6c)

This field is a file control block built by DOS if the command line that executes a program has a file name as its second parameter.

The previous two fields are used only by programs that use the DOS File Control Block disk file functions. Most contemporary programs use the system of file handles supported by DOS.

Command Tail / Disk Transfer Area (PSP:80)

When the program is executed, everything on the command line, beginning with the second character after the program's name, is fed into a string of words in the command tail. Leading and any extra white space is eliminated. The first byte of the command tail is a count of characters the tail contains.

Once the program is underway, this field is the Disk Transfer Area, the read and write buffer for files opened under the File Control Block DOS functions. This field is also used by the DOS functions that manipulate file directories.

Finding Your Program's Files

There are many times when your program's executable files are on a drive or in a subdirectory other than the one currently logged. For example, you might have a test editor program in one place and your text files in another. You would log into the drive:directory where you keep your files and run the program from where you keep it.

If the only program file involved is the .EXE file, there is no problem. You maintain a DOS path to the program's location, or you give its location as an unambiguous DOS path ahead of the program's name on the command line. But often a program needs other files not related to the data files but related specifically to the program. Examples are files with configuration tables, on-line help text files, and program overlays. The program needs to determine at run time where these files are.

You have three different ways to find your program files. You can name the program's path in an environment variable dedicated to the program, you can search the DOS path, or you can derive the path from the manner in which the program is executed.

From an Environment Variable

To use an environment variable, you give it a name and require the user to issue the DOS SET command either from the startup AUTOEXEC.BAT file or the command line prior to running the program. Then your program uses the **getenv** function to read the path and stick it on the front of the file name. This approach has problems, however. If you put the SET command in the AUTOEXEC.BAT file, the environment variable becomes a permanent fixture in the environment space of all programs, not just the one that needs it. It is not uncommon to find programs from different sources using the same environment variable mnemonic name. Many language products use the INCLUDE environment variable name to tell the compiler where the included files are to be found, for example. If you try to issue the SET command from the command line before the program is run, you might find that there is no room for it. The environment space begins with the greater of 256 bytes or the size allocated before any programs are executed. If you fill it up in the AUTOEXEC and then load some TSR programs, you will find that the environment space cannot grow to accept any more variables.

From the Path

You can read the PATH environment variable and search the paths specified in there. Paths are separated by semicolons in the text of the PATH variable. This approach has a few drawbacks. Your program's path gets into the path searched by all programs and DOS. There is a perceptible performance penalty whenever you execute a program. The more paths to look through, the longer it takes. If your program is run frequently, it might be worth it. If it is run only occasionally, you might not want to take this tack.

From the Command Line

The most foolproof way to find your program files is to search in this sequence. First look in the current logged on subdirectory. The user might be logged into where the program lives. If the files are not there, Search the DOS path. At the user's option, the program could be in the path. If the path does not help you find the files, you next figure out where the program was run from. This is a matter of interpreting the string passed to your program as **argv[0]**. This string (in DOS 3.x) is the unambiguous path to where the program's executable .EXE or .COM file is located followed by the program's file name. For example, if your program is on the C: drive in subdirectory \BIN\LOCAL and is named YOURPROG.EXE, the **argv[0]** parameter points to this string:

```
C:\BIN\LOCAL\YOURPROG.EXE
```

As you can see, the characters ahead of the program's name are the path. This position can be found by searching for the last (right-most) occurrence of the backslash that terminates the last subdirectory name.

Listing 5.15 is findpath.c, a program that searches for a named file following the sequence just described. You run it by naming the file you want on the command line. The **main** function calls the **findpath** function, which returns a pointer to the path in which the file is found or a NULL pointer if the file cannot be found. To use this function in your own programs, delete the **main** function from findpath.c and call the **findpath** function in the same manner.

Listing 5.15: findpath.c

```
/* ------------- findpath.c --------------- */

/*
 * A function to find where a file is located.
 */

#include <stdio.h>
#include <stdlib.h>
#include <dos.h>
#include <string.h>
#include <io.h>
#include <dir.h>

static char path[65];

char *findpath(char *fname)
{
    char *pp, *pathenv;

    /* ---- see if the file is in the current directory ---- */
    if (access(fname, 0) == 0)  {
        getcwd(path, 64);
        if (path[strlen(path) - 1] != '\\')
            strcat(path, "\\");
        return path;
    }
    /* --------- search the path for the file ---------- */
    if ((pathenv = getenv("PATH")) != NULL) {
        while (*pathenv)    {
            pp = path;
            memset(path, '\0', sizeof path);
            while (*pathenv && *pathenv != ';')
                *pp++ = *pathenv++;
            if (*pathenv)
                pathenv++;
            if (*(pp - 1) != '\\')
                *pp++ = '\\';
            strcpy(pp, fname);
            if (access(path, 0) == 0)   {
                *pp = '\0';
```

continued...

...from previous page

```
                return path;
            }
        }
    }
    /* --- check the directory where the program was run --- */
    strcpy(path, *_argv);
    pp = strrchr(path, '\\') + 1;
    strcpy(pp, fname);
    if (access(path, 0) == 0)   {
        *pp = '\0';
        return path;
    }
    return NULL;
}

#ifdef DEMOPATH
void main(int argc, char *argv[])
{
    char *fp;

    if (argc > 1)   {
        fp = findpath(argv[1]);
        printf("\nThe path is %s",
            fp ? fp : "nowhere to be found");
    }
}
#endif
```

Getting More Than 20 Handles for Your Program

The designers of DOS decided that your program needs no more than 20 files open at a time. Well, not exactly. What they really decided was that they could support a finite number of files per program, and 20 is the number they chose. The Program Segment Prefix has room for 20 open handles in its handle array. The first five handles are opened by DOS when your program starts up. These five handles are given over to the **stdin**, **stdout**, **stderr**, **stdaux**, and **stdprn** system handles. The remaining 15 handles are yours to do with as you choose—unless, of course, your program is the child process of a parent with open handles, in which case you inherit the open condition of the parent's handles.

DOS itself can support 255 open handles at a time, which indicates that the DOS designers had some idea of multiple resident programs. However, if you do not put a FILES= statement in your CONFIG.SYS file in the root directory of your boot volume, you will get the default of eight files open for all the programs resident at one time. The installation procedures for most software systems require a minimum FILES=20 statement in CONFIG.SYS.

Twenty open handles is not enough for many applications. The typical small data base will have a number of data and index files, and those requirements can easily exceed the limit of 20 concurrent open handles. To get around it, many programs use a pattern of opens and closes, closing handles to make room in the PSP's handle array for new files. This thrashing of handle opens and closes exacts a performance cost.

DOS 3.3 added a feature where you can specify a different handle array, one with more than twenty entries, but many software developers do not want to restrict their programs to 3.3 and greater; there are plenty of 2.0, 2.1, 3.0, 3.1, and 3.2 DOS installations, and the developers do not want to limit their market.

There is a trick to getting yourself additional handles up to the limit specified in the FILES= command. When you open a file, DOS finds an available entry in your handle array and appropriates it. Available entries are marked with the value 255. Then DOS finds an available entry in its handle array and writes the offset to that entry into the entry in your array that it just grabbed. The DOS handle values are from 0 to 254. When DOS returns a handle to your program, it returns a value from 0 to 19, the offset to the entry in your PSP's handle array. Here is what you do: After you have opened the 20th file, you pick one of the handles and tell DOS to reuse it. You do this by saving the DOS handle from the PSP handle you have chosen. Then you assign the value 255 to the PSP entry and open the file. DOS thinks the 255-value handle is available and uses it. In subsequent accesses of the two files, you copy their respective DOS handles into the PSP handle before each read, write, or seek. Then you address the file to DOS by using the single handle you picked.

Listing 5.16 is handles.c, a program that demonstrates this technique. The **main** function of the program opens twenty-five files, writes a text message to each of them, and closes them. To use this technique in your programs, you would remove the **main** function from handles.c and link the rest of it to your code. Before opening any files, call the **init_handles** function. Before your program exits and after all files have been closed, call the **return_handles** function. This technique does not work with the Turbo C FILE stream functions because Turbo C includes code that limits the open FILE pointer count to 20. If you want to include those functions, you must acquire the Turbo C runtime library source code and recompile it with the OPEN_MAX and SYS_OPEN variables in stdio.h set to a higher number. The following paragraphs describe how the technique works.

The first item to address is the MAXFILES global in handles.c. Set it to the largest number of files that you will have open at one time. The **_openfd** integer array replaces one with the same name that the Turbo C file I/O functions use. The Turbo C version of the array contains only enough entries for the default 20 handles. This book's version compiles to enough entries to accommodate the MAXFILES global. The **handles** array is where you save the internal handles that DOS writes into the PSP handle array. There are two tables of DOS function codes. One, **dosfuncs**, is a table of those INT 21 functions that pass handles to DOS in the **bx** register. The other, **handlefuncs**, is a table of functions that return handles in the **ax** register.

You must call the **init_handles** function to use this technique. It initializes the handle arrays for the program and attaches the DOS INT 21 interrupt vector to the **newdos** interrupt function. The **return_handles** function restores the INT 21 vector. You must call this function when your program is done. Be cautious when testing programs that use this technique. If your program blows up before calling **return_handles**, you will need to reboot your computer because the vector will still point to where your **newdos** function was resident.

The **close** function replaces the Turbo C **close** function. The Turbo C version checks the handle to see that it is within the maximum 20 limit. You don't want this version to do that, so it is replaced with the simple one shown here.

The **newdos** interrupt function is where the handle extension is managed. This function is executed whenever any part of your program calls INT 21. First, you'll see how the handle extension technique opens files when there are no handles available.

The **newdos** function first tests to see if the DOS function being requested is one of those that returns a handle. These are the file open and create functions. If the function is one of these, the program tests to see if your PSP handle array has an available handle as indicated by a -1 value in the handle slot in the array. If so, DOS is allowed to function normally. If not, the program looks at its own **handles** array to see if there is an available entry with the -1 value. If not, DOS functions normally. If so, the program wants to trick DOS into thinking that the program has an available handle. The value that is stored in the 20th handle entry is saved in the **savehandle** variable. Then a -1 is written into that entry. This way, DOS will think that the 20th handle is available even though it was already used.

Before calling DOS, you must restore the registers to what they contained when you entered the interrupt function. Remember that the logic just processed could have used some of them; they must be put back to their original values so the caller's parameters to DOS are intact. You chain to the DOS INT 21 interrupt function by calling through the **olddos** function pointer. When DOS returns, the registers contain return values from DOS. Because a Turbo C **interrupt** function pops all the registers from the stack, you must assign those stacked registers the values returned in the actual registers by DOS.

Look now at the code following the return from DOS and its register assignments. When DOS returns, the offset to the **handles** array is put into the **ax** register for return to the caller. The handle that DOS put into the 20th array entry is stored in the **handles** array. Then the original value of the 20th handle is restored to the array in the PSP.

Now you can see how the technique manages a function call that passes a handle to DOS: If the handle is one of the extended ones, it will have a value greater than 19. Before chaining one of these calls to DOS, you must substitute the DOS handle that was returned when the file was open. First, the 19th PSP handle entry is saved in the **holdhandle** variable. The file's DOS handle was saved in the **handles** array when the file was opened. Now, using the caller's handle as a subscript, you write that value into the 19th array entry in the PSP and set the **bx** register to 19 so DOS will refer the function to the 20th array entry in the PSP. When DOS returns, you put the 20th entry back into the **handles** array. Normally, the value has not changed, but, in the case of a close, DOS has changed the array's entry to -1, and you need to free up the corresponding entry in **handles**. You restore the original 20th entry from **holdhandle** and return to the caller.

Your program must be reasonably well-behaved to use this handle-extending technique. You should always explicitly close all files before exiting the program. Do not expect DOS to close them by default as it does when you use the conventional file handle processes. Do not chain to a child program and expect the extended handles to be inherited either. DOS does not know about your tricks here and will not cooperate.

Listing 5.16: handles.c

```
/* ----------- handles.c ------------------- */

/*
 * A function set to extend the number of handles a
 * program can have open at one time.
 */

#include <stdio.h>
#include <io.h>
#include <sys\stat.h>
#include <fcntl.h>
#include <dos.h>
#include <mem.h>
#include <string.h>
#include "interupt.h"

#define MAXFILES 30

unsigned int _openfd[MAXFILES] = {
    O_RDONLY | O_DEVICE,
    O_WRONLY | O_DEVICE,
    O_WRONLY | O_DEVICE,
    O_RDWR   | O_DEVICE | O_BINARY,
    O_WRONLY | O_DEVICE | O_BINARY
};

static int handles[MAXFILES];
static void interrupt (*olddos)(void) = NULL;
static void interrupt newdos(IREGS);

/* ------- dos functions that use handles ----------- */
```

continued...

...from previous page

```
static char dosfuncs[] = {
    62,63,64,66,92
};

/* ---- dos functions that return handles in ax --- */
static char handlefuncs[] = {
    60,61,90,91
};

static unsigned psp;  /* psp of the handle-extending program */

/* ------ initialize the handle extension process ------ */
void init_handles(void)
{
    psp = getpsp();
    setmem(_openfd+5, (MAXFILES-5) * sizeof(int), -1);
    if (_osmajor > 3 || (_osmajor == 3 && _osminor >= 30))  {
        _BX = MAXFILES;
        _AH = 0x67;
        geninterrupt(0x21);
    }
    else    {
        setmem(handles, sizeof handles, -1);
        olddos = getvect(DOS);
        setvect(DOS, newdos);
    }
}

/* ------ turn off the handle extension process ------ */
void return_handles(void)
{
    if (olddos != NULL) {
        setvect(DOS, olddos);
        olddos = NULL;
    }
}

/* ----- replacement for the Turbo C close function ----- */
int close (int handle)
{
```

continued...

...from previous page

```
    _openfd[handle] = -1;
    return _close(handle);
}

/* -------- INT 21 interrupt service routine ---------- */
static void interrupt newdos(IREGS ir)
{
    void interrupt (*myolddos)(void);
    int i, j, k;
    char func;
    char savehandle = -1, holdhandle = -1;
    char newhandle  = -1, thishandle = -1;
    unsigned myds;

    func = (ir.ax >> 8) & 255;
    if (_psp == psp)    {
        /*  test for a DOS function that returns a handle  */
        for (i = 0; i < sizeof handlefuncs; i++)    {
            if (func == handlefuncs[i]) {
                /* handle func, test for all handles in use */
                for (j = 0; j < 20; j++)
                    if (peekb(_psp, 0x18 + j) == -1)
                        break;
                if (j == 20)    {
                    /* --- all PSP handles are in use --- */
                    for (k = 20; k < sizeof handles; k++)    {
                        /* test for an available pseudohandle */
                        if (handles[k] == -1)    {
                            savehandle = peekb(_psp, 0x18 + 19);
                            pokeb(_psp, 0x18 + 19, -1);
                            newhandle = k;
                            break;
                        }
                    }
                }
                break;
            }
        }
        /* --- test for a DOS function that uses a handle --- */
```

continued...

...from previous page

```
        for (i = 0; i < sizeof dosfuncs; i++)    {
            if (func == dosfuncs[i] && ir.bx > 19)  {
                /* --- handle function above the max --- */
                holdhandle = peekb(_psp, 0x18 + 19);
                pokeb(_psp, 0x18 + 19, handles[ir.bx]);
                thishandle = ir.bx;
                ir.bx = 19;
                break;
            }
        }
    }
    myolddos = olddos;  /* so the hook is from BP not DS */
    myds = _DS;         /* save ds */
    _SI = ir.si;        /* how the caller had the registers */
    _DI = ir.di;
    _ES = ir.es;
    _DS = ir.ds;
    _DX = ir.dx;
    _CX = ir.cx;
    _BX = ir.bx;
    _AX = ir.ax;
    (*myolddos)();      /* chain to INT 21 */
    ir.ax = _AX;        /* how DOS returned the registers */
    ir.fl = _FLAGS;
    ir.bx = _BX;
    ir.cx = _CX;
    ir.dx = _DX;
    ir.ds = _DS;
    ir.es = _ES;
    _DS = myds;         /* DS = newdos's version */
    if (_psp == psp)    {
        /* ----- was this a handle-returning function? ------ */
        if (newhandle != -1)    {
            /* ------ return our extended handle in ax ------ */
            ir.ax = newhandle;
            /* ----- save the handle returned by DOS -------- */
            handles[newhandle] = peekb(_psp, 0x18 + 19);
            /* ---- restore the original handle 19 value ---- */
            pokeb(_psp, 0x18 + 19, savehandle);
        }
```

continued...

...from previous page

```
        /* ----- was this a handle-passing function? -------- */
        if (thishandle != -1)   {
            /*  save the handle returned by DOS (might be -1) */
            handles[thishandle] = peekb(_psp, 0x18 + 19);
            /* ---- restore the original handle 19 value ---- */
            pokeb(_psp, 0x18 + 19, holdhandle);
        }
    }
}

/* -------- example main: your program goes here ----------- */
void main(void)
{
    int i;
    int fd[MAXFILES-5];
    char fname[13], data[80];

    init_handles();
    for (i = 0; i < MAXFILES-5; i++)    {
        sprintf(fname, "testfile.%03d", i);
        fd[i] =
            open(fname,O_CREAT|O_TRUNC|O_RDWR,S_IREAD|S_IWRITE);
        if (fd[i] != -1)
            printf("\nHandle for testfile.%03d is %d",i,fd[i]);
    }
    for (i = 0; i < MAXFILES-5; i++)
        if (fd[i] != -1)    {
            sprintf(data, "Writing to testfile.%03d\n", i);
            write(fd[i], data, strlen(data));
        }
    for (i = 0; i < MAXFILES-5; i++)
        if (fd[i] != -1)
            close(fd[i]);
    return_handles();
}
```

SUMMARY

In the next chapter, you will add a bit of functionality to the window library by introducing a simple menu manager. The menu manager will support the example programs in later chapters, but you can use it in your own programs as well.

CHAPTER 6

WINDOW MENUS

This chapter is about video menus. The windows from Chapter 4 are not just for applications. They are the foundation for other general-purpose library routines as well, and the menu manager is one of them. In this chapter, you will learn how to put menu bars and pop-down menus in your programs.

What you need to understand:

- The Turbo C text display routines
- Video windows

New subjects discussed:

- Table-driven menus
- Sliding menu bar
- Pop-down menus

WINDOW MENUS

Most programs use menus to let the user select from the modes and options in the system. There are many different formats for menus, but most of them have similar purposes. The most common menu format is the menu bar with pop-down menus. The menu bar is a single line across the top of the screen with a set of commands displayed across the bar. Each command has an associated pop-down menu that has a series of second-level commands. When you select from those pop-down commands, you tell the system to do something.

The process is universal enough that it can be supported with a general-purpose menu manager program, one that is driven by a table. You define the table in your application program. The table says what commands are on the bar, what commands are in the pop-down menus, and what functions are to be called when the commands are issued.

The Menu Manager

Listing 6.1 is menu.h, which contains the structure definition for menus and the prototype for the menu manager executive function. Menu.h also has the definitions for the menu colors. To use the system, you describe an array of MENU structures where each entry in the array is a command on a menu bar. The structure entry contains **mname**, a pointer to the string that displays the menu selection; **mselcs**, a pointer to an array of character pointers that point to the pop-down menu selections; and **func**, a pointer to an array of function pointers that point to the functions to be executed when the command is executed. When you define the strings for the pop-down menu selection names, leave two spaces at the end of each string for the flags that disable and toggle the selections. If neither of these features is in your menu, you do not need to reserve the space.

If the function pointer for a menu selection is NULL, the command is taken to be an toggle option, and its use is toggled on and off by the appearance and disappearance of a check mark in the selection's display. The **test_option** macro tests the setting of an option in the following manner:

```
if (test_option(menu, hsel, vsel))
```

You can set and clear options with the **set_option** and **clear_option** macros as shown here:

```
set_option(menu, hsel, vsel);

clear_option(menu, hsel, vsel);
```

The **menu** parameter in these macros is the address of the array of MENU structures. The **hsel** and **vsel** parameters are integers relative to one that indicate which horizontal menu bar selection and which vertical pop-down menu selections are being addressed.

A pop-down menu selection can be temporarily disabled and reenabled by these macros:

```
disable_selection(menu, hsel, vsel);

enable_selection(menu, hsel, vsel);
```

A selection is disabled if the last character of its name has an asterisk. A disabled selection is displayed with the DISABLEFG color. This next macro tests to see if a selection is enabled:

```
enabled(menu, hsel, vsel);
```

The cursor will not stop on a disabled selection. For that reason, do not disable all the selections on a pop-down menu because the **executive** function will go into a loop looking for a selection to land the cursor on.

Listing 6.2 is menu.c, which contains the menu manager program. When your program calls the **executive** function, you pass the address of the array of MENU structures. The menu bar is displayed, and the selection named in the call (1, 2, 3. . .) is highlighted with its menu popped down. You can move the cursor bar up and down with the arrow keys, press the first letter of the menu selection name, or use the right and left arrow keys to move among the pop-down menus. When you press the Enter key, the highlighted selection is executed, and the function it points to is called, or, if the function pointer is NULL, its toggle indicator is changed. When you press the Esc key, the menus disappear and the **executive** function returns to its caller.

Here is how the **executive** function works. The function opens a single-line window at the top of the screen. Using the MENU array pointer that your program passes, **executive** displays the names of the menu bar selections in the bar window and calls the **light** function to highlight the first selection on the bar. The highlight is the display of the selection name in the colors specified as SELECTFG and SELECTBG in menu.h. The **while** loop processes pop-down menus. As long as the user does not press the Esc key and the functions called by selections do not return a true value, the **while** loop continues. Each iteration of the loop calls the **getvmn** function, which pops down the menu under the current bar selection. The function calls **dimension** to compute the pop-down menu's size and uses the current horizontal selection to compute its placement.

The selections are displayed from the array of selection strings pointed to by the MENU entry. If a selection is marked as disabled with an asterisk in its last character position, the selection is displayed with the DISABLEFG color. Now the program lets the user type keystrokes and moves up and down the menu or from side to side to other pop-down menus, according to the key that is pressed. If the user presses the first letter of a selection, that selection is executed. If the user presses the Enter key, the currently marked selection is executed. If the selection has a NULL function pointer associated with it, the program toggles the option marker (a check mark in the second position from the end of the selection's name on the menu). Otherwise the **getvmn** functions returns to the **executive** function with the number of the selection or zero if the user pressed the Esc key. The **executive** program calls the function associated with a selection and continues in the **while** loop.

When the user presses Esc or a selection function returns a true value, the **executive** function breaks out of the **while** loop to terminate the menu process by closing the menu bar window. During menu processing, the cursor is hidden by a call to the **hidecursor** function. This action keeps the cursor from blinking at you while you are looking at menus. Every time a selection function is called and when menu processing is done, a call to the **unhidecursor** functions redisplays the cursor.

Listing 6.1: menu.h

```
/* ----------- menu.h ---------- */

typedef struct {
    char *mname;          /* menu bar selection names       */
    char **mselcs;        /* the pop-down menu selections   */
    int (**func)(void);   /* the functions to execute       */
} MENU;

void executive(MENU *);

/* ---------- menu colors ---------- */
#define MENUBG BLUE
#define MENUFG WHITE
#define SELECTBG WHITE
#define SELECTFG BLACK
#define DISABLEFG LIGHTGRAY

#define endname(m,h,v) \
    (&(m[h-1].mselcs[v-1][strlen(m[h-1].mselcs[v-1])]))
#define selector(m,h,v) (*(endname(m,h,v)-2))
#define enabler(m,h,v)  (*(endname(m,h,v)-1))

#define CHECK '\xfb'
#define test_option(m,h,v)         (selector(m,h,v)==CHECK)
#define set_option(m,h,v)          (selector(m,h,v)=CHECK)
#define clear_option(m,h,v)        (selector(m,h,v)=' ')
#define enable_selection(m,h,v)    (enabler(m,h,v)=' ')
#define disable_selection(m,h,v)   (enabler(m,h,v)='*')
#define enabled(m,h,v)             (enabler(m,h,v)!='*')
```

Listing 6.2: menu.c

```
/* ----------- menu.c ----------- */

#include <stdio.h>
#include <conio.h>
#include <stdlib.h>
#include <string.h>
#include <ctype.h>
#include "window.h"
#include "menu.h"
#include "keys.h"
#include "cursor.h"

#define ON 1
#define OFF 0

static int getvmn(MENU *, int *);
static void dimension(char **,int *,int *);
static void light(MENU *, int, int);
static void vlight(MENU *, int, int, int);

static int lastvsel[] = {1,1,1,1,1,1};

/* ------------ display & process a menu ---------- */
void executive(MENU *mn)
{
    int hsel=1, vsel, frtn = FALSE;
    int i = 0;

    open_window(1,1,80,1,MENUFG,MENUBG,0,0);
    hidecursor();
    cprintf("    ");
    while ((mn+i)->mname)
        cprintf(" %-10.10s ", (mn+i++)->mname);
    light(mn, hsel, ON);
    while (!frtn && ((vsel = getvmn(mn, &hsel)) != 0))  {
        light(mn,hsel,OFF);
        unhidecursor();
        frtn = (*(mn+hsel-1)->func [vsel-1])();
        hidecursor();
        light(mn, hsel, ON);
```

continued...

...from previous page

```
    }
    close_window();
    unhidecursor();
}

/* ---------pop down a vertical menu --------- */
static int getvmn(MENU *mn, int *hsel)
{
    int ht, wd, vx, sel = 0, vsel, vs;
    char **selcs;

    while (sel != ESC && sel != '\r')   {
        dimension((mn+*hsel-1)->mselcs, &ht, &wd);
        vx = 5+(*hsel-1)*12;
        open_window(vx, 2, vx+wd+1, ht+3, MENUFG, MENUBG,1,0);
        selcs = (mn+*hsel-1)->mselcs;
        for (vsel = 1; *selcs; vsel++)  {
            textcolor(enabled(mn,*hsel,vsel)?MENUFG:DISABLEFG);
            cprintf(vsel == 1 ? " %s" : "\r\n %s",*selcs++);
        }
        textcolor(MENUFG);
        sel = 0;
        vsel = lastvsel[*hsel-1];
        while (sel != ESC && sel != '\r' &&
                    sel != FWD && sel != BS)    {
            vlight(mn, *hsel, vsel, ON);
            sel = enabled(mn, *hsel, vsel) ?
                    getkey() :
                    (sel == UP ? UP : DN);
            selcs = (mn+*hsel-1)->mselcs;
            for (vs = 1; *selcs; vs++, selcs++) {
                if (enabled(mn,*hsel,vs) &&
                        tolower(**selcs) == tolower(sel))   {
                    vsel = vs;
                    vlight(mn, *hsel, vsel, ON);
                    sel = '\r';
                    break;
                }
            }
            switch (sel)    {
```

continued...

...from previous page

```
                    case UP:
                        vlight(mn, *hsel, vsel, OFF);
                        if (vsel > 1)
                            --vsel;
                        else
                            vsel = ht;
                        vlight(mn, *hsel, vsel, ON);
                        break;
                    case DN:
                        vlight(mn, *hsel, vsel, OFF);
                        if (vsel < ht)
                            vsel++;
                        else
                            vsel = 1;
                        vlight(mn, *hsel, vsel, ON);
                        break;
                    case '\r':
                        if ((mn+*hsel-1)->func [vsel-1] == NULL)    {
                            if (test_option(mn,*hsel,vsel))
                                clear_option(mn,*hsel,vsel);
                            else
                                set_option(mn,*hsel,vsel);
                            vlight(mn, *hsel, vsel, ON);
                            sel = 0;
                        }
                        else
                            close_window();
                        break;
                    case FWD:
                        close_window();
                        light(mn, *hsel, OFF);
                        if ((mn+*hsel)->mname)
                            (*hsel)++;
                        else
                            *hsel = 1;
                        light(mn, *hsel, ON);
                        break;
                    case BS:
                        close_window();
                        light(mn, *hsel, OFF);
```

continued...

...from previous page

```
                    if (*hsel == 1)
                        while ((mn+*hsel)->mname)
                            (*hsel)++;
                    else
                        --(*hsel);
                    light(mn, *hsel, ON);
                    break;
                case ESC:
                    close_window();
                    break;
                default:
                    putch(BELL);
                    break;
            }
        }
    }
    return sel == ESC ? 0 : vsel;
}


/* ---------- compute a menu's height & width --------- */
static void dimension(char *sl[], int *ht, int *wd)
{
    *ht = *wd = 0;

    while (sl && sl [*ht])  {
        *wd = max(*wd, (unsigned) strlen(sl [*ht]) + 2);
        (*ht)++;
    }
}

/* --------- accent a horizontal menu selection ---------- */
static void light(MENU *mn, int hsel, int onoff)
{
    textcolor(onoff ? SELECTFG : MENUFG);
    textbackground(onoff ? SELECTBG : MENUBG);
    gotoxy((hsel-1)*12+6, 1);
    cprintf((mn+hsel-1)->mname);
}

```

continued...

...from previous page

```
/* --------- accent a vertical menu selection ---------- */
static void vlight(MENU *mn, int hsel, int vsel, int onoff)
{
    textcolor(onoff ? SELECTFG :
        enabled(mn,hsel,vsel) ? MENUFG : DISABLEFG);
    textbackground(onoff ? SELECTBG : MENUBG);
    gotoxy(1, vsel);
    cprintf(" %s", *((mn+hsel-1)->mselcs+vsel-1));
    lastvsel[hsel-1] = vsel;
}
```

A Sample Menu Program

Listing 6.3 is demomenu.c, a demonstration of the use of the menu manager. The first part of the program describes the menus. Look down at the MENU array named **mn**. It defines three selections on the menu bar. Above it are the three corresponding arrays of function pointers. These point to stub functions in the program that simply display notices to the effect that they have been called and then return. The function pointers for the options menu are NULL. This causes those selections to be treated as toggles. The three arrays at the top of the program describe the text in the pop-down menus. The Save selection on the Files menu is marked disabled by the asterisk appearing as the final character of its name. The New selection will enable the Save selection. The Open selection will disable it. These actions are taken in the **save** and **new** stub functions in demomenu.c.

To get the menu displayed and executed, the program calls the **executive** function with the address of the MENU array as a parameter. The menu manager takes over from there, operating the menu and calling the proper functions as the user makes selections.

Listing 6.3: demomenu.c

```
/* ------- demomenu.c --------- */

#include <stdio.h>
#include <string.h>
#include "window.h"
#include "menu.h"

char *fselcs[] = {
    "Open    ",
    "New     ",
    "Save   *",
    "Quit    ",
    NULL
};

char *eselcs[] = {
    "Move     ",
    "Copy     ",
    "Delete   ",
    NULL
};

char *oselcs[] = {
    "Insert    ",
    "Justify   ",
    NULL
};

int open(void),new(void),save(void),quit(void);
int move(void),copy(void),delete(void);

static int (*ffuncs[])()={open,new,save,quit,quit};
static int (*efuncs[])()={move,copy,delete};
static int (*ofuncs[])()={NULL,NULL};

static MENU mn[] = {
    {"File",    fselcs, ffuncs},
    {"Edit",    eselcs, efuncs},
    {"Options", oselcs, ofuncs},
    {NULL}
```

continued...

...from previous page

```
};

void main(void)
{
    executive(mn);
}

int open(void)
{
    disable_selection(mn, 1, 3);
    notice(" -- open -- ");
    return 0;
}
int new(void)
{
    enable_selection(mn, 1, 3);
    notice(" -- new -- ");
    return 0;
}
int save(void)
{
    notice(" -- save -- ");
    return 0;
}
int quit(void)
{
    return 1;
}
int move(void)
{
    notice(" -- move -- ");
    return 0;
}
int copy(void)
{
    notice(" -- copy -- ");
    return 0;
}
int delete(void)
{
    notice(" -- delete -- ");
    return 0;
}
```

SUMMARY

With a window and menu manager in the bag, you will next proceed to the last of the window libraries, the data entry template feature. This capability allows you to describe a data entry screen format in program tables and use the data entry routines to collect your user's formatted text input.

CHAPTER 7

WINDOW DATA ENTRY TEMPLATES

This chapter discusses window data entry templates. When the user types in data, your program must engage some manner of text collection software. It is best if the data collection technique is consistent throughout the program, so data entry is a natural candidate for a general-purpose function library. Because you've used windows for everything else in this book, you will use a window to gather the user's input strings.

What you need to understand:	New subjects discussed:
• Video windows	• Data entry templates

DATA ENTRY

Many old C programs read the user's text inputs by calling an abomination called the **scanf** function. Other than as a study in the worst way to read text, the **scanf** function has no use. Yet the purveyors of C language standards continue to specify **scanf** for no reason but to keep those old programs compiling.

Readers of this book can abandon **scanf**. You do not need it, and it will not be used in this book. Instead, you are offered an improved technique for collecting the user's input data values. You will develop a simple system of data entry template screens and provide a general-purpose collector function to use them.

The Data Entry Template

A data entry template is a window display that contains places for the user to fill in the blanks to enter text. Each place on a template where the user can type data is called a "field." The template consists of fields and prompting text. The prompting text is whatever it takes to tell the user what the field represents. The field position is where the user types in data. You define the template by specifying where the prompts and the fields are located in the window and the size of each field. The collector function manages the placement of the cursor in each field and allows the user to move from field to field, type data, and specify when the data entry is done.

Data entry templates have their roots in the paper forms that everyone fills out from time to time. Data entry systems often collect data from forms that were filled out by people. Other times the data values are originated at the keyboard. Either way, the techniques are very much the same.

A common technique for data entry is to pop up a window for the collection of a small number of fields related to what the program needs to know. Perhaps the user needs to identify a file name or give the date of an event. A window pops up with some prompting information and a field or two for the user to fill in. The user types the data, presses the assigned "form complete" function key, and the program has the data it needs. By using a window, the program can collect the data without needing a dedicated part of the screen.

THE WINDOW DATA ENTRY MANAGER

Listings 7.1 and 7.2 are entry.h and entry.c, the source files that implement the data entry template windows. Entry.h defines the structures that you fill out to describe fields and prompts in the window. Each FIELD structure represents one field, and you build an array of them with one entry for each field in the window and a terminating NULL entry. The elements in the structure give the row and column position of the field's first character and the field's length. The coordinates are relative to one within the window. The structure includes a pointer to the place where the program will store the data string when the user enters it. Your program supplies the collection buffer, which must be one character greater than the length.

Data Field Prompts

Each PROMPT structure represents a string of text that will be written into the window before data entry begins. The prompts are in an array of PROMPT structures with a terminating NULL entry. Usually, you will have one of these prompts for each field, but it is not required. The structure contains the row and column coordinates where the prompt string begins and a pointer to the text of the prompt.

Data Entry Fields

The **data_entry** function in entry.c collects the data values into the current window. You pass to the function a pointer to the array of FIELDs and a pointer to the array of PROMPTs. If the collection buffers contain string values, those values are displayed in the fields before data entry begins. The user can type new values or use the Tab, Enter, Home, End, and arrow keys to move from field to field. The order in which the cursor moves from field to field is determined by the placement of the fields in the array of FIELD structures. When the user presses a function key or the Esc key, the **data_entry** function returns the terminating key to its caller. When the user is looking at a field to key in some data, the field appears to be blank. If the user keys any text, that text replaces the text that had been in the field. If the user enters no text and presses Enter, Esc, or a function key, the previous text is not replaced.

You can use the **clear_template** function to set all your collection buffers to spaces. You can use the **field_tally** function to display the current fields and prompts in a window prior to calling **data_entry**.

The colors in entry.h define the screen colors for a data entry window. You should have opened the window with the ENTRYFG and ENTRYBG colors before calling **field_tally** or **data_entry**. The FIELDFG and FIELDBG symbols define the colors for the field into which text is being entered. As the user moves from field to field, this color combination highlights the field to call attention to it. The cursor also moves to the new field.

Listing 7.1: entry.h

```
/* --------- entry.h ---------- */

typedef struct {        /* data entry field description*/
    int frow;           /* field row                   */
    int fcol;           /* field column position       */
    int flen;           /* field length                */
    char *fbuff;        /* field buffer                */
} FIELD;

typedef struct {        /* prompt descriptor           */
    int prow;           /* prompt row                  */
    int pcol;           /* prompt column               */
    char *ptext;        /* prompt text                 */
} PROMPT;

void field_tally(FIELD *, PROMPT *);
int data_entry(FIELD *, PROMPT *);
void clear_template(FIELD *, PROMPT *);

/* --------- data entry screen colors ---------- */
#define ENTRYFG WHITE
#define ENTRYBG BLUE
#define FIELDFG BLACK
#define FIELDBG WHITE
```

Listing 7.2: entry.c

```
/* --------- entry.c ---------- */

#include <string.h>
#include <conio.h>
#include <bios.h>
#include <mem.h>
#include "window.h"
#include "entry.h"
#include "keys.h"
#include "cursor.h"

/* ------ blank a field on the template -------- */
static void blank_field(FIELD *fld)
{
    int i;

    gotoxy(fld->fcol, fld->frow);
    for (i = 0; i < fld->flen; i++)
        putch(' ');
    gotoxy(fld->fcol, fld->frow);
}

/* ------ display all the fields in a window ------- */
void field_tally(FIELD *fld, PROMPT *pt)
{
    int i;

    /* ----- display the field prompts in the window ----- */
    while (pt->prow)    {
        gotoxy(pt->pcol,pt->prow);
        cputs(pt++->ptext);
    }
    for (i = 0; (fld+i)->frow; i++) {
        blank_field(fld+i);
        gotoxy((fld+i)->fcol, (fld+i)->frow);
        cputs((fld+i)->fbuff);
    }
}

```

continued...

...from previous page

```
/* ------- clear a template to all blanks ------ */
void clear_template(FIELD *fld, PROMPT *pt)
{
    int i;

    for (i = 0; (fld+i)->frow; i++)
        setmem((fld+i)->fbuff, (fld+i)->flen, ' ');
    field_tally(fld, pt);
}

/* ---------- read a field into its buffer ------- */
static int get_field(FIELD *fld)
{
    char buff[80];

    textcolor(FIELDFG);
    textbackground(FIELDBG);
    *buff = fld->flen+1;
    *(buff+1) = 0;
    blank_field(fld);
    cputs(fld->fbuff);
    gotoxy(fld->fcol, fld->frow);
    unhidecursor();
    while (bioskey(1) == 0)
        ;
    blank_field(fld);
    cgets(buff);
    hidecursor();
    if (cgets_returnkey != ESC && *(buff+1) > 0)
        strcpy(fld->fbuff, buff+2);
    textcolor(ENTRYFG);
    textbackground(ENTRYBG);
    blank_field(fld);
    cputs(fld->fbuff);
    return cgets_returnkey;
}

/* ----- Process data entry for a screen template. ---- */
int data_entry(FIELD *fld, PROMPT *pt)
{
```

continued...

...from previous page

```
    int exitcode = 0, done = FALSE;
    FIELD *fhead, *ftail;

    hidecursor();
    fhead = ftail = fld;
    while (ftail->frow)
        ftail++;
    field_tally(fld, pt);
    /* ---- collect data from keyboard into screen ---- */
    while (done == FALSE)   {
        exitcode = get_field(fld);
        switch (exitcode)   {
            case DN:
            case '\r':
            case FWD:   done = (ftail == fhead+1);
                        fld++;
                        if (fld == ftail)
                            fld = fhead;
                        break;
            case UP:    if (fld == fhead)
                            fld = ftail;
                        --fld;
                        break;
            case HOME:  fld = fhead;
                        break;
            case END:   fld = ftail-1;
                        break;
            case ESC:
            case F1:
            case F2:
            case F3:
            case F4:
            case F5:
            case F6:
            case F7:
            case F8:
            case F9:
            case F10:   done = TRUE;
                        break;
            default:    putch(BELL);
```

continued...

...from previous page

```
                                break;
                }
        }
        unhidecursor();
        return (exitcode);
}
```

AN EXAMPLE OF DATA ENTRY

Listing 7.3 is demoentr.c, a program that demonstrates the use of the data entry template functions. The first item of interest is the array of PROMPT structures. These structures describe the static text that is displayed in the window when a data entry is processed. Each entry includes the column and row coordinates within the window and relative to one where the corresponding prompting text is displayed.

The **nad** structure named **nd** represents the collection buffers for the fields on the data entry template. Each buffer is one greater than the field length to handle the null-terminating byte.

The array of FIELD structures has one entry for each of the data entry fields. Each entry includes the window column and row coordinates for the first byte of the field, the length of the field not including the null terminating byte, and the address of the collection buffer.

The **main** function of the demoentr.c program opens a window, calls **clear_template** to clear all the fields, and calls **data_entry** to collect data values into the fields. If this was a production program, you would do something with the values after the function returned. You might also put values into some of the collection buffer strings before you call **data_entry**. This method would display those values on the screen while data entry is being processed.

When the **data_entry** function returns, the program closes the window and exits.

Listing 7.3: demoentr.c

```
/* -------- demoentr.c ---------- */

/*
 * Demonstrate the data entry template
 */

#include <stdio.h>
#include <conio.h>
#include "window.h"
#include "keys.h"
#include "cursor.h"
#include "entry.h"

PROMPT prompts[] = {
    { 2, 10, "--- NAME AND ADDRESS RECORDS ---"},
    { 4,  2, "Name"                            },
    { 5,  2, "Address"                         },
    { 6,  2, ""                                },
    { 7,  2, "City"                            },
    { 7, 40, "State"                           },
    { 8,  2, "Zip"                             },
    { 8, 18, "Phone"                           },
    { 0,  0, NULL                              }
};

struct nad {
    char name[36];
    char addr1[36];
    char addr2[36];
    char city[26];
    char state[3];
    char zip[6];
    char phone[25];
} nd;

FIELD template[] = {
    { 4, 12, 35, nd.name  },
    { 5, 12, 35, nd.addr1 },
    { 6, 12, 35, nd.addr2 },
```

continued...

...from previous page

```
        { 7, 12, 25, nd.city  },
        { 7, 46,  2, nd.state },
        { 8, 12,  5, nd.zip   },
        { 8, 24, 10, nd.phone },
        { 0,  0,  0, NULL     }
};

void main(void)
{
        open_window(10,5,62,16,ENTRYFG,ENTRYBG,1,2);
        clear_template(template, prompts);
        data_entry(template, prompts);
        close_window();
}
```

SUMMARY

This chapter concludes the collection of window functions. Later chapters will use these functions as required for their examples. Next, Chapter 8 describes how to use the PC's serial input/output port and a modem to communicate and exchange data files between processors.

CHAPTER 8

SERIAL COMMUNICATIONS AND THE MODEM

This chapter is about serial communications and modems. Entire books have been devoted to these subjects, and if you want to know everything there is to learn about it, see the bibliography for some comprehensive works. In this chapter, you will learn enough to get your PC's serial port working with your modem by using Turbo C and the new functions included here. In addition, the popular XMODEM file transfer protocol is explained and implemented in a set of programs.

What you need to understand:

- Interrupt functions
- Direct port input/output

New subjects discussed:

- Serial Communications
- Modems
- File Transfer Protocols (XMODEM)

COMMUNICATING

Computer-to-computer communications are a routine part of our daily lives. Most programmers have, at one time or another, used a computer and a modem to send or receive data files. Many other people use computers in networks of one kind or another to move data around. Bulletin board systems, on-line services, electronic mail, and shared data base systems are only a few of the applications for computer links.

In this chapter, you look at the most often-used method for computer communications: the serial port and modem. Serial ports are input/output devices that process serial bit streams of data between processors. Modems are devices that translate the serial bit streams to and from tonal signals and transmit and receive those signals on voice-grade telephone lines.

The standard PC configuration includes up to two serial ports. DOS addresses these devices with the device names COM1 and COM2. DOS and BIOS include minimum support for these devices primarily so that a user can connect serial printers to them. But the strength in a serial port is its ability to transmit and receive data between computer systems either with a direct connection or through modems. For these purposes, the levels of support afforded by DOS and BIOS are inadequate primarily because of performance limitations. The software overheads imposed by the BIOS and DOS serial port functions cannot cope with the demands of the faster data rates that are possible with modems.

Serial Input/Output

Consider the basics of serial data transmissions first. Asynchronous serial communications are typically achieved with serial ports that conform to the RS232C standard specification for data transmission. A serial port transmits and receives bytes one at a time to and from another serial port. In the computer, a byte is represented as a row of eight bits on the system bus. Each bit is 0 or +5 volts, representing the 0 and 1 states that programmers are accustomed to. The strength of the bus signal is relatively low, reflecting the low power levels of integrated circuits. If you extended the bus beyond a certain distance, the voltage drop of the bus conductor itself would reduce the +5 value to a level that could not be electrically discerned from the 0 value by the devices that must read them.

An RS232C serial port translates the bus voltages into +12 and -12 volts and increases their strength (the load they will drive) so that the devices can be farther apart. At the same time, the serial port takes the eight parallel signals of each byte and converts them into a single stream of ones and zeros, or, in other words, a serial pattern. To allow the sending and receiving devices to synchronize with one another, this serial bit pattern is framed by start and stop bits in a manner that both devices recognize. To allow a limited amount of error correction, the devices can agree that a parity bit is included and that it will coerce the data byte into even or odd parity. The devices agree on the number of bits in each data byte. Finally, the speed at which the bits are transmitted is agreed to by both devices and is expressed in bits per second, commonly called the "baud rate." Common baud rates are 300, 1200, 2400, 4800, 9600, and 19,200 bits per second. Because each character is typically 10 bits—usually one start bit, seven data bits, a parity bit, and one stop bit—the baud rates can be estimated to deliver a rate of characters per second, computed as the baud rate divided by ten. Therefore a serial port operating at 1200 baud can transmit at up to 120 characters per second. Usually, the number is less than that because of the two systems' overheads of buffer and file management and file transfer protocols.

The serial port hardware consists of a Universal Asynchronous Receiver Transmitter (UART) device and line drivers. The UART manages the translation of the parallel bus byte into a properly framed serial stream. The line drivers convert the signal strengths between the 0 and +5 volt bus levels and the +12 and -12 line levels.

Serial Ports

The IBM PC can have zero, one, or two serial ports. (The PS/2 can have three, and a number of third-party serial boards allow a PC to have as many as 32 serial ports. This chapter restricts its discussions to the standard PC's two serial ports.) A program communicates with these serial ports in one of four ways: by reading and writing the port registers directly, by using the serial I/O ROM BIOS functions, by calling the DOS auxiliary input/output functions, or by reading and writing a DOS file opened with the names COM1 or COM2. The functions in this chapter will directly address the serial ports, using polled I/O for serial transmissions and an interrupt service routine for the serial receiver. The port numbers are standard among the PC family, and the Intel 8250 is the standard UART device.

The Modem

If two computers are about twenty-five feet apart, they can be connected directly by cable through their serial ports. The RS232C standard does not guarantee greater distances although systems have been known to work with 75- and 100-foot lengths of cable. When the two computers are on opposite sides of the continent, another method is needed. Enter the modem.

A modem is connected to a local computer's serial port on one side and to the telephone line on the other. This computer can, with adequate software, communicate with a similarly equipped computer anywhere else in the world. The modem reads the RS232C bits from the computer and translates them into tones that it sends across the voice-grade telephone line. The remote modem translates the tones it hears into RS232C bits and sends them into the remote computer through its serial port. In this manner, the two computers converse.

Today's modems have their own programming language. The language that has come to be accepted as a standard is the one originally introduced in the Hayes Smartmodem. Other modem makers must strive for compatibility with the Hayes command set if they want to sell modems.

The PC sends the commands and data to the modem. The commands tell the modem how to act; the data is transmitted to whomever or whatever is on the other end of the telephone line. The modem can dial the phone for the originator of the call and answer the phone for the receiver of the call. The Hayes command set provides a wealth of functionality. Its original design allowed users of dumb terminals to type the commands into the modem from the terminal keyboard.

Every Hayes command is preceded by the AT prefix. For example, if the phone is ringing and you want the modem to answer it, you type ATA. To reset the modem, you type ATZ. When the modem is powered up or reset, it is in command mode, expecting commands. Certain commands place the modem into data mode where characters are transmitted and received. There is a character sequence (+++) combined with a time delay that tells the modem to return to the command mode. The rest of the commands are cryptic and abstruse. With luck, you will never need to learn them because the PC can know and manage them for you. Many commercial and shareware communications programs manage the modem commands for the user. It is not uncommon for a user to have no idea whatsoever of how the modem works.

(The explanations of serial ports and modems just given are about all you can expect in the way of advanced communications theory from this book, and they are more than you need to know to use the software that follows. But programmers, being what we are, exhibit unusual curiosity about our tools, and most of us would not be content with that poor fragment of an explanation. If you do not already understand the serial port, you are encouraged to do further research with the books listed in the bibliography.)

The Serial Port Software

Listings 8.1 and 8.2 are serial.h and serial.c, respectively. These source files implement the serial port transmissions. They include functions to initialize and release the serial port and to send and receive characters.

Serial.c contains a group of variables that you initialize to the configuration of the serial port. These variables are SERIALPORT, PARITY, STOPBITS, WORDLEN, and BAUD. They are coded as variables rather than defined as globals so that you can change them from within a program. Serial.h contains definitions of the serial port registers. These definitions adjust themselves to whichever port (COM1, COM2) you select. Other definitions in serial.h relate to the various signals and register values that are used to manage the transmissions, including those of the 8259 Programmable Interrupt Controller.

Interrupt-Driven Serial Input

The software in this chapter writes to the serial port by polling it when a character is ready for transmission. But while serial input can be read that way, it should not be. You could poll the serial receiver port for input if your program has little to do but watch the serial line. Most communications programs, however, have other tasks. They echo the input to the screen or write it to a disk file. These operations involve some execution time during which the program cannot be watching the serial port. The sending program is transmitting characters at its own speed, expecting the receiver to keep up. At the faster baud rates, a program that ignores the serial input line long enough to do anything significant will experience a loss of input characters. For this reason, the software in this chapter receives serial input with an interrupt function. As the characters are received, each one generates an interrupt. The interrupt function reads the character and places it in a buffer. As the program needs characters, it reads them from the buffer.

The serial input buffer is circular with two pointers. One pointer points to the next place for the serial input interrupt function to write a character. The other pointer points to the next character for the application program to take from the buffer. When these two pointers point to the same character position, the buffer is empty.

The XON/XOFF Protocol

The interrupt processing just described will sufficiently manage most data receptions only if the buffer is big enough. If large bursts of high-speed receptions occur, it is possible for the receiving program to fall behind in relieving the buffer. In this case, the buffer would fill up, and you'd be losing characters again.

To deal with this possibility, most communications programs use a technique where the receiver can tell the sender to stop sending for a while. When the receiver is ready to receive again, it tells the sender to start sending. This technique is called the XON/XOFF protocol because the ASCII character XOFF (Ctrl-S) is used to stop the sender, and XON (Ctrl-Q) is used to restart the sender. The receiver interrupt service routine watches the condition of the receiver buffer. When the buffer reaches a specified threshold, the receiver sends the sender the XOFF character. The sender, seeing this character, suspends transmitting. The receiving program now watches the buffer from inside the function that applications programs call to read serial characters. When the buffer is at a specified safety level, the receiver sends the XON character. The sender sees that character and begins sending again. If the margin between the threshold and the buffer capacity is wide enough, no data characters are lost.

You can observe this process while communicating manually with any on-line service or bulletin board system. While the service is transmitting a message to your terminal, press Ctrl-S and watch the transmission stop. Wait a while and press Ctrl-Q. The transmission will resume.

The serial.h file includes the SERIALBUFFERSIZE definition to specify the size of the buffer. The SAFETYLEVEL definition defines the level at which the XON will be sent following an XOFF. This level is set at one quarter the size of the buffer. The THRESHOLD definition sets the level at which the XOFF is sent at three quarters the size of the buffer.

The Serial Functions

A program uses the functions in serial.c to communicate with another program in another computer or perhaps to drive a serial printer. Following are the functions that the programs call and descriptions of how they work.

initserialport

You call this function prior to sending or receiving data with the serial port. The function initializes the values in a bit-field parameter byte that is used to initialize the port. These values set the parity, number of stop bits and the word length. The parameter byte is written to the Line Control register of the UART.

To set the baud rate, the program must initialize a value in the UART that divides the baud rate clock down to the desired bit rate. The baud rate is divided into the constant value 115,200, and the quotient result is written into the UART's Divisor Latch registers. There is a register for the most significant byte and one for the least significant byte. To write these values, the program must strobe the Divisor Latch Access Bit in the Line Control register. The bit is set to its on state (one); the two Divisor Latch values are written; and then the bit is set to its off state (zero).

Next, the program attaches the serial input interrupt vector to the interrupt service routine, **newserialint**. So that interrupts will work, the Data Terminal Ready signal, Request To Send signal, and an odd signal named OUT2 must be set in the UART's Modem Control Register. The serial Interrupt Request Line is asserted in the 8259 Programmable Interrupt Controller's PIC01 register, and the Data Ready signal is set in the UART's Interrupt Enable register. An End Of Interrupt signal is sent to the PIC00 register. Finally, any interrupts left over from earlier operations are flushed by reads to the Receive Data, Interrupt Ident, Line Status, and Modem Status registers.

restore_serialint

This function is used to restore the serial receiver interrupt vector to its previous setting. You call this function when you are done with the port. If you fail to call the function, the vector will not be restored, and a stray interrupt could cause problems.

clear_serial_queue

This function clears out the serial receiver buffer. The modem software described later uses it.

input_char_ready

This is a macro that returns a true value if there are unread characters in the serial input buffer.

readserial

This function reads the next character from the serial input buffer. If no characters are in the buffer, the function waits for one by calling the **input_char_ready** macro. This wait can be terminated by a timeout, in which case a false value is returned. When a character is ready to be read, the function tests to see if the sender is waiting for the XON character. If so, and if the serial receiver buffer is below the safety level, the function transmits the XON character to the sender.

writeserial

This function writes to the serial output line that the character passed as its parameter. If the remote computer has previously sent the XOFF character and the local computer is still waiting for the XON character, this function simply waits. Then it tests the UART to see if it is ready for an output character. When it is, the function sends the character to the serial output port.

newserialint

This function is not called from your program. It is the interrupt service routine for serial input. It reads the character that caused the interrupt and processes it. If the character is the XOFF control, the function sets a flag that tells the transmitter to suspend transmissions. If the character is the XON control, the function clears the flag. These tests are made only if the XON/XOFF protocol is enabled. Many transmissions do not use this function because the transmissions involve binary data and the XON and XOFF characters are valid data values. Most such transmissions use file transfer protocols that involve error-correction and packet management. These protocols do not have the problems of unbridled input overrun associated with the text transmissions that use the XON/XOFF protocol.

The **newserialint** function writes data characters into the serial input buffer. If the buffer reaches the threshold and XON/XOFF is enabled, the function transmits the XOFF character to the sender.

Listing 8.1: serial.h

```
/* ---------- serial.h --------------- */

/*
 * Serial Port Definitions
 */

extern SERIALPORT;
extern char *nextserialin, *nextserialout;

/* ----------- serial prototypes ----------- */
void initserialport(void);
int readserial(void);
int writeserial(int);
void clear_serial_queue(void);
void restore_serialint(void);

/* ----------------- serial macros ------------------- */
#define serialstat() (inp(LINESTATUS))
#define input_char_ready() (nextserialin!=nextserialout)
```

continued...

...from previous page

```
#define XON  17
#define XOFF 19

/* ---------------- serial port addresses ---------------- */
/* - 8250 UART base port address:  COM1 = 3f8, COM2 = 2f8 - */
#define BASE        (0x3f8-((SERIALPORT-1)<<8))
#define TXDATA       BASE       /* transmit data          */
#define RXDATA       BASE       /* receive data           */
#define DIVLSB       BASE       /* baud rate divisor lsb */
#define DIVMSB      (BASE+1)    /* baud rate divisor msb */
#define INTENABLE   (BASE+1)    /* interrupt enable       */
#define INTIDENT    (BASE+2)    /* interrupt ident'n      */
#define LINECTL     (BASE+3)    /* line control           */
#define MODEMCTL    (BASE+4)    /* modem control          */
#define LINESTATUS  (BASE+5)    /* line status            */
#define MODEMSTATUS (BASE+6)    /* modem status           */

/* --------------- serial interrupt values ----------------- */
#define IRQ      (4-(SERIALPORT-1))      /* 0-7 = IRQ0-IRQ7     */
#define SERIALINT  (12-(SERIALPORT-1)) /* interrupt vector    */
#define SERIALIRQ  (~(1 << IRQ))
#define PIC01    0x21 /*8259 Programmable Interrupt Controller*/
#define PIC00    0x20 /* "        "              "        "   */
#define EOI      0x20 /* End of Interrupt command             */
#define TIMER    0x1c /* PC timer interrupt vector            */

/* --------------- line status register values ------------- */
#define XMIT_DATA_READY    0x20

/* ------------ modem control register values -------------- */
#define DTR   1
#define RTS   2
#define OUT2  8

/* ----------- ASCII serial control characters ------------- */
#define SOH      1
#define EOT      4
#define ACK      6
#define NAK      0x15
#define CAN      0x18
```

continued...

...from previous page

```

/* ---------- interrupt enable register signals ---------- */
#define DATAREADY 1

/* ------------ serial input interrupt buffer ------------ */
#define SERIALBUFFERSIZE 1024
#define SAFETYLEVEL (SERIALBUFFERSIZE/4)
#define THRESHOLD (SAFETYLEVEL*3)
```

Listing 8.2: serial.c

```
/* --------- serial.c -------------- */

/*
 * Serial Port Communications Functions
 */

#include <stdio.h>
#include <conio.h>
#include <dos.h>
#include "serial.h"
#include "timer.h"

#define TRUE  1
#define FALSE 0

static char serial_buffer[SERIALBUFFERSIZE];
char *nextserialin = serial_buffer;
char *nextserialout = serial_buffer;
int buffer_count;

int SERIALPORT  = 1;    /* COM1 or COM2                     */
int PARITY      = 0;    /* 0 = none, 1 = odd, 2 = even      */
int STOPBITS    = 1;    /* 1 or 2                           */
int WORDLEN     = 8;    /* 7 or 8                           */
int BAUD        = 2400; /* 110,150,300,600,1200,2400        */
int TIMEOUT     = 10;   /* number of seconds to time out */

```

continued...

...from previous page

```
int xonxoff_enabled = TRUE;
static int XON_input_pending;
static int XON_output_pending;

/* ----- serial port initialization parameter byte ------ */
static union    {
    struct {
        unsigned wordlen  : 2;
        unsigned stopbits : 1;
        unsigned parity   : 3;
        unsigned brk      : 1;
        unsigned divlatch : 1;
    } serial_initial_bits;
    char serial_initial_char;
} initserial;

static void (interrupt far *oldserialint)(void);
static void interrupt far newserialint(void);

/* -------- initialize the serial port ----------- */
void initserialport(void)
{
    initserial.serial_initial_bits.parity   =
        PARITY == 2 ? 3 : PARITY;
    initserial.serial_initial_bits.stopbits = STOPBITS-1;
    initserial.serial_initial_bits.wordlen  = WORDLEN-5;
    initserial.serial_initial_bits.brk      = 0;
    initserial.serial_initial_bits.divlatch = 1;
    outp(LINECTL, initserial.serial_initial_char);
    outp(DIVLSB, (char) ((115200L/BAUD) & 255));
    outp(DIVMSB, (char) ((115200L/BAUD) >> 8));
    initserial.serial_initial_bits.divlatch = 0;
    outp(LINECTL, initserial.serial_initial_char);
/* ------ attach to the serial interrupt vector --------- */
    if (oldserialint == NULL)
        oldserialint = getvect(SERIALINT);
    setvect(SERIALINT, newserialint);
    outp(MODEMCTL, (inp(MODEMCTL) | DTR | RTS | OUT2));
    outp(PIC01, (inp(PIC01) & SERIALIRQ));
    outp(INTENABLE, DATAREADY);
```

continued...

...from previous page

```
    outp(PIC00, EOI);
/* ----- flush existing serial interrupts ------ */
    inp(RXDATA);
    inp(INTIDENT);
    inp(LINESTATUS);
    inp(MODEMSTATUS);
}

/* ------ restore the serial interrupt vector ---------- */
void restore_serialint(void)
{
    if (oldserialint)
        setvect(SERIALINT, oldserialint);
}

/* ------- clear the serial input buffer --------- */
void clear_serial_queue(void)
{
    nextserialin = nextserialout = serial_buffer;
    buffer_count = 0;
}

/* ---- serial input interrupt service routine ------- */
static void interrupt far newserialint(void)
{
    int c;
    outp(PIC00,EOI);
    if (nextserialin == serial_buffer+SERIALBUFFERSIZE)
        nextserialin = serial_buffer;
    c =   inp(RXDATA);
    if (xonxoff_enabled)
        if (c == XOFF)
            XON_input_pending = 1;
        else if (c == XON)
            XON_input_pending = 0;
    if (!xonxoff_enabled || (c != XON && c != XOFF))    {
        *nextserialin++ = (char) c;
        buffer_count++;
    }
    if (xonxoff_enabled && !XON_output_pending &&
```

continued...

...from previous page

```
                buffer_count > THRESHOLD)    {
            while ((inp(LINESTATUS) & XMIT_DATA_READY) == 0)
                ;
            outp(TXDATA, XOFF);
            XON_output_pending = 1;
        }
}

/* ---- read a character from the input buffer ----- */
int readserial(void)
{
    set_timer(TIMEOUT);
    while (!input_char_ready())
        if (timed_out())
            return FALSE;
    if (nextserialout == serial_buffer+SERIALBUFFERSIZE)
        nextserialout = serial_buffer;
    --buffer_count;
    if (XON_output_pending && buffer_count < SAFETYLEVEL)    {
        XON_output_pending = 0;
        writeserial(XON);
    }
    return *nextserialout++;
}

/* ---- write a character to the serial port ----- */
int writeserial(int c)
{
    while (XON_input_pending)
        ;
    set_timer(TIMEOUT);
    while ((inp(LINESTATUS) & XMIT_DATA_READY) == 0)
        if (timed_out())
            return FALSE;
    outp(TXDATA, c);
    return TRUE;
}
```

The Modem Software

Listings 8.3 and 8.4 are modem.h and modem.c, respectively. These files contain the functions that programs use to communicate with the modem. Modem communications imply serial port input/output, so the modem functions themselves use the functions in serial.c.

There are a lot of modem commands and modes, but the software in modem.c is restricted to just what you need to make a connection and transmit and receive some data. Modem.h defines the string commands to initialize a Hayes-compatible modem and allow it to place and answer calls. The cryptic command set is documented in the user manuals that come with most modems. You do not need to learn the commands to use this software unless the strings in modem.h do not work with your modem. Even though modem manufacturers attempt to achieve compatibility with the Hayes command set, some differences can creep in. You might need to experiment with the strings to make them work. The special curly character in the strings is not a part of the command set. It tells the modem software to wait for one second during the transmission.

Following is a discussion of each of the modem functions.

initializemodem

This function initializes the modem and attaches the timer interrupt. It also initializes the serial port and clears the serial input buffer.

release_modem

This function resets the modem, the timer interrupt, and the serial port. You must call this function when you are done with the modem to assure that the interrupt vectors are restored.

call_remote

This function tells the modem to call the phone number that is passed as its parameter. It uses the string encoded in the DIAL definition as the call command prefix. As coded, it assumes a touch tone phone. To use rotary dialing, change the string to ATDP.

answer_modem

This function puts the modem into automatic answer mode. If the phone rings when the modem is in this mode, the modem will answer and transmit a carrier signal. If the caller is a computer that called in the manner used by **call_remote**, the modem connection is complete, and the modem goes into its transmission and reception mode, allowing data to be sent and received.

hangup

This function hangs up the phone.

Listing 8.3: modem.h

```
/* -------- modem.h ------------
 * Modem Definitions
 */
/* -------- Hayes modem control strings --------- */
#define RESETMODEM "ATZ\r~"
#define INITMODEM  "AT&C1E0M1S7=60S11=55V1X3S0=0\r~"
#define HANGUP     "~+++~ATH0\r~ATS0=0\r~"
#define ANSWER     "ATS0=1\r"
/* --------- prototypes ---------- */
void initializemodem(void);
void call_remote(char *);
void answer_modem(void);
void hangup(void);
void release_modem(void);
```

Listing 8.4: modem.c

```
/* ------------ modem.c --------- */

#include <stdio.h>
#include <dos.h>
#include <conio.h>
#include "serial.h"
#include "modem.h"
#include "timer.h"

char DIAL[] = "ATDT";

/* ----------- send a string to the modem ------------ */
static void modem_out(char *s)
{
    while(*s)    {
        if (*s == '~')
            sleep(1);
        else if (!writeserial(*s))
            break;
        s++;
    }
}

/* ----------- initialize the modem ---------- */
void initializemodem(void)
{
    intercept_timer(NULL);
    initserialport();
    modem_out(RESETMODEM);
    modem_out(INITMODEM);
    clear_serial_queue();
}

/* -------- release the modem --------- */
void release_modem(void)
{
    modem_out(RESETMODEM);
    restore_timer();
    initserialport();
```

continued...

...from previous page

```
        restore_serialint();
        clear_serial_queue();
}

/* ----------- place a call -------------- */
void call_remote(char *phoneno)
{
        modem_out(DIAL);
        modem_out(phoneno);
        modem_out("\r");
        clear_serial_queue();
}

/* ------------- answer a call ------------ */
void answer_modem(void)
{
        modem_out(ANSWER);
        clear_serial_queue();
}

/* ------------ hang up the call ----------------- */
void hangup(void)
{
        modem_out(HANGUP);
        clear_serial_queue();
}
```

Example Programs: SENDER and RECEIVER

To demonstrate the use of the modem and serial functions, Listings 8.5 and 8.6 are sender.c and receiver.c, respectively. These are simple modem connection programs that will allow you to use the keyboard and screen to talk to someone at another computer. The originator of the call runs the sender.c program, and the answerer runs the receiver.c program. The only difference between the two programs is that sender.c places a call and receiver.c answers it. Once the connection is made, the two programs poll the keyboard for keystrokes and watch the serial input line for characters. Each program echoes its own keystrokes and sends them to the other. Each program locally echoes characters read from the other. With these programs, you can carry on a two-way conversation. Run sender.c by typing its name and a phone number on the command line. Just type the digits of the phone number. Run receiver.c at the other location by typing its name on the command line.

Listing 8.5: sender.c

```
/* ------ sender.c ---------- */

/*
 * Use the modem/serial functions to call a friend
 */

#include <conio.h>
#include <bios.h>
#include "serial.h"
#include "modem.h"
#include "keys.h"

void main(int argc, char *argv[])
{
    int c;

    initializemodem();
    if (argc > 1)   {
        call_remote(argv[1]);  /* dial the phone number */
        while (1)    {
            /* ------ poll for a keystroke --------- */
            if (bioskey(1))    {
                if ((c = getch()) == ESC)
                    break;
                putch(c);
                if (c == '\r')
                    putch('\n');
                writeserial(c);      /* transmit the keystroke */
            }
            /* ------- poll for serial input ---------- */
            if (input_char_ready())    {
                c = readserial();
                putch(c);
                if (c == '\r')
                    putch('\n');
            }
        }
        hangup();
    }
    release_modem();
}
```

Listing 8.6: receiver.c

```
/* ------ receiver.c ---------- */

/*
 * Use the modem/serial functions to
 * answer a call from a friend
 */

#include <conio.h>
#include <bios.h>
#include "serial.h"
#include "modem.h"
#include "keys.h"

void main(void)
{
    int c;

    initializemodem();
    answer_modem();
    while (1)    {
        /* ------ poll for a keystroke --------- */
        if (bioskey(1))    {
            if ((c = getch()) == ESC)
                break;
            putch(c);
            if (c == '\r')
                putch('\n');
            writeserial(c);       /* transmit the keystroke */
        }
        /* ------- poll for serial input ---------- */
        if (input_char_ready())    {
            c = readserial();
            putch(c);
            if (c == '\r')
                putch('\n');
        }
    }
    hangup();
    release_modem();
}
```

XMODEM

XMODEM is a public domain file transfer protocol that provides for error correction during the transmission of data files between computers. It was developed in the early days of home computers and modems to solve the problems caused by line hits when programmers tried to exchange binary files across the phone lines. The protocol and its programs were made widely available at no cost, and the technique caught on. Its acceptance was so widespread that now virtually all communications programs support it.

A sending XMODEM program transmits a file to a receiving XMODEM program. The two programs are different, one supporting the transmission and one the reception. Often the two processes are combined into a single program.

The sending program does not begin sending until the receiver is ready to receive. The receiver sends either a NAK character (0x15) to say that it can handle checksums or a "C" to say that it can handle the CRC. This protocol allows compatibility between older and newer different implementations of XMODEM. An older sending program waits for a NAK; a newer version waits for either the NAK or a "C". For a NAK, the sender retreats to the checksum; otherwise, it uses the CRC.

An older receiving program sends the NAK when it is ready to receive. A newer one does not know if the sender can support the CRC, so it sends the "C" and waits. If the SOH (0x01) character doesn't show up to identify the start of the first block from the sender, the receiver tries a few more "C"s and then switches to the NAK. Eventually the SOH shows up followed by the first block. The receiver thus knows whether to expect a checksum or a CRC, based on this exchange.

Each block consists of the following components:

- the SOH character
- the one-byte consecutive block number relative to one
- the ones complement of the block number
- 128 bytes of data
- either the one-byte checksum or the two-byte CRC

After transmitting this format, the sender waits for a NAK or ACK (0x06) from the receiver. After the last block, the sender sends the single EOT (0x04) character.

The sending program adds the error-detecting character sequence to each transmission, and the receiving program checks it for validity. The character sequence is computed from the data stream. The receiver makes the same computation and compares the result to the sequence received from the sender. If they match, the assumption is made that the data stream was received without error. Early XMODEM programs used an eight-bit checksum of the data characters. Later versions of XMODEM use a 16-bit Cyclic Redundancy Check (CRC) value instead of a character checksum.

If the checksum or CRC is matched correctly, the receiving program sends an ACK character to the sending program. If the check character is incorrect, the receiver sends a NAK. The sending program sends more data in response to the ACK or resends the previous data record in response to a NAK. The XMODEM protocol sends the file in fixed-length, 128-byte blocks, and the ACK/NAK logic is applied to each block in turn.

The receiver analyzes each block that comes in. The first byte must be the SOH or EOT character. The EOT means the transmission is complete and the receiver sends the ACK. Following the SOH is the block number and the ones complement of the block number. The block number must be either the last block number plus one or, the last block number, signifying a retransmission of the last block. Next come 128 data bytes followed by a checksum or CRC. The checksum must be the 8-bit sum of the 128 data bytes. The CRC is computed from the 128 data bytes plus two more bytes of a zero value. If the check character is correct, the receiver writes the data to the file and sends an ACK. If not, the receiver sends the NAK, whereupon the sender resends the block.

Timeouts and error detections are all reported with NAKs. After a number of consecutive NAKs, both the sender and receiver terminate the transmission. The first timeout is 10 seconds waiting for each SOH to start a block. The other characters in the transmission are assumed lost if a one-second timeout occurs.

During an XMODEM transmission, the XON and XOFF protocols are disabled because binary data bytes can include the values assigned to XON and XOFF. The XON/XOFF protocol is unnecessary because of the ACK/NAK packet protocol.

The 16-bit CRC is built from the string of 8-bit bytes. The CRC starts with a zero value. Each data byte is concatenated to the right of the CRC to form a 24-bit value. This value is shifted left eight bits. For each one-bit shift, if the most significant bit of the 24-bit value before the shift is a one, the value 0x1021 is XORed with the left-most 16 bits of the new 24-bit value. When all bytes have been processed this way, the left-most 16 bits are the CRC.

The XSEND and XRECV Programs

Listings 8.7 and 8.8 are xsend.c and xrecv.c, respectively. These programs will transmit a file from one computer to another by using the XMODEM protocol. You run the xsend.c program by typing its name, a file name, and the receiver's telephone number on the command line. You run the xrecv.c program at the receiving computer by typing its name and the file name to be created. The xrecv.c program initializes the modem to answer the phone and prompts you to type "r" when the connection is made. The xsend.c program calls the number and prompts you to type "s" when the telephone connection is made. You will see the connection made when the modem's CONNECT message appears on the screen. When both users have typed their respective single-letter commands, the programs manage the transmission of the file. As the file is being transmitted, the block number is displayed. Errors and their retries are reported as they occur. When the file transmission is complete, the programs exit.

You can use the xsend.c and xrecv.c programs as they appear here, or you can use the XMODEM protocol functions in both programs for a larger, more ambitious communications program.

Listing 8.7: xsend.c

```
/* ------------- xsend.c -------------- */

/*
 * Transmit a file using the XMODEM file transfer protocol
 */

#include <stdio.h>
#include <conio.h>
#include <stdlib.h>
#include <ctype.h>
#include <mem.h>
#include "timer.h"
#include "serial.h"
#include "modem.h"
#include "keys.h"

#define RETRIES  12
#define TRUE 1
#define FALSE 0

#define PADCHAR  0x1a
#define CRC      'C'

/* ------- external data ---------- */
extern int TIMEOUT;
extern int xonxoff_enabled;

/* -------- local data ----------- */
static int tries;    /* retry counter */
static char bf [130]; /* i/o buffer   */
static FILE *fp;

/* ------- prototypes ------------- */
unsigned compute_crc(char *, int);
void send_xmodem(void);

void main(int argc, char *argv[])
{
    int c = 0;

```

continued...

...from previous page

```
    if (argc != 3)  {
        cprintf("\r\nUsage: xsend <filename> <phoneno>");
        exit(1);
    }
    if ((fp = fopen(argv[1], "r")) == NULL) {
        cprintf("\r\nNo such file as %s", argv[1]);
        exit(1);
    }
    initializemodem();
    cprintf("\r\nPress 's' after CONNECT to send");
    cprintf("\r\nPress Esc any time to abort\r\n");
    call_remote(argv[2]);
    while (tolower(c) != 's' && c != ESC)   {
        /* ------- poll for keyboard input ---------- */
        if (kbhit())
            c = getch();
        /* ------- poll for serial input ---------- */
        if (input_char_ready())
            putch(readserial());
    }
    if (tolower(c) == 's')
        send_xmodem();
    fclose(fp);
    hangup();
    release_modem();
}

/* ---------- transmit with xmodem protocol ------------- */
void send_xmodem(void)
{
    int i, chksum, endoffile = FALSE, ans = 0, ln, crcout = 0;
    unsigned crc;
    char blck_no = 1;

    xonxoff_enabled = FALSE;
    tries = 0;

    /* ----- wait for the go-ahead from the receiver ------ */
    TIMEOUT = 6;
    while (tries++ < RETRIES && crcout != NAK && crcout != CRC)
```

continued...

...from previous page

```
            crcout = readserial();
        TIMEOUT = 10;

        /* -------- send the file to the receiver ----------- */
        while (tries < RETRIES &&
                !endoffile && ans != CAN && !timed_out())     {

            /* ---- read the next data block ----- */
            setmem(bf, 128, PADCHAR);
            if ((ln = fread(bf, 1, 128, fp)) < 128)
                endoffile = TRUE;
            if (ln == 0)
                break;
            cprintf("\rBlock %d  ", blck_no);
            chksum = 0;
            if (kbhit())
                if (getch() == ESC) {
                    writeserial(CAN);
                    break;
                }
            writeserial(SOH);       /* SOH            */
            writeserial(blck_no);       /* block number  */
            writeserial(~blck_no);      /* 1s complement */

            /* ------- send the data block ------ */
            for (i = 0; i < 128; i++)    {
                writeserial(bf[i]);
                chksum += bf[i];        /* checksum calculation */
            }

            /* -- send error-correcting value (chksum or crc) -- */
            if (crcout == NAK)
                writeserial(chksum & 255);
            else    {
                crc = compute_crc(bf, 130);
                writeserial((crc >> 8) & 255);
                writeserial(crc & 255);
            }

            /* ----- read ACK, NAK, or CAN from receiver ----- */
```

continued...

...from previous page

```
            ans = readserial();
            if (ans == ACK) {
                blck_no++;
                tries = 0;
            }

            if (ans == NAK) {
                endoffile = FALSE;
                cprintf("\r\n%2d tries", ++tries);
                /* ---- position to previous block ----- */
                if (fseek(fp, -128L, 1) == -1)
                    fseek(fp, 0L, 0);
            }
        }
        if (endoffile)    {
            writeserial(EOT);                       /* send the EOT    */
            readserial();                           /* wait for an ACK */
            cprintf("\r\nTransfer Completed");
        }
        else
            cprintf("\r\nTransfer Aborted");
        xonxoff_enabled = TRUE;
    }

    /* --------- compute the crc ------------ */
    unsigned compute_crc(char *bf, int len)
    {
        int i;
        long crc = 0;
        while (len--)    {
            crc |= (*bf++) & 255;
            for (i = 0; i < 8; i++) {
                crc <<= 1;
                if (crc & 0x1000000L)
                    crc ^= 0x102100L;
            }
        }
        return (unsigned) (crc >> 8);
    }
```

Listing 8.8: xrecv.c

```
/* -------------- xrecv.c --------------- */

/*
 * Receive a file using the XMODEM file transfer protocol
 */

#include <stdio.h>
#include <conio.h>
#include <stdlib.h>
#include <ctype.h>
#include <dos.h>
#include "timer.h"
#include "serial.h"
#include "modem.h"
#include "keys.h"

#define RETRIES  12
#define CRCTRIES 2
#define TRUE 1
#define FALSE 0

#define CRC      'C'

/* -------- external data ---------- */
extern int TIMEOUT;
extern int xonxoff_enabled;

/* --------- local data ------------ */
static int tries;    /* retry counter */
static char bf [130]; /* i/o buffer   */
FILE *fp;

/* -------- prototypes ------------- */
void receive_xmodem(void);
static void receive_error(int, int);
unsigned compute_crc(char *, int);

/* --------- error messages ----------- */
static char *errs[] = {
    "Timed Out            ",
```

continued...

...from previous page

```
    "Invalid SOH        ",
    "Invalid block #    ",
    "Invalid chksum/crc"
};

void main(int argc, char *argv[])
{
    int c = 0;

    if (argc != 2)  {
        cprintf("\r\nUsage: xrevc <filename>");
        exit(1);
    }
    if ((fp = fopen(argv[1], "w")) == NULL) {
        cprintf("\r\nCannot open %s", argv[1]);
        exit(1);
    }
    initializemodem();
    cprintf("\r\nPress 'r' after CONNECT to receive");
    cprintf("\r\nPress Esc any time to abort");
    answer_modem();
    while (tolower(c) != 'r' && c != ESC)   {
        /* ------- poll for keyboard input ---------- */
        if (kbhit())
            c = getch();
        /* ------- poll for serial input ---------- */
        if (input_char_ready())
            putch(readserial());
    }
    if (tolower(c) == 'r')
        receive_xmodem();
    fclose(fp);
    hangup();
    release_modem();
}

/* ---------- receive with xmodem protocol ------------- */
void receive_xmodem(void)
{
    int blk=0, soh= 0;
```

continued...

...from previous page

```
    int blck_no, neg_blckno;
    int i;
    int crcin = TRUE, fst = TRUE;
    unsigned chksum, cs, cs1;

    xonxoff_enabled = FALSE;

    /* - send Cs then NAKs until the sender starts sending - */
    tries = 0;
    TIMEOUT = 6;
    while (soh != SOH && tries < RETRIES)   {
        crcin = (tries++ < CRCTRIES);
        writeserial(crcin ? CRC : NAK);
        soh = readserial();
        if (!timed_out() && soh != SOH)
            sleep(6);
    }
    while (tries < RETRIES) {
        if (timed_out())
            receive_error(0, NAK);

        /* -- Receive the data and build the file -- */
        cprintf("\rBlock %d   ", blk + 1);
        if (!fst)   {
            TIMEOUT = 10;
            soh = readserial();
            if (timed_out())
                continue;
            if (soh == CAN)
                break;
            if (soh == EOT) {
                writeserial(ACK);
                break;
            }
        }
        fst = FALSE;
        TIMEOUT = 1;
        blck_no  = readserial() & 255;    /* block number   */
        neg_blckno = readserial() & 255;  /* 1's complement */
        chksum = 0;
```

continued...

...from previous page

```
        /* ---- data block ----- */
        for (i = 0; i < 128; i++)   {
            *(bf + i) = readserial();
            if (timed_out())
                break;
            chksum = (chksum + (*(bf + i)) & 255) & 255;
        }
        if (timed_out())
            continue;
        /* ---- checksum or crc from sender ---- */
        cs = readserial() & 255;
        if (crcin)  {
            cs1 = readserial() & 255;
            cs = (cs << 8) + cs1;
        }
        if (timed_out())
            continue;
        if (soh != SOH) {       /* check the SOH */
            receive_error(1, NAK);
            continue;
        }
        /* --- same as previous block number? --- */
        if (blck_no == blk)
            fseek(fp, -128L, 1);
        /* --- no, next sequential block number? --- */
        else if (blck_no != ((blk + 1) & 255)) {
            receive_error(2, CAN);
            break;
        }
        blk = blck_no;
        /* --- test the block # 1s complement --- */
        if ((neg_blckno & 255) != (~blk & 255))    {
            receive_error(2, NAK);
            continue;
        }
        if (crcin)
            chksum = compute_crc(bf, 130);
        /* --- test chksum or crc vs one sent --- */
        if (cs != chksum)   {
            receive_error(6, NAK);
```

continued...

...from previous page

```
                continue;
            }
            soh = blck_no = neg_blckno = cs = 0;
            tries = 0;
            /* --- write the block to disk --- */
            fwrite(bf, 128, 1, fp);
            if (kbhit())
                if (getch() == ESC) {
                    writeserial(CAN);
                    break;
                }
            writeserial(ACK);
        }
        if (soh == EOT)
            cprintf("\r\nTransfer Complete");
        else
            cprintf("\r\nTransfer Aborted");
        xonxoff_enabled = TRUE;
}

/* ------------- send a nak ------------ */
static void receive_error(int erno, int rtn)
{
    ++tries;
    if (TIMEOUT == 1)
        cprintf("\r\n%s (%d tries)", errs[erno], tries);
    writeserial(rtn);
}

/* --------- compute the crc ------------ */
unsigned compute_crc(char *bf, int len)
{
    int i;
    long crc = 0;
    while (len--)   {
        crc |= (*bf++) & 255;
        for (i = 0; i < 8; i++) {
            crc <<= 1;
            if (crc & 0x1000000L)
                crc ^= 0x102100L;
```

continued...

...from previous page

```
        }
    }
    return (unsigned) (crc >> 8);
}
```

SUMMARY

This chapter discusses serial ports and modems. Chapter 9 explains and implements memory-resident pop-up programs and uses a Personal Dialer utility program to demonstrate the techniques needed to write a Terminate-and-Stay-Resident (TSR) program.

CHAPTER 9

MEMORY-RESIDENT PROGRAMS

This chapter is about writing memory-resident programs with Turbo C. Memory-resident programs—also called TSRs—are widely used and just as widely misunderstood. There are specific problems associated with their development and no sure way to make all such programs work in harmony together or in the company of some nonresident programs. There are, however, a set of guidelines for writing TSRs that you can use in their development. Programs developed with these techniques have a good chance of being compatible with most operating environments.

What you need to understand:

- Interrupt functions
- DOS Memory Control Blocks
- The Program Segment Prefix

New subjects discussed:

- Heap and stack sizes
- DOS reentrance
- The InDOS flag
- Interrupt 0x28
- The Disk Transfer Area (DTA)
- Critical errors
- Breaks

MEMORY-RESIDENT PROGRAMS

Chapter 1 discussed the Turbo C **interrupt** function type, and Chapter 2 used it in interrupt service routines, providing a timer library that your programs can use to time events. But Chapter 2 went one step farther by providing a memory-resident utility that blanks the screen after a period of time with no keyboard activity. This utility is an example of a kind of program that is widely used to extend the user interface of the computer—the Terminate-and-Stay-Resident, or TSR, program.

Two of the most popular types of TSR programs are the keyboard enhancer program and the desktop accessory. Keyboard enhancers, such as ProKey and SuperKey, allow the user to assign sequences of characters to a function key, an <Alt> key combination, or any other key. Desktop accessories, such as SideKick and Homebase, provide notepads, calculators, calendars, telephone dialers, and other desktop aids that pop up at the press of a key.

Other TSR programs include spelling checkers, outline processors, print spoolers, extensions to the DOS command processor, debugging aids, and alarm clocks. These programs and many other resident processes are readily available from commercial vendors, from public domain software sources, or from source code published in magazines.

The TSR program is known by several names, among them pop-up, memory-resident utility, and desktop accessory. Usually, though, they are known among programmers as, simply, TSRs. Such programs are unique because when one is executed, it remains resident in memory and often does not go away until you reboot the computer. While resident, it executes (or pops up) when called.

A typical TSR program is started by an external event—usually the press of a hot key. A hot key is a keystroke formed when the user presses a combination of keys that are reserved for the execution of the utility program. Obviously, this keystroke must be one that is not commonly used for other tasks.

Starting a TSR program causes any other program to be suspended while the TSR executes. When the TSR terminates, the interrupted program resumes. This interrupted process can be a transient program, another TSR program, or DOS itself.

The TSR Environment

The section called "DOS Memory Structure" in Chapter 5 describes the environment under which nonresident, transient programs operate under DOS. Nothing in DOS provides for the co-residency of user programs, co-execution of user programs, or cognizance by DOS of more than one task in memory at a time. The only way that more than one task can be active in memory is for all but one task to be memory resident. According to DOS, such programs are not tasks but interrupt service routines to support the current single running task. DOS allows a task to spawn a subordinate task, but only one task can be active at a time. The spawning task remains dormant until the spawned task terminates.

When DOS is running and at the command processor prompt, TSR programs are executed as if they were normal transient programs. Neither DOS nor the command processor has any way of knowing that these programs will become resident until they terminate by using the Turbo C **keep** function. When the program terminates, it tells DOS how much memory to reserve. As far as DOS is concerned, this action simply increases the lower address of the TPA to just above the memory-resident program, decreasing the amount of memory available to a user program by the size of the resident program. Figure 9.1 shows the system memory map with two TSR programs in place.

Memory-resident programs respond to a defined hot key to run their processes. The programs preserve the condition of the computer when they interrupt it and restore the previous condition when done. A typical memory-resident utility program uses window techniques to communicate with the user because the pop-up nature of a window lends itself to a process that must restore everything to an undisturbed state when it is finished.

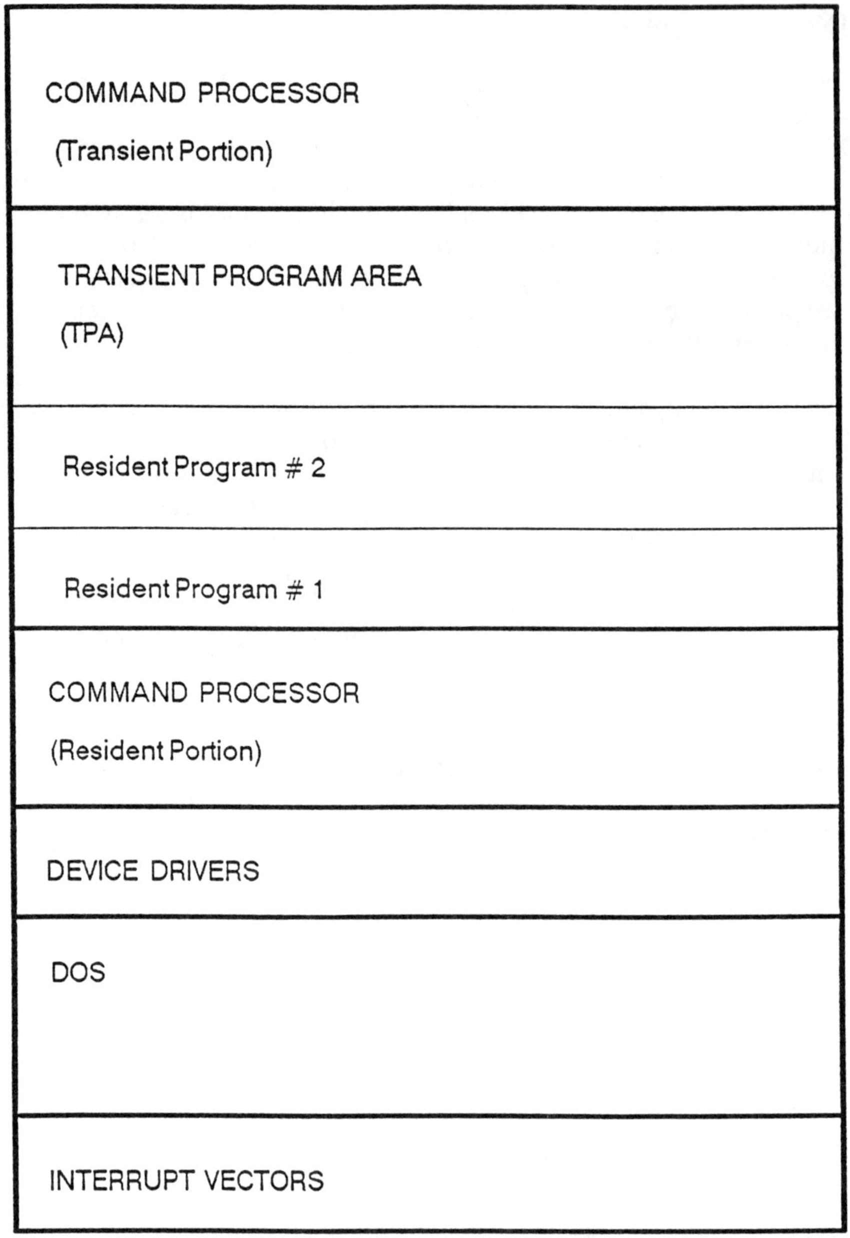

Figure 9.1 The DOS memory map with two TSRs

What Should Be Resident?

As you proceed with this chapter, you will learn how to write TSR utilities in Turbo C. You might develop a tendency to build everything as a resident program and have everything available at the touch of a hot key, but restrain yourself. Not everything can or should be resident.

Remember, as you add resident programs, the size of the TPA is decreased. You can shrink it to a point where not enough memory remains to run normal programs. You might find yourself rich in pop-up utilities but without enough memory to build a small spreadsheet or compose a memo in your word processor.

Remember also that you are straining the design limits of DOS when you insert the first resident program into memory. It is not surprising that TSR programs from different sources do not coexist peacefully. Further, some TSRs do not perform well when certain transient programs are run.

A programmer needs guidelines for deciding whether a utility program should be a TSR or a normal, transient program. Following are tests to apply to programs you are writing:

- **How big is the program?** If the program cannot be compiled and linked with the small memory model—64K code, 64K data and stack—then it probably should not be a TSR. This self-imposed restraint might prevent you from loading memory with utilities at the expense of other programs the user needs.

- **How often is the program needed?** Don't write a resident income tax preparation utility. A program run as infrequently as once a day should not be resident. A program run once an hour could be memory-resident. Do not overload the system with seldom-used TSR programs.

- **What resources are needed by the program?** If a program must allocate much memory or its performance is degraded when memory is limited, it should not be resident. A resident program can be popped up while any other program is running; the other program might have all or most of the memory itself. If the current transient program is a COM file, DOS thinks the current program has all the memory. You might not be able to get any memory at all without a lot of dark byte-twiddling.

- **What is the nature of the program's task?** If the program is used as an adjunct to other programs that the user runs, it is a good candidate to be a TSR. For example, an outline processor is a handy pop-up while you are running a word processor. The same is true for an on-line thesaurus. A calculator and notepad are relevant any time. Not all utility programs, however, should be on-line at the touch of a key.

- **What is the execution time for the program?** The advantage of a pop-up utility is that it is available instantly, and you can run it without closing down whatever else you are doing. The time savings are irrelevant if the utility program takes all day to run.

Getting Resident

To be a TSR, a program must declare itself resident and reserve enough memory to accommodate its size. To know the size of the program, you must know how Turbo C programs are built, which will be explained shortly. Once a program has executed, attached itself to its interrupt vectors, and done everything that is required for a resident program, it calls the **keep** function as follows:

```
#include dos.h
unsigned int sizeprogram;

keep(0, sizeprogram);
```

The sizeprogram integer must be initialized to the length of the program in paragraphs. A paragraph is 16 bytes.

How Big Is the TSR Program?

When your program declares itself resident, it must specify its size so that DOS knows how much memory to set aside for it. You could be safe and declare every program to be 64K bytes, but this strategy would unnecessarily consume memory. It is easy to figure the size of an assembly language program, but the configuration of a C program is somewhat hidden from the programmer. To compute the program's size, you must look at how the Turbo C compiler builds your program.

Figure 9.2 shows the memory map of a typical Turbo C small-model program. The Program Segment Prefix (PSP), explained in Chapter 5, is at the beginning of every program. The code, which is the machine language that executes the functions, follows the PSP. Next come data variables declared as static or external and initialized when they are declared. Uninitialized static and external variables follow the initialized variables.

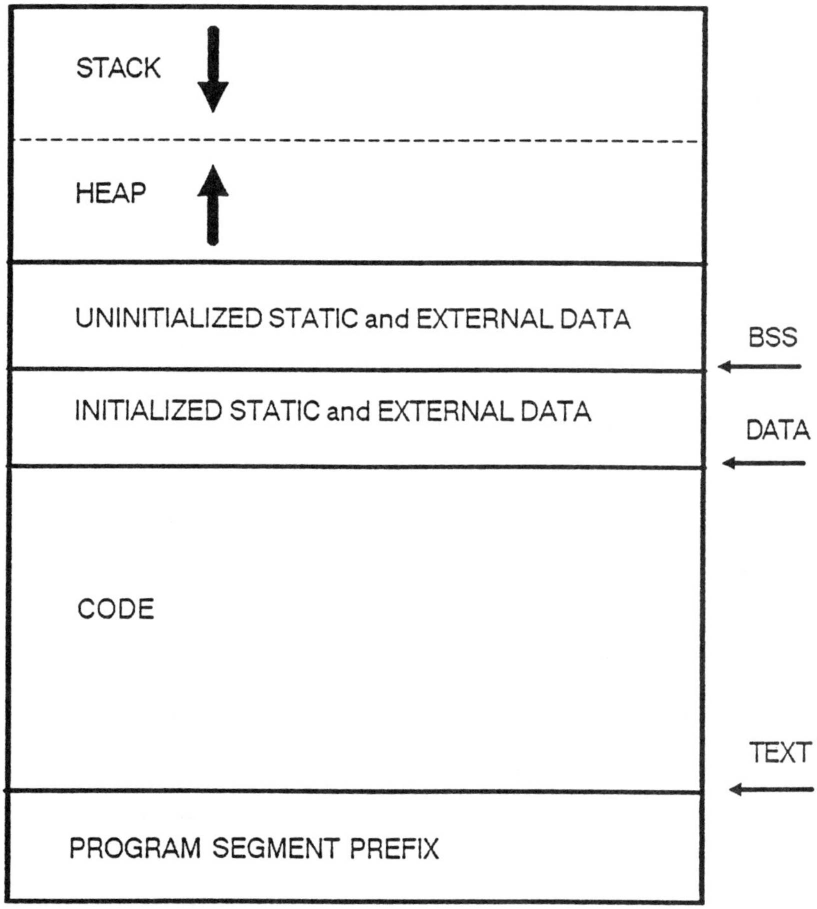

Figure 9.2 Turbo C program memory map

The heap is next and is the block of memory from which dynamic memory allocations are made. The size of the heap depends on how much memory your program is going to allocate.

The stack is next and grows downward. As the program uses stack space, the stack pointer grows downward. The amount of stack required by the program depends on the depth to which function calls are nested and the amount of local data used by those functions. Each call to a function pushes the parameters for that function on the stack and causes some registers to be saved on the stack. If the function has local, automatic variables, the stack pointer is moved farther down because these variables are also stored on the stack. A function that is called recursively and that has a lot of parameters and automatic variables will use a lot of stack. In a TSR, you want to specify as small a stack as is safe.

You specify the program's heap and stack sizes by initializing the Turbo C global variables named **_stklen** and **_heaplen**. These initializations must be done with initializers rather than assignments. Computing the TSR program's size is then a matter of computing the distance between the PSP address and the top of the stack. The problem is in figuring out what the sizes of the heap and stack should be. If you specify them to be smaller than they need to be, then your program will probably crash. If you make them too big, you are wasting resident memory.

To estimate your heap size, examine your use of the Turbo C memory allocation functions. If you are using the window functions from Chapter 4, you can estimate your heap requirements by estimating the size and number of windows that will be concurrently established. Each window allocates a save buffer equal to its height multiplied by its width multiplied by two. The heap buffer for a window is returned to the heap when the window is closed, so the important consideration is the maximum number of windows that are opened at one time. You must estimate the other heap demands of your program by reviewing your own use of the Turbo C memory allocation functions. If your program allocates memory as a function of external influences, such as data dependencies or user inputs, be sure that your error-checking is thorough and your error-handling is appropriate.

One way to find the optimum size of the stack and heap is by trial and error. First, get your program working with a large stack and heap. Next, reduce the **_stklen** and **_heaplen** initializers in your program. With each experimental reduction, stress the program with tests that use the most heap and stack. Continue these experiments until the program begins to crash the system or behave in peculiar ways. Then, increase the stack and heap lengths back to a safe value. Do this iteratively until you have what you believe to be a safe configuration. Now use the program extensively before you believe that it is correct. You are striving for the most memory-efficient program. Because it is a resident program, any memory it reserves that it does not need is wasted because the memory is unavailable to other programs.

Another way is to build your TSR program with an oversized stack and heap. Run it for a while in ways that use a lot of stack and heap. Then use the Turbo Debugger to examine the memory between the stack and the heap. The block of bytes that are set to zero values is the memory that was not used.

Chapter 12 discusses the use of the Turbo Debugger for TSR programs.

Is the TSR Program Already Resident?

Remember, DOS does not know that your program is resident after it terminates. If you execute a TSR program several times, several copies of it will be resident unless it has a way to test to see if a copy of itself is already in memory.

There is a common way for a TSR program to test to see if it is already resident. Each TSR is coded with a unique string array signature. When a TSR is loaded, it must search memory for other resident programs, looking at each one to see if it has the signature. If the search ends at the signature of the newly loaded transient copy of the TSR, then no other copy is resident. If the signature is found in another program, the TSR is assumed to be already resident.

Searching memory for the contents of other resident programs involves walking through the chain of memory blocks that DOS has allocated. The techniques for finding the DOS memory block chain and walking through it are described in Chapter 5.

Attaching and Chaining Interrupts

You will need to attach all the interrupt vectors that will allow your TSR to be executed once it is resident. Attaching an interrupt vector is easy in Turbo C. The **setvect** function provides a one-line way to do the job. You must have declared an interrupt function, and you must know which vector you are going to attach to the vector. Then, issue the **setvect** function call, which is described in Chapter 2.

If you attach your programs to interrupts that are used by other programs, you must chain those interrupts so that all programs that need them will see them. For example, if you attach your program to the timer interrupt and make no provision for the rest of the system to use the interrupt, the other processes that are timer-event-driven will be disabled for as long as your program is installed. If that happens, the system clock will shut down.

Other interrupts you might attach are the keyboard interrupt, the BIOS disk function interrupt, and other interrupts that exist to support the TSR. In each of these cases, you must chain the interrupt to the other processes that need it.

Attaching and chaining interrupts are discussed in detail in Chapter 2.

Popping Up

Once the TSR is resident, it must be able to pop up. This operation is usually the result of a hot key press by the user. The program has a number of things it must do once it decides it wants to pop up, but you should first look at the mechanisms by which the program decides that it can pop up.

The Keyboard Interrupt

When the user presses the hot key, the TSR must interrupt whatever the system is doing and start itself. To do this, the program must watch the keyboard for the hot key. An understanding of this process requires an understanding of how keyboard interrupt and data scan codes work.

A key press generates interrupt 9, and processing takes over at the function pointed to by the interrupt 9 vector. The function must read the keyboard data port and process the keystroke. The PC keyboard does not generate the ASCII value your program sees when it issues the **getchar** function; the keyboard generates a scan code that can be read from the keyboard's input data port. Each key on the keyboard has its own value. The function must determine from this value which key or keys are pressed and what to make of them.

The ROM-BIOS has a keyboard interrupt service routine that reads the scan codes, translates them into ASCII values, and inserts them into a keyboard buffer. Programs (including DOS) that read the keyboard read from this buffer. The ROM-BIOS maintains a status byte that tells whether the Alt, Right Shift, Left Shift, or Ctrl keys are being pressed. A program can read the current value of these keys by retrieving that status byte from the ROM-BIOS.

A TSR can attach itself to the interrupt 9 vector. The interrupt 9 function in the TSR must chain to the previous contents of the interrupt 9 vector so that the ROM-BIOS keyboard services continue. Before chaining, however, the TSR's interrupt service routine can read the scan code and status byte to see if the hot key has been pressed.

If the TSR avoids all DOS function calls, the interrupt 9 function can execute the pop-up function immediately. If the TSR wants to use DOS functions, the interrupt service routine must not execute the pop-up but must flag the presence of the hot key and return. Other interrupt service routines will observe the hot key flag and execute the pop-up when it is safe to do so. One function that watches for an acceptable time to execute the pop-up is the timer interrupt service routine.

The Timer Interrupt

The PC is interrupted 18.2 times a second by the system timer, which uses interrupt vector 8 to execute the timer function. Chapter 12 includes a resident clock program run by the timer interrupt. Hot key TSRs also must use the timer interrupt, so they will attach a timer function to interrupt vector 8. Because the program cannot execute until it is safe to use DOS functions, the keyboard function sets a flag when the hot key is pressed as just described. The TSR uses a timer interrupt to see if the flag is set and, if the flag is set, to see if it is safe to use DOS functions. If these two conditions are met, the timer function can call the TSR's pop-up functions.

As with the keyboard interrupt, the timer function of a TSR must chain the timer interrupt to other programs that have it attached ahead of the TSR.

The DOS Reentrance Problem

A TSR program must avoid DOS function calls if it can be executed as the result of an interrupt of DOS itself. The TSR must either never call DOS or make sure it never interrupts DOS to pop up.

As long as a program reads the keyboard by using ROM-BIOS functions and writes the screen with either ROM-BIOS calls or direct video memory accesses, the program runs without problems, but if a TSR program, having interrupted DOS, attempts to use DOS functions, the system crashes. This is because DOS functions are not reentrant. This non-reentrant characteristic of DOS would seem to restrict TSR programs to operations that can be done within the limits of memory and ROM-BIOS resources. That restriction is no big sacrifice for console operations. As you learned from the way the window functions are built, you can get along nicely without DOS if you only need the keyboard and the screen. But this approach excludes file operations from a resident program, and programs need files.

The Many DOS Stacks

DOS maintains several stacks. When DOS is executing one of the lower functions numbered 0 to 12, it uses one stack; when it is executing any other function, it uses another stack. In either case, DOS saves the caller's stack segment and pointer registers in a single location for each group; therefore, neither of the groups is reentrant.

DOS is better described as semi-reentrant. When functions 0 to 12 are interrupted, it is safe to call any of the other functions. When any of the other functions is interrupted, it is safe to use functions 0 to 12.

There is no problem avoiding DOS functions 0 to 12. These functions manage the DOS console input and output. They are easy to forsake because there are other ways to manage the screen and keyboard, and those other ways offer better performance than the DOS functions. The upper functions are not so easy to avoid. They do everything else, including file management, which is necessary in a resident program.

Because you can avoid functions 0 to 12 but need the others, the two-stack situation will work for you. If you can be sure that your interrupts will always occur outside of the upper DOS functions, no reentrance problem will exist. You manage the problem by flagging a hot key interrupt and delaying its process until DOS is outside of an unsafe function. The unsafe functions are fast functions; they do their operation and return quickly, so there is no undue wait.

Because the TSR is triggered by a hot key interrupt, and because keyboard interrupts occur regardless of what DOS is doing, you need a way to determine if DOS is unsafe. The InDOS Flag provides that information.

The InDOS Flag (0x34)

DOS Function 0x34 returns the DOS segment address and an offset to a special flag that DOS maintains. That flag is called the InDOS Flag. When DOS is about to go into one of the unsafe functions, it sets this flag. When the unsafe function completes, DOS clears the flag.

When a resident program first executes, it uses DOS function 0x34 to find the address of the InDOS Flag. When the hot key is pressed, the keyboard function sets a flag. At every tick of the system clock, the timer function examines the hot key flag. If the hot key flag is set, the timer function looks at the InDOS Flag. If that flag is set, the timer function returns, doing nothing for the resident program. At each successive tick of the clock, the timer function watches the InDOS Flag. When the flag finally says that DOS is no longer busy, the timer function clears the hot key flag and pops up the TSR.

This procedure works some of the time. At other times, DOS stays busy until the user does something other than press the hot key—for example, when the command processor is waiting at the system prompt for the user to type a command. If the user presses the hot key, the keyboard function sets the hot key flag, but, because DOS is busy, the timer function never pops up the TSR. To cope with this condition, DOS uses the 0x28 interrupt vector.

The 0x28 Interrupt

There are frequent periods during which DOS is busy when DOS knows that you can use the upper DOS functions. One of these times is while DOS is waiting for a keystroke. When DOS knows that it is busy but that it is safe to use its upper functions, DOS calls the 0x28 interrupt. The purpose of the interrupt is to tell TSRs that they can use the upper DOS functions.

TSRs can attach themselves to the 0x28 interrupt vector. The TSR's 0x28 interrupt service routine tests for the hot key flag. If the hot key flag is set, the program pops up the TSR. If not, the interrupt service routine returns to the program that called the interrupt. In either case, the program chains the interrupt vector to any other TSR that might be attached to it.

The 0x28 interrupt is called when DOS is busy; however, a TSR executed from this function cannot be interrupted by another TSR unless the running TSR also makes occasional calls to INT 0x28. The reason for this limitation is that when DOS calls the interrupt, the InDOS Flag is set. While the TSR is running, the InDOS Flag will remain set, and if the user presses the hot key for another TSR, that program's timer interrupt service routine will wait for the InDOS Flag to be reset, which will not happen while the TSR is running. This condition will always exist when the first TSR is popped up while the DOS command processor is waiting for a user command.

To allow a second TSR to interrupt a first, each TSR can call the 0x28 interrupt while waiting for a keystroke.

The Disk ROM-BIOS Interrupt (0x13)

You never want to interrupt a disk operation. If your TSR is allowed to interrupt the system while a disk seek, read, or write operation is underway, the latent time used by the TSR can generate disk errors for the interrupted program. If the TSR is allowed to interrupt a seek-read operation or a seek-write operation, particularly after the seek and before the read/write, the TSR's use of the disk system could throw the interrupted program's disk processing out of whack. To avoid these circumstances, a TSR attaches the ROM-BIOS disk interrupt vector 0x13. If any process calls this interrupt, the TSR sets a flag and then chains to the prior interrupt vector for 0x13. When the 0x13 interrupt is completed, the TSR's interrupt service routine clears the flag. This flag is tested by the timer interrupt service routine. If disk operations are in effect, the TSR is not allowed to pop up.

Context Switching

When the TSR is first executed, it enjoys all the resources that DOS provides to a normal task. After it has declared itself resident and terminated, those resources are given to other programs or, when no program is running, to the DOS command processor. When the TSR is executed as the result of the hot key, the program is a parasite to the interrupted program. DOS does not realize that a different task is running; those resources still belong to the interrupted task. Somehow, the system pointers to those resources must be changed so that the TSR is the acknowledged running task. Changing such resources among tasks is called context switching in a multitasking environment, and a multitasking DOS switches the context. In the single-task DOS of the PC, however, DOS does no context switching, so the interrupting task must switch its own context in and out.

The Stack

All programs need a stack. The TSR has a stack when it terminates, but when it interrupts another program, the PC's stack segment and stack pointer registers point to the interrupted program's stack. Because stacks push down and pop up, and because such a device promotes reentrant programs, you might reason that the best approach is to use the interrupted program's stack. Many assembly language TSRs do just that, but to do so, they must severely restrict their use of stack space. First, you have no idea how much stack the interrupted program will provide. Second, DOS guarantees that it will have a stack with enough space for the registers only. C is a stack-intensive language, and you need more stack space than DOS guarantees, which means that a TSR must switch to its own stack when it interrupts another process.

Switching to your own stack means you must save the stack segment and pointer registers before you make the switch. These saved values are returned to the registers before the TSR returns to the interrupted program. When the TSR declares itself resident, it saves its own stack segment and stack pointer registers. When the TSR is popped up and has saved the stack context of the interrupted program, the TSR reestablishes its own stack.

If the TSR is reentrant (i.e., if it can interrupt itself), this stack switching can fail. The second time you switch the stack, you overwrite the save area for the stack register. To avoid this, you must write resident programs that are not reentrant. This restriction is no great loss; most memory-resident utilities do not need to be reentrant.

To prevent a TSR from being reentrant, you set a flag when the TSR is popped up. The flag remains set until the TSR returns to the interrupted process. If the TSR is requested a second time (by a chance bump of the hot key, perhaps), it senses the setting of the flag and declines to run. Such flags are called "semaphores."

The Program Segment Prefix (PSP)

The PSP is a 256-byte control area at the front of every program in memory. The prefix contains many fields that DOS uses to manage the processing environment of the program. Chapter 5 contains a discussion of the PSP and describes its contents.

Each program has a PSP. To DOS, the only real PSP is the one at the front of the last program executed. DOS allows programs to spawn the execution of other programs, and the new program inherits PSP values from its parent, but, because DOS only recognizes one active task at a time, it knows about only one PSP.

The PSP contains several interesting fields, but the one of most interest for this discussion is the array of 20 file handles. As discussed in Chapter 5, a program can open 20 files at a time. Each file is assigned a handle, and that handle is an element of the array in the PSP. The array has room for 20 handles, and the first five entries are assigned to the stdin, stdout, stderr, stdaux, and stdprn logical devices when the program is first executed. As a program opens files, the new handles are stored in the PSP array. Array entries that have not been used contain a -1 value. The program addresses the files as subscripts into the array. The array values are subscripts into a DOS table of files.

If a TSR loads, opens a file, then declares itself resident and terminates, the handle for that file is stored in the TSR's PSP. When the TSR is popped up, DOS thinks the interrupted program is still running. If the TSR makes a DOS call for the file it opened when it was first executed, DOS looks into the PSP of the interrupted program for the handle. This action will confuse matters; if the corresponding array entry in the interrupted program's PSP contains an entry, the file reference will be to the interrupted program's file and not to the TSR's file. If the interrupted program has not used that entry in its PSP, DOS will think that it is being asked to refer to an unopened file.

The solution would seem to be one of the following:

- Don't open files at initialization of the TSR; open them when the TSR interrupts the other program. This method uses entries from the interrupted program's PSP for the TSR's files.
- Don't use the handle files of DOS 2.0 and above. Use the older File Control Block (FCB) logic from DOS 1.1. Those functions do not use PSP array entries. The FCB tables are maintained in the data space of the programs that use them.
- Switch the PSP address in DOS when the TSR interrupts, and switch it back when the TSR returns.

Each of these approaches has its disadvantages:

- There are two disadvantages to using the interrupted program's PSP array for TSR file handles. First, the nature of the TSR might be such that opening and closing files presents an unacceptable performance penalty each time the program is popped up. Second, there is no way to be sure that the interrupted program's PSP will have enough handle array space for the TSR's handles.
- Using FCB functions has two disadvantages. First, a file opened with FCB functions must be in the logged-on subdirectory of the system when the file is opened. No DOS path subdirectories may be used in the file specification when the file is opened. Second, all Turbo C standard library file operations assume the use of the more flexible handle files. To use FCB functions, you must develop equivalent functions to replace the standard open, close, read, write, fopen, fclose, fget, fput, fprintf, etc., functions.

- There are no documented DOS functions for modifying the address of the PSP as DOS recognizes it. There is a documented DOS function for reading the current PSP address (INT 0x21, Function 0x62), but it is available only with DOS versions 3.0 and higher. Two undocumented DOS INT 0x21 functions (0x50 and 0x51) set and get the address of the PSP, but they are not reliable in DOS versions 2.0, 2.1, and 2.11 for use in TSR programs. They share a stack with certain DOS functions that might be interrupted by a TSR, and if the TSR uses functions 0x50 and 0x51 while interrupting these other DOS functions, the system will crash. You may use these functions only if your TSR is to run with DOS versions 3.0 and higher. The two undocumented DOS functions are called GetPSP and SetPSP in this chapter.

The solution is none of the above. A TSR must be able to use files, but all the obvious solutions have disadvantages. Working substitutes for the GetPSP and SetPSP functions are needed if the program is to work with DOS 2.0, 2.1, and 2.11.

The approach taken here is to use the Turbo C global variable **_osmajor** to see if the program is running under DOS 2.0, 2.1, or 2.11. If so, you can determine the PSP address holders at run-time when the TSR is executed. You find where DOS stores the PSP address and do your own getting and setting of the PSP.

The Disk Transfer Area (DTA)

The second half of the PSP is the DTA, a 128-byte buffer where DOS reads and writes any disk files that are opened for use with the FCB functions. DOS also uses this area for functions that deal with directory searches.

A TSR must save the DTA address of the program it interrupts and establish its own DTA address if the TSR will use any DOS functions that write to the DTA. Upon return to the interrupted program, the TSR must restore the DTA address to the address of the interrupted program. The interrupt might have occurred after the interrupted program set the DTA address and before the program was done with it.

Because the TSR will be in C, you cannot be certain that it will not change or use the DTA. Actions of functions in the C library are not necessarily known, and the best course is the safe one. The Turbo C **getdta** and **setdta** functions are used to safely modify the DTA.

Video Switching

Most TSR programs use the screen to communicate with the user. The TSR can pop up at any time, so the screen contents must be preserved for whatever was using it before the pop-up. If you do all screen output by using a window package such as the one in Chapter 4, the prior screen images are saved as windows are opened on areas of the screen.

Most window packages are text-based. That is, they do not work if the system is in one of the many possible PC graphics modes. There are many graphics modes, and a significant amount of memory is required to save blocks of graphics screens so that pop-up windows can be displayed. These are problems that can be addressed but that are beyond the scope of this book. The advised approach is to test the current video mode and not pop up unless the computer is using one of the text modes.

The Cursor

In Chapter 5, you learned a number of cursor tricks. Among them were ways to change the configuration of the cursor. It follows that a TSR program must save the current configuration of the cursor, set it to whatever the TSR needs, and restore it before popping down.

The cursor.c file in Chapter 5 includes functions to perform such tasks. The **savecursor** function reads and saves the current cursor configuration. The **normalcursor** function sets the cursor shape to the normal blinking underline style. The **restorecursor** function restores the cursor to the configuration it had at the time of the last **savecursor** call.

The DOS Critical Error Interrupt (0x24)

When DOS encounters a critical error, it calls the Critical Error Interrupt, number 0x24. For example, if you try to access a diskette with the drive door open, DOS senses a not ready condition and calls the critical error interrupt. If a program does not attach itself to the 0x24 interrupt vector, all critical errors are handled by an interrupt service routine in the DOS command processor. The command processor writes the "Abort, Retry, or Ignore" message on the screen. The function returns a value to DOS that specifies what DOS should do about the error.

Assume that no program has attached itself to the 0x24 vector. Your TSR interrupts a transient program. Your TSR tries to read a diskette, and the drive door is open. The DOS command processor takes over and asks the user whether it should abort, retry, or ignore. If the user types "A," DOS attempts to abort. Because TSRs swap PSP addresses, DOS tries to abort the TSR. DOS does not know that there is a transient program in an interrupted condition and does not return to it, even though its memory is still allocated by DOS. The system is amuck. If your TSR did not swap PSP addresses, DOS aborts the transient program and does not return to the TSR.

A TSR must attach the 0x24 interrupt vector regardless of whether it intends to do anything about the errors. The vector is attached when the TSR program is popped up and restored when the TSR program is about to return to the interrupted program. Under no circumstance should the TSR tell DOS to abort the process. Most TSR programs simply ignore the errors and tell DOS to also ignore the errors, figuring that the user can tell when something is wrong. The critical error interrupt is not chained.

The DOS Ctrl-Break Interrupt and Ctrl-C Interrupt

When the user presses the Ctrl-Break key combination, BIOS calls interrupt 0x1a, which usually vectors into DOS. When this happens or when the user presses the Ctrl-C key, DOS displays the ^C token at the current cursor location on the screen and calls interrupt 0x23. The 0x23 function provided by DOS causes immediate termination of the current program. You do not want the TSR program terminated in this fashion; it has too many interrupt vectors attached to it, and a transient program might be above it in memory. If you merely intercept the interrupt, you run the risk that another program loaded behind yours attached itself to the interrupt and will do something inappropriate with the Ctrl-Break while your TSR program is running.

Turbo C includes the **getcbrk** and **setcbrk** functions that allow a program to read the current status (enabled/disabled) of the Ctrl-Break process and to set the status. When a TSR program is popped up, it should read the current status of the Ctrl-Break process. Then, the TSR should disable the Ctrl-Break process. When the TSR program is ready to return to the interrupted process, the TSR program should restore the Ctrl-Break status to its former setting.

If you disable the Ctrl-Break process in the manner just described and the user presses Ctrl-Break when the TSR program is running, the interrupted program will be terminated when the TSR program returns. If all TSRs use the same logic, only transient programs will be terminated by the Ctrl-Break interrupt.

To completely disable the effects of either break key while the TSR is popped up, a TSR should attach interrupt vectors 0x23 and 0x1a to its own interrupt service routine, one which does nothing. The attaching is done when the TSR is popped up, and the interrupts are restored when the TSR pops down.

Unloading a TSR Program

There will be occasions when you will want to unload a TSR program, which is not a simple procedure. Remember, DOS does not know about the program because to DOS, the program terminated when it became resident; therefore, to unload a TSR program, you must do what DOS would have done if the program had been transient.

Unloading a TSR program involves the following steps:

- **Decide To Unload.** Decide from within the TSR program that it is to unload. Some programs use a menu selection to tell the TSR to unload. Other programs use special unload hot keys.

- **Restore Interrupt Vectors.** The TSR program may not be able to perform this task. If another TSR program was loaded after yours and it chained interrupts, you will effectively disable it if you replace the old vectors. Also, the other TSR, if it is terminated later, will replace the vectors with pointers into the space formerly occupied by your program. Before you can restore interrupt vectors, you must determine if your program still owns them. To determine if you still own the interrupts, you must compare the vectors to the addresses of your interrupt service routines. If any vector has changed, you do not own it; therefore, you cannot terminate the program—you must merely suspend it.

- **Close Files.** When a transient program terminates, DOS automatically closes all files by scanning the program's file handle array in the PSP and closing any entries still in use. Remember, these entries are offsets to an array DOS maintains. When a TSR program terminates to stay resident, DOS does not close the TSR's open files; therefore, your TSR termination routine must do it. If you do not close the files, the DOS file table entry is not released and is not available for later use by other programs. Successive loading and termination of a TSR program that does not close its files will exhaust the DOS file table and crash the system.

  Entries in the PSP file handle array represent files at the handle level. These entries are equivalent to the low-level unbuffered input/output functions in C. The C language functions that do buffered stream input/output maintain their own internal buffers and pointers and might require flushing before closing. Flushing is a C library operation rather than a DOS operation. You will want to close all such files by calling the standard **fclose** function. Files that the TSR opened with the **open** and **creat** functions can be closed with the **close** function.

- **Return TSR Memory to DOS.** You can use the Turbo C **freemem** function for this process. There are usually only two blocks allocated. One is the program's environment block; its address is in the PSP at offset 0x2c. The other block is the PSP itself.

TSR.C: THE TURBO C TSR ENGINE

Up to now, this chapter has described how a TSR program works and what you must do to write one. Now, you will get the tools to do that. Listings 9.1 and 9.2 are tsr.h and tsr.c, a TSR engine that you link with your program to make it a memory-resident pop-up utility program. You write a program that declares the hot key value and calls the **tsr** function after it has initialized. The program provides the **exec_popup** function for the TSR engine to call when the pop-up is to occur. Other than those interfaces, the program appears to be a normal nonresident program. Its association with tsr.c is what makes it resident. All the concerns of TSR processing are managed from within the engine itself.

Components of tsr.c

The following discussion addresses the parts of tsr.c that will explain how it works. The subjects are presented in the order in which they appear in the listing.

The Hot Key

The tsr.c program includes two variables, **scancode** and **keymask**, that define the hot key that pops up the program. The program that you attach to the TSR engine must initialize these values. Following is a discussion of what the values should be.

When a key is pressed, the 09 interrupt occurs and the keyboard interrupt service routine reads the keyboard input port, which returns a scan code. Each key on the keyboard has a scan code. Figure 9.3 shows these scan codes. At the same time, the interrupt service routine looks at the BIOS shift key status byte. This byte is described in Chapter 5 in the section named "The Case of the Missing Keys." The byte is located at address 0:417 and contains bits for the Ctrl, Alt, Shift, Ins, Caps Lock, and Scroll Lock keys. Figure 9.4 shows the position of these key bit values in the status byte. If the bit corresponding to the key is set to one, the key is being pressed. By sensing the specified scan code and determining that the specified toggle/shift key is depressed, the TSR keyboard function can determine that the hot key combination has been pressed. To specify these values, you initialize the **scancode** and **keymask** variables.

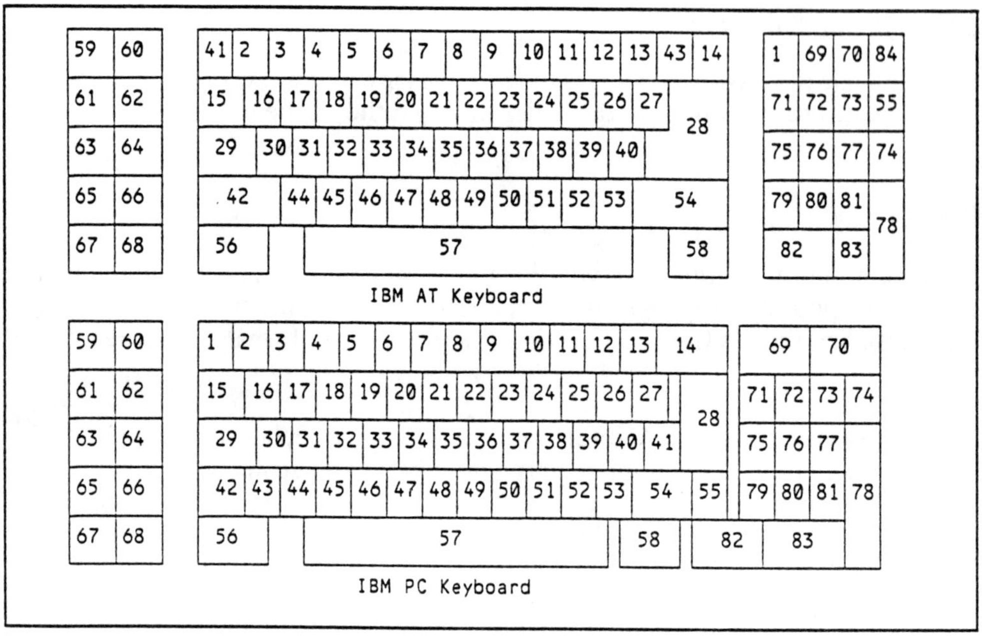

Figure 9.3 *The keyboard scan codes*

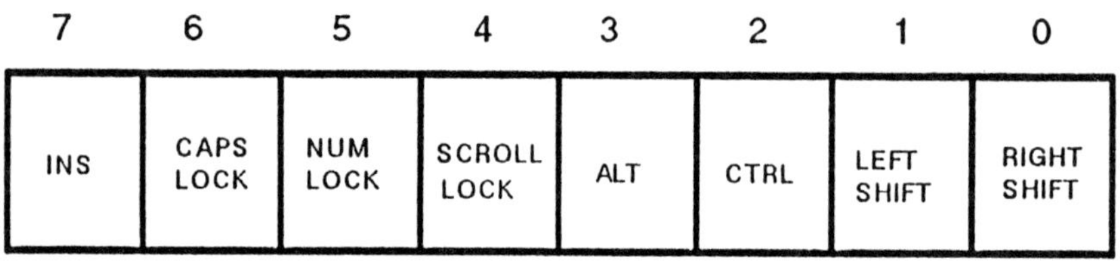

Figure 9.4 *The keyboard status mark*

The TSR Signature

The character array named **signature** in tsr.c must be initialized by your TSR application program. Each TSR needs a unique signature. When you run the TSR from the command line, it needs to know if it is already resident, and this signature is used for that purpose.

The unloading Variable

The integer variable named **unloading** is originally set to a false value. If your TSR decides to unload itself from memory, it will set this variable to a true value before returning from its **exec_popup** function to pop down.

The tsr Function

The tsr.c source file includes the **tsr** function. Your program calls this function to become a TSR. The **tsr** function first calls the tsr_init function to initialize several control values. Then it calls **resident** to see if the TSR is already in memory. If not, it calls the **resinit** function to set itself up as a TSR. Note the DEBUG variable. If you compile with this variable defined, the program will execute as a one-time nonresident program rather than a TSR. This is a method for testing the TSR that is discussed at the end of this chapter.

The tsrinit Function

This function establishes several startup variables. It uses the undocumented DOS function 0x34 to get the address of the InDOS flag discussed earlier. It uses the DOS function 0x52 to get the address of the first Memory Control Block. This structure is discussed in Chapter 5. The function calls the Turbo C **getdta** function to save the address of the TSR's DTA for context switching. If version 2 of DOS is being used, the **pspaddr** function is called to locate the places in DOS where the PSP is stored.

The resinit Function

This function turns the program into a TSR. It saves the TSR's stack segment and pointer registers for context switching. Next it saves the current values of the interrupt vectors for the system timer, the keyboard, DOS interrupt 0x28, and the BIOS disk interrupt. These saved values are used to chain the interrupts and to restore them when the TSR unloads. Next the function attaches those interrupt vectors to its own interrupt service routines. The size of the program is computed as the number of bytes from the address of the PSP to the end of the stack. This value is divided by 16 to produce the number of paragraphs to reserve when the program terminates to stay resident. The Turbo C **keep** function is called to complete the function, and the program is now a TSR.

The newbreak Function

The interrupt function named **newbreak** is the TSR's Ctrl-C and Ctrl-Break function. It is not attached when the TSR declares itself resident, but only temporarily while the TSR is popped up. Its purpose is to disable breaks. It does nothing and does not chain to the previous interrupt service routine.

The newcrit Function

The interrupt function named **newcrit** is the TSR's critical error function. It is not attached when the TSR declares itself resident, but only temporarily, while the TSR is popped up. Its purpose is to avoid the confusion of an abort by a critical error while the TSR has contexts switched from where DOS had them. The critical error function returns a zero value in the ax register to DOS. This value tells DOS to ignore the error.

The newdisk Function

As the computer runs programs and the programs use DOS, DOS uses the ROM-BIOS disk interrupt vector (0x13) to read and write sectors of disk data. The **newdisk** function protects the disk operations from being interrupted by your TSR. A flag is set upon entry to the chained function and cleared when the function returns. If that flag is set when the TSR is otherwise ready to pop up, the TSR will delay its execution until the flag is cleared.

The testhotkey Function

This function tests the scancode passed to it for a match on the programmed hot key scan code. If they match, the function tests the BIOS shift key status byte to see if the programmed hot key value matches. If both are true, the function sets the **hotkey_flag** and returns the true value. Otherwise, the function returns a false value. This function is called by the keyboard and timer interrupt functions.

The newkb Function

The interrupt function named **newkb** is the keyboard function for the TSR. If a scan code has been specified, **newkb** reads the keyboard data port and calls **testhotkey** to see if the scan code from the key press and the BIOS shift status byte match the TSR's hot key. If so, the function resets the keyboard hardware so that it will not interrupt again. If not, the function chains to the earlier keyboard interrupt service routine.

The timer Function

Each tick of the timer causes an execution of the timer function **newtimer** in resident.c. Before it does anything else, it chains to the earlier address of the timer interrupt vector. Then, the function calls **testhotkey** with a key value of 0. This allows the use of key combinations from the BIOS shift status byte without an associated scan code. With this method, you can program such hot keys as Alt/Right Shift. If the hot key was pressed, the function tests the InDOS flag. If DOS is not busy, **newtimer** tests to see if a disk BIOS operation is in process. If not, it resets the timer interrupt, turns off the flag that says the hot key was pressed, and calls the **dores** function to get the TSR utility running.

The new28 Function

The 0x28 interrupt is serviced by the function named new28. It chains to any earlier 0x28 function and tests the hot key flag. If the hot key has been pressed, it tests to make sure that the InDOS flag is set. If so, it resets the hot key flag and calls **dores**.

The resident_psp and interrupted_psp Functions

These functions change the current PSP when the TSR is about to pop up or down. If the program uses DOS 2.x, the values from the PSP table are used to find the places where the old PSP is found and the new PSP value is to be stored. Otherwise, the program uses the Turbo C **getpsp** function and the DOS 0x50 function to set the PSP.

The dores Function: Executing the TSR Program

The **dores** function is called when the TSR has determined that it is safe to execute the TSR. **Dores** first sets the **running** semaphore to prevent another press of the hot key from starting the TSR in a reentrant fashion. Then, the interrupted program's stack registers are saved, and the stack is pointed to the TSR's local stack.

The critical error and break interrupt vectors are saved, and the TSR's functions are attached to the vectors. The current Ctrl-Break setting is saved, and Ctrl-Break interrupts are disabled.

The interrupted program's DTA address is saved, and the DTA is set to that of the TSR. The same process is done for the PSP address. Then, the TSR function named **exec_popup** is called. This function is in your program. You will learn about its operation when you get to the example TSR program.

Note that the **dores** function does not manage any video or cursor context switching. The TSR engine does not know what your program needs in the way of video support and does not attempt video management. That process will be the responsibility of each individual TSR program.

When the **exec_popup** function returns, the PSP address, DTA address, critical error interrupt vector, break vectors, and Ctrl-Break setting are restored to the values they contained before the TSR took over. The **dores** function then restores the interrupted program's stack and tests to see if the TSR set the **unloading** flag. If so, **dores** calls the **unload** function. The **running** semaphore is reset, and **dores** returns to the interrupted program.

The resident Function: Testing to See If the TSR Is Already Resident

The **resident** function tests to see if the TSR is already in memory. It uses the TSR's signature to make this test. The program that is running is a transient copy of the TSR. It has the signature in it. If a resident copy exists, it too has the signature. Both copies of the program will have the signature at the same offset from their respective PSP addresses. First the function computes the difference between the data segment register and the PSP. Then it walks through the DOS Memory Control Block chain looking for PSPs. A PSP can be recognized by the value 0x20cd in its first word. This value is explained in Chapter 5. If the value is a PSP, the program compares its address to the Turbo C **_psp** global variable. If the values are the same, the search has terminated on the PSP of the transient copy of the program, and no resident copy exists. If the values are not the same, the block is the PSP of some other program, perhaps a resident copy of the TSR. Using the offset address of the signature and the difference computed between the data segment and the PSP address, the program compares its signature with the corresponding memory location in the other program. If they match, the program assumes that a resident copy of itself exists.

The pspaddr Function: Finding DOS 2.x PSP Place Holders

This function locates where DOS 2.x keeps the PSP by using the following procedure. First, the present PSP address is taken from the Turbo C **_psp** global variable. Next, the memory occupied by DOS is searched for a copy of the PSP address. Once such a value is found, its address is saved, and the PSP is changed to an artificial value by using the DOS 0x50 function. The value at the found address is examined to see if it has changed to the artificial PSP. If so, an address of where a PSP address is stored in DOS has been identified and is now saved in the table named **psps**. The original PSP address is restored with DOS 0x50, and the search proceeds. DOS 2.0, 2.1, and 2.11 keep the PSP address in two locations. These addresses are used by the **resident_psp** and **interrupted_psp** functions.

The unload and resterm Functions: Unloading the TSR

The **unload** function determines if the TSR can be unloaded by testing to see if any of the interrupt vectors have changed. If so, the TSR cannot be unloaded. If not, the TSR can be unloaded, and the **resterm** function is called.

Termination of a TSR program involves four procedures:

- closing files
- restoring interrupt vectors
- erasing the TSR's signature
- de-allocating program memory

First, all files must be closed. When DOS terminates a program, it closes all open files by checking all 20 entries in the PSP's file handle array. This action closes files at the handle level and does not account for stream files that are open and might need to be flushed. Because the TSR **unload** function cannot use the DOS program termination process, the TSR program must close its own files. This part of the unload procedure is the responsibility of the TSR program itself and is not dealt with by the TSR engine.

The second TSR termination procedure is to restore all interrupt vectors to their original values before the TSR attached itself to them.

The third TSR termination procedure is to erase the TSR's signature. If the TSR is unloaded and the signature is not erased, that string remains in memory. If a different TSR is loaded and its memory usage does not initialize the first TSR's signature, then the signature remains undisturbed. A later attempt to reload the first TSR will find its signature in the memory owned by the second, and a false positive test for residency will result. To avoid this condition, the termination procedure sets the signature to a null-terminated string.

The fourth and final TSR termination procedure is to de-allocate the memory blocks that have been allocated to the TSR. At least two blocks of memory are allocated to a program by DOS when the program is loaded. One block contains the program's environment variables, and the other is the program itself. The address of the environment variables is in the PSP for the program, and the address of the PSP is the address of the program. If the TSR is 64K or less, the Turbo C **freemem** function can be called to free just these two blocks. If, however, the program is larger than 64K, then the program consists of multiple memory blocks. To deal with this possibility, the procedure walks through the DOS memory allocation chain and frees all memory blocks that are owned by the TSR program.

When the TSR returns to the interrupted process through the interrupt service routine that popped it up, the TSR will be removed from memory.

Listing 9.1: tsr.h

```
/* ---------- tsr.h ----------- */

void tsr(void);

/* -------- application-dependent prototype --------- */
void exec_popup(void);  /* popup execution code */
```

Listing 9.2: tsr.c

```
/* --------- tsr.c --------- */

/*
 * A Turbo C Terminate and Stay Resident (TSR) engine
 */

#include <dos.h>
#include <stdlib.h>
#include <stdio.h>
#include <conio.h>
#include "interupt.h"
#include "tsr.h"

#define TRUE 1
#define FALSE 0

/* --- vectors ---- */
#define DISK     0x13
#define INT28    0x28
#define CRIT     0x24
#define CTRLC    0x23
#define CTRLBRK 0x1b

/* INITIALIZE THESE VALUES HERE OR AT RUNTIME BEFORE TSR */
unsigned scancode;  /* Keyboard (INT 9) scan code */
unsigned keymask;   /* BIOS Shift Status Byte       */

extern char signature[];     /* the TSR's signature */

```

continued...

...from previous page

```
/* ------ global variable for popup to set and test ------ */
int unloading;                  /* TSR unload flag                  */

/* ------ interrupt vector chains ------ */
static void interrupt (*oldbreak)(void);
static void interrupt (*oldctrlc)(void);
static void interrupt (*oldtimer)(void);
static void interrupt (*old28)(void);
static void interrupt (*oldkb)(void);
static void interrupt (*olddisk)(void);
static void interrupt (*oldcrit)(void);
/* ------ ISRs for the TSR ------- */
static void interrupt newtimer(void);
static void interrupt new28(void);
static void interrupt newkb(void);
static void interrupt newdisk(IREGS);
static void interrupt newcrit(IREGS);
static void interrupt newbreak(void);

static unsigned sizeprogram;/* TSR's program size              */
static unsigned dosseg;     /* DOS segment address             */
static unsigned dosbusy;    /* offset to InDOS flag            */
static unsigned psps[2];    /* Table of DOS PSP addresses      */
static int pspctr;          /* # of DOS PSP addresses          */
static int diskflag;        /* Disk BIOS busy flag             */
static unsigned mcbseg;     /* address of 1st DOS mcb          */

static char far *mydta;     /* TSR's DTA                       */
static unsigned myss;       /* TSR's stack segment             */
static unsigned mysp;       /* TSR's stack pointer             */
static unsigned intpsp;     /* Interrupted PSP address         */
static int running;         /* TSR running indicator           */
static int hotkey_flag;     /* Hot key pressed flag            */

/* ------- local prototypes -------- */
static void tsr_init(void);
static void resinit(void);
static void unload(void);
static void resterm(void);
static void pspaddr(void);
```

continued...

...from previous page

```
static void dores(void);
static void resident_psp(void);
static void interrupted_psp(void);
static int resident(char *);

#define signon(s) printf("\n%s %s.", signature, s);

void tsr(void)
{
    tsr_init();
    if (resident(signature) == FALSE)   {
        /* ------ initial load of TSR program ------ */
        signon("is now available");
#ifdef DEBUG
        exec_popup();
        return;
#else
        /* ------ Terminate & Stay Resident ------ */
        resinit();
#endif
    }
    signon("is already resident");
}

/* ---------- initialize TSR control values ---------- */
static void tsr_init(void)
{
    unsigned es, bx;
    /* ------ get address of DOS busy flag ---- */
    _AH = 0x34;
    geninterrupt(DOS);
    dosseg = _ES;
    dosbusy = _BX;
    /* ---- get the seg addr of 1st DOS MCB ---- */
    _AH = 0x52;
    geninterrupt(DOS);
    es = _ES;
    bx = _BX;
    mcbseg = peek(es, bx-2);
    /* ----- get address of resident program's dta ----- */
```

continued...

...from previous page

```
    mydta = getdta();
    /* -------- get addresses of PSP in DOS 2.x ------- */
    if (_osmajor < 3)
        pspaddr();
}

/* -------- establish & declare residency --------- */
static void resinit(void)
{
    myss = _SS;
    mysp = _SP;
    oldtimer = getvect(TIMER);
    old28 = getvect(INT28);
    oldkb = getvect(KYBRD);
    olddisk = getvect(DISK);
    /* ----- attach vectors to resident program ----- */
    setvect(TIMER, newtimer);
    setvect(KYBRD, newkb);
    setvect(INT28, new28);
    setvect(DISK, newdisk);
    /* ------ compute program size ------- */
    sizeprogram = myss + ((mysp+50) / 16) - _psp;
    /* ----- terminate and stay resident ------- */
    keep(0, sizeprogram);
}

/* ---------- break handler ------------ */
static void interrupt newbreak(void)
{
    return;
}

/* -------- critical error ISR ---------- */
static void interrupt newcrit(IREGS ir)
{
    ir.ax = 0;          /* ignore critical errors */
}

/* ------ BIOS disk functions ISR ------- */
static void interrupt newdisk(IREGS ir)
```

continued...

...from previous page

```
{
    diskflag++;
    (*olddisk)();
    ir.ax = _AX;        /* for the register returns */
    ir.cx = _CX;
    ir.dx = _DX;
    ir.fl = _FLAGS;
    --diskflag;
}

/* ------ test for the hot key ------ */
static int test_hotkeys(int ky)
{
    static unsigned biosshift;

    biosshift = peekb(0, 0x417);
    if (ky == scancode && (biosshift & keymask) == keymask)
        /* ---- set hotkey indicator ---- */
        hotkey_flag = !running;
    return hotkey_flag;
}

/* ----- keyboard ISR ------ */
static void interrupt newkb(void)
{
    static int kbval;
    if (test_hotkeys(inportb(0x60)))    {
        /* --- reset the keyboard ---- */
        kbval = inportb(0x61);
        outportb(0x61, kbval | 0x80);
        outportb(0x61, kbval);
        outportb(0x20, 0x20);
    }
    else
        (*oldkb)();
}

/* ----- timer ISR ------- */
static void interrupt newtimer(void)
{
```

continued...

...from previous page

```
    (*oldtimer)();
    test_hotkeys(0);
    if (hotkey_flag && peekb(dosseg, dosbusy) == 0) {
        if (diskflag == 0)  {
            outportb(0x20, 0x20);
            hotkey_flag = FALSE;
            dores();
        }
    }
}

/* ----- 0x28 ISR -------- */
static void interrupt new28(void)
{
    (*old28)();
    if (hotkey_flag && peekb(dosseg, dosbusy) != 0) {
        hotkey_flag = FALSE;
        dores();
    }
}

/* ------ switch psp context from interrupted to TSR ----- */
static void resident_psp(void)
{
    int pp;

    if (_osmajor <  3)  {
        /* --- save interrupted program's psp (DOS 2.x) --- */
        intpsp = peek(dosseg, *psps);
        /* ----- set resident program's psp ----- */
        for (pp = 0; pp < pspctr; pp++)
            poke(dosseg, psps [pp], _psp);
    }
    else    {
        /* --- save interrupted program's psp --- */
        intpsp = getpsp();
        /* ----- set resident program's psp ----- */
        _AH = 0x50;
        _BX = _psp;
        geninterrupt(DOS);
```

continued...

...from previous page

```
    }
}

/* ---- switch psp context from TSR to interrupted ---- */
static void interrupted_psp(void)
{
    int pp;

    if (_osmajor <  3)  {
        /* ---- reset interrupted psp (DOS 2.x) ---- */
        for (pp = 0; pp < pspctr; pp++)
            poke(dosseg, psps[pp], intpsp);
    }
    else    {
        /* ---- reset interrupted psp ---- */
        _AH = 0x50;
        _BX = intpsp;
        geninterrupt(DOS);
    }
}

/* ------ execute the resident program ------- */
static void dores(void)
{
    static char far *intdta;    /* interrupted DTA           */
    static unsigned intsp;      /*     "       stack pointer */
    static unsigned intss;      /*     "       stack segment */
    static unsigned ctrl_break; /* Ctrl-Break setting        */

    running = TRUE;     /* set TSR running metaphore */
    disable();
    intsp = _SP;
    intss = _SS;
    _SP = mysp;
    _SS = myss;
    oldcrit = getvect(CRIT);/* redirect critical error    */
    oldbreak = getvect(CTRLBRK);
    oldctrlc = getvect(CTRLC);
    setvect(CRIT, newcrit);
    setvect(CTRLBRK, newbreak);
```

continued...

...from previous page

```
    setvect(CTRLC, newbreak);
    ctrl_break = getcbrk(); /* get ctrl break setting      */
    setcbrk(0);             /* turn off ctrl break logic   */
    intdta = getdta();      /* get interrupted dta         */
    setdta(mydta);          /* set resident dta            */
    resident_psp();         /* swap psps                   */
    enable();
    exec_popup();           /* call the TSR C program here */
    disable();
    interrupted_psp();      /* reset interrupted psp       */
    setdta(intdta);         /* reset interrupted dta       */
    setvect(CRIT, oldcrit); /* reset critical error        */
    setvect(CTRLBRK, oldbreak);
    setvect(CTRLC, oldctrlc);
    setcbrk(ctrl_break);    /* reset ctrl break            */
    _SP = intsp;            /* reset interrupted stack     */
    _SS = intss;
    enable();
    if (unloading)          /* if TSR set the unload flag  */
        unload();
    running = FALSE;        /* reset TSR running metaphore */
}

/* ---- test to see if the program is already resident ---- */
static int resident(char *signature)
{
    char *sg;
    unsigned df;
    unsigned blkseg, mcbs = mcbseg;

    df = _DS - _psp;
    /* ---- walk thru mcb chain & search for TSR ----- */
    while (peekb(mcbs, 0) == 0x4d)  {
        blkseg = peek(mcbs, 1);
        if (peek(blkseg, 0) == 0x20cd)  {
            /* --- this is a psp --- */
            if (blkseg == _psp)
                break;          /* if the transient copy */
            for (sg = signature; *sg; sg++)
                if (*sg != peekb(blkseg+df,(unsigned)sg))
```

continued...

...from previous page

```
                    break;
            if (*sg == '\0')
                /* ---- TSR is already resident --- */
                return TRUE;
        }
        mcbs += peek(mcbs, 3) + 1;
    }
    return FALSE;
}

/* -------- find address of PSP (DOS 2.x) ---------- */
static void pspaddr(void)
{
    unsigned adr = 0;

    disable();
    /* ---- search for matches on the psp in dos ---- */
    while (pspctr < 2 &&
            (unsigned)((dosseg<<4) + adr) < (mcbseg<<4))    {
        if (peek(dosseg, adr) == _psp)  {
            /* --- matches psp, set phoney psp --- */
            _AH = 0x50;
            _BX = _psp + 1;
            geninterrupt(DOS);
            /* --- did matched psp change to the phoney? --- */
            if (peek(dosseg, adr) == _psp+1)
                /* --- this is a DOS 2.x psp placeholder --- */
                psps[pspctr++] = adr;
            /* ---- reset the original psp ------ */
            _AH = 0x50;
            _BX = _psp;
            geninterrupt(DOS);
        }
        adr++;
    }
    enable();
}

/* --------- unload the resident program --------- */
static void unload(void)
```

continued...

...from previous page

```
{
    if (getvect(DISK) == (void interrupt (*)()) newdisk)
        if (getvect(KYBRD) == newkb)
            if (getvect(INT28) == new28)
                if (getvect(TIMER) == newtimer) {
                    resterm();
                    return;
                }
    /* ---- another TSR is above us, cannot unload ---- */
    putch(7);
}

/* ------- TSR unload function ----------- */
static void resterm(void)
{
    unsigned mcbs = mcbseg;
    /* ----- restore the interrupt vectors ----- */
    setvect(TIMER, oldtimer);
    setvect(KYBRD, oldkb);
    setvect(INT28, old28);
    setvect(DISK, olddisk);
    /* ----- obliterate the signature -------- */
    *signature = '\0';
    /* ---- walk thru mcb chain &
        release memory owned by the TSR ----- */
    while (peekb(mcbs, 0) == 0x4d)  {
        if (peek(mcbs, 1) == _psp)
            freemem(mcbs+1);
        mcbs += peek(mcbs, 3) + 1;
    }
}
```

THE TSR APPLICATION PROGRAM

The program that becomes the TSR does so by calling the **tsr** function in tsr.c and by providing the **exec_popup** function to be called when the program is popped up. In addition, the program specifies the hot key and the size of the stack and heap. To operate in this environment, the program must adhere to certain conventions as follows:

- The program must not use the DOS functions 0 to 12. This eliminates the use of most of the stdio.h functions. The program must not use the Turbo C **getch** function either because this function calls DOS. The other conio.h functions are safe.

- If the program changes the current working disk drive or directory, it must restore the original drive and directory before returning to the interrupted program.

- The program should avoid floating point operations. The Turbo C floating point package uses several interrupt vectors, which are attached in Turbo C's startup code. The vectors are not restored until after a C program exits and returns to the startup code. If successive TSRs were loaded this way, the last one would be doing the floating point operations for all of them.

- The program must never terminate or exit to DOS.

Other than these restrictions, the program is a complete Turbo C program, able to do anything any other program can do.

A TSR UTILITY PROGRAM: THE PERSONAL DIALER

Listing 9.3 is dialer.c, a TSR program that maintains a data base of names, addresses, and phone numbers and that will dial the phone number through the modem.

The dialer program initializes the TSR signature and sets the **_stklen** and **_heaplen** variables. It uses the data entry functions from Chapter 7 to display and maintain the records of names and addresses.

When you run the dialer program, it checks for a file name on the command line. If there is one, that file is used for the name and address data base. If no file name is given, the program uses DIALER.DAT as a default. It sets up the hot key as Alt-Period by setting **scancode** to 52 and **keymask** to 8. Then it calls the **tsr** function.

The **exec_popup** function is called from within tsr.c when the program is about to pop up. First, it saves the cursor context by calling **savecursor**. Then, it calls **normalcursor** just in case the interrupted program is using an unconventional cursor configuration. Because the program begins with a static display, it then calls **hidecursor**.

The dialer program opens its data base file such that if it does not exist, it is created. This TSR opens its data base file each time it is popped up and closes the file when it is popped down. This way, all changes are recorded in the file, and no records are lost if the user powers down without unloading the TSR. The program keeps track of where the file is pointed from pop-up to pop-up and seeks to that location each time.

The program displays data base records in a data entry template window. It opens that window and calls the **nextrecord** function to cause the next record to be read and displayed. Then, the program waits for a keystroke. The user can press Home, End, PgUp, and PgDn to move throughout the records. The F2 key causes the program to dial the phone number of the current record. The F3 key lets the user search the names for a match on a text substring. The Ins key sets up the insert of a new record in the data base, and the F4 key lets the user modify the current record. The Del key deletes the current record after first verifying that the user wants to do it. The F10 key is used to unload the dialer TSR from memory. The Esc key pops the program down.

When the user pops the TSR down, the program closes the window and the file and restores the cursor configuration to its value at pop-up.

The data base is maintained in the coincidental order in which records are inserted. The text search facility allows a rapid location of a desired record. If you want to find Sam, search for Sam. If more than one Sam exists, repeat the search from the location where the first Sam is found.

Following is a discussion of each of the user functions and how they are implemented in the program.

The **delete_record** function works by reading the records following the deleted record and writing them, starting at the position of the deleted record. When the last record is written over the next-to-last record position, the Turbo C **chsize** function reduces the file size by the length of one record. This operation would be slow if the data base was big. Most personal phone books have a reasonable number of entries, and this process works well.

Dialing the number consists of calling **initializemodem** and **call_remote**. The user is prompted to pick up the phone and press any key. When the key is pressed, the program calls the **hangup** function, which disconnects the modem from the phone line. Because the user has the phone off its hook, the user can now hear the ringing and talk when the called party answers.

The **text_search** function uses a data entry template that consists of the name field only. When the user enters a text string, the **searchstr** function takes over. It first normalizes the search string by calling the **normalize** function. Normalization consists of translating all letters to lowercase. Then the function begins reading data base records from the current location and comparing the string to a normalized copy of the data base name. The search is a success if the search string appears as a substring anywhere in the data base name. The Turbo C **strstr** function makes this comparison. The search continues until a hit is found or until the entire data base has been searched.

The **insert_record** function clears the data entry template and the record buffer by calling the **clear_template** function. It seeks to the end of the file and then calls the **change_record** function.

The **change_record** function uses the **data_entry** function to allow the user to enter data into the record. If the user presses the F2 key after the entry is complete, the new record is written to the data base.

The **next_record**, **prev_record**, **first_record**, and **last_record** functions position the file to the record requested, read the record, and display it on the template.

Listing 9.3: dialer.c

```
/* --------- dialer.c ---------- */

/*
 * A Personal Dialer TSR program
 */

#include <stdio.h>
#include <fcntl.h>
#include <conio.h>
#include <io.h>
#include <sys/stat.h>
#include <string.h>
#include <ctype.h>
#include <dir.h>
#include "window.h"
#include "keys.h"
#include "cursor.h"
#include "entry.h"
#include "modem.h"
#include "tsr.h"

/* ====== INITIALIZE THESE VALUES BEFORE COMPILING ======= */
char signature[] = "Personal Dialer";
extern unsigned _heaplen = 2048;
extern unsigned _stklen  = 1024;

/* -------- prompts for the dialer window --------- */
static PROMPT prompts[] = {
    { 2, 23, "PERSONAL DIALER"},
    { 4,  2, "Name"                             },
    { 5,  2, "Address"                          },
    { 6,  2, ""                                 },
    { 7,  2, "City"                             },
    { 7, 40, "State"                            },
    { 8,  2, "Zip"                              },
    { 8, 18, "Phone"                            },
    { 0,  0, NULL                               }
};

/* --------- dialer file record ----------- */
```

continued...

...from previous page

```
static struct nad {
    char name[36];
    char addr1[36];
    char addr2[36];
    char city[26];
    char state[3];
    char zip[6];
    char phone[15];
} nd;

static char schname[36];        /* text name to search for */
static char nameinfile[36];     /* name from file record   */

/* -------- text search data entry template ---------- */
static FIELD search[] = {
    { 4, 12, 35, schname  },
    { 0,  0,  0, NULL     }
};

/* ------------ dialer data entry template ------------- */
static FIELD template[] = {
    { 4, 12, 35, nd.name  },
    { 5, 12, 35, nd.addr1 },
    { 6, 12, 35, nd.addr2 },
    { 7, 12, 25, nd.city  },
    { 7, 46,  2, nd.state },
    { 8, 12,  5, nd.zip   },
    { 8, 24, 14, nd.phone },
    { 0,  0,  0, NULL     }
};

/* --------- hotkey arrays ----------- */
extern unsigned scancode[], keymask[];

char filename[65];
extern int unloading;    /* set to unload the TSR */
static int fd;           /* dialer data file descriptor */
static long curr_rcd;    /* file position just past current */

/* ------- local prototypes ---------- */
```

continued...

...from previous page

```
static void delete_record(void);
static void dial_phone(void);
static void text_search(void);
static void insert_record(void);
static void change_record(int);
static void first_record(void);
static void last_record(void);
static void prev_record(void);
static void next_record(void);
static void this_record(void);
static void seek_this_record(void);
static void specprompt(char *);
static void dialprompt(void);
static void searchstr(void);
static void normalize(char *);

void main(int argc, char *argv[])
{
    if (argc > 1)
        strcpy(filename, argv[1]);
    else    {
        getcwd(filename, 64);
        if (filename[strlen(filename) - 1] != '\\')
            strcat(filename, "\\");
        strcat(filename, "dialer.dat");
    }
    *scancode = 52;     /* set Alt-period as the hot key */
    *keymask = 8;
    tsr();              /* set up dialer as a TSR */
}

/* -------- this code is executed upon popup -------- */
void exec_popup(void)
{
    int code = 0;

    savecursor();
    normalcursor();
    hidecursor();
    fd = open(filename, O_RDWR|O_CREAT|O_BINARY,S_IWRITE);
```

continued...

...from previous page

```
        lseek(fd, curr_rcd, SEEK_SET);
        open_window(5,5,68,16,ENTRYFG,ENTRYBG,1,2);
        clear_template(search, prompts);
        clear_template(template, prompts);
        dialprompt();
        next_record();
        while (code != ESC) {
            /* ------- read user command key ------ */
            code = getkey();
            if (filelength(fd) == 0L)   {
                if (code != INS && code != F10 && code != ESC)  {
                    notice(" Empty File ");
                    continue;
                }
            }
            switch (code)   {
                case HOME:                  /* go to first record */
                    first_record();
                    break;
                case END:                   /* go to last record */
                    last_record();
                    break;
                case PGUP:                  /* go to previous record */
                    prev_record();
                    break;
                case PGDN:                  /* go to next record */
                    next_record();
                    break;
                case F2:                    /* dial the number */
                    dial_phone();
                    break;
                case F3:                    /* search names for text */
                    text_search();
                    break;
                case INS:                   /* insert a new record */
                    insert_record();
                    break;
                case F4:                    /* change current rcd */
                    change_record(F4);
                    break;
```

continued...

...from previous page

```
            case DEL:                  /* delete current rcd */
                if (yesno(" Delete this name?"))
                    delete_record();
                break;
            case F10:                  /* unload dialer */
                unloading = yesno(" Unload Personal Dialer?");
                if (unloading)
                    code = ESC;
                break;
            default:
                break;
        }
    }
    /* ------- pop down ---------- */
    prev_record();
    close_window();
    close(fd);
    unhidecursor();
    restorecursor();
}

/* ---------- delete the current record ------------ */
static void delete_record(void)
{
    int done = FALSE;
    long here = tell(fd);
    while (done == FALSE)   {
        if ((done = eof(fd)) == FALSE)  {
            read(fd, &nd, sizeof nd);
            done = eof(fd);
            lseek(fd,-((long)sizeof nd*2),SEEK_CUR);
            write(fd, &nd, sizeof nd);
        }
        else
            lseek(fd,-((long)sizeof nd),SEEK_CUR);
        if (done)
            chsize(fd, tell(fd));
        else
            lseek(fd,(long)sizeof nd,SEEK_CUR);
    }
```

continued...

...from previous page

```
    lseek(fd, here, SEEK_SET);
    this_record();
}

/* ---- call the phone number from the current record ------ */
static void dial_phone(void)
{
    char phoneno[25];
    char *cp1 = nd.phone;
    char *cp2 = phoneno;

    while (*cp1)    {
        if (isdigit(*cp1) || *cp1 == ',')
            *cp2++ = *cp1;
        cp1++;
    }
    *cp2 = '\0';
    open_window(32,12,45,14,WHITE,GREEN,1,2);
    cputs("Dialing ...");
    initializemodem();
    call_remote(phoneno);
    close_window();
    notice(" Pick up phone and press ");
    hangup();
    release_modem();
}

/* ----- text match search on names in the file -------- */
static void text_search(void)
{
    int dcode = 0;
    clear_template(template, prompts);
    specprompt("Enter search string");
    while (dcode != ESC && dcode != '\r')    {
        dcode = data_entry(search, prompts);
        hidecursor();
        if (dcode == '\r')
            searchstr();
    }
    dialprompt();
```

continued...

...from previous page

```
        this_record();
}

/* --------- insert a new record into the file -------- */
static void insert_record(void)
{
        lseek(fd, 0L, SEEK_END);
        clear_template(template, prompts);
        change_record(INS);
}

/* ------ change an existing record in the file ------ */
static void change_record(int code)
{
        int dcode = 0;

        specprompt("(F2 to Save, Esc to Ignore)");
        while (dcode != ESC && dcode != F2) {
                dcode = data_entry(template, prompts);
                if (dcode == F2)    {
                        if (code == F4)
                                seek_this_record();
                        write(fd, &nd, sizeof nd);
                        curr_rcd = tell(fd);
                }
        }
        if (code == INS && dcode == ESC)    {
                lseek(fd, curr_rcd, SEEK_SET);
                this_record();
        }
        field_tally(template, prompts);
        hidecursor();
        dialprompt();
}

/* -------- go to the first record in the file -------- */
static void first_record(void)
{
        lseek(fd, 0L, SEEK_SET);
        next_record();
```

continued...

...from previous page

```
}

/* -------- go to the last record in the file -------- */
static void last_record(void)
{
    lseek(fd, 0L, SEEK_END);
    this_record();
}

/* -------- go to the previous record in the file -------- */
static void prev_record(void)
{
    seek_this_record();
    if (tell(fd) == 0L)
        lseek(fd, 0L, SEEK_END);
    this_record();
}

/* -------- go to the next record in the file -------- */
static void next_record(void)
{
    if (eof(fd))
        lseek(fd, 0L, SEEK_SET);
    clear_template(template, prompts);
    read(fd, &nd, sizeof nd);
    curr_rcd = tell(fd);
    field_tally(template, prompts);
}

/* -------- point to and display the current record -------- */
static void this_record(void)
{
    seek_this_record();
    next_record();
}

/* ---- seek to the beginning of the current record ---- */
static void seek_this_record(void)
{
    if (tell(fd) != 0L)
```

continued...

...from previous page

```
        lseek(fd, -((long) sizeof nd), SEEK_CUR);
}

/* -------- display a help prompt in the window ------ */
static void specprompt(char *s)
{
    int pad = (61 - strlen(s)) /2, p;
    gotoxy(1,10);
    for (p = 0; p < pad; p++)
        putch(' ');
    cputs(s);
    for (p = 0; p < pad; p++)
        putch(' ');
}

/* -------- the window command prompt --------- */
static void dialprompt(void)
{
    specprompt("Ins=Add,F2=Dial,F3=Sch,"
               "F4=Chg,Del=Delete,Esc=Quit,F10=Unload");
}

/* -------- string search through the file --------- */
static void searchstr(void)
{
    normalize(schname);
    while (TRUE)    {
        if (eof(fd))
            lseek(fd, 0L, SEEK_SET);
        read(fd, &nd, sizeof nd);
        strcpy(nameinfile, nd.name);
        normalize(nameinfile);
        if (strstr(nameinfile, schname) != NULL)
            break;
        if (tell(fd) == curr_rcd)
            break;
    }
    if (tell(fd) == curr_rcd)
        error_message("String not found");
    curr_rcd = tell(fd);
```

continued...

...from previous page

```
    field_tally(template, prompts);
}

/* ---- normalize a string to all lower case ------- */
static void normalize(char *s)
{
    while (*s)  {
        *s = tolower(*s);
        s++;
    }
}
```

TESTING A TSR PROGRAM

If you write a TSR program and try to test it as a TSR program, you will experience some inconvenience. First, you will not be able to use the Turbo C Integrated Development Environment for interactive testing. A TSR program is installed from the command line and run with a hot key. Next, until the terminate function is working or if other programs are installed above the TSR, you must remove the TSR program by rebooting the computer. Further, because it has attached itself to interrupt vectors, its loops and aborts can hang up your system. The TSR program is not easy to test in its resident configuration.

A better approach is to test the TSR program as a transient program. The DOS interfaces that establish and operate the TSR in the memory-resident environment are all managed by tsr.c. Why not bypass these operations until your program is reasonably well tested?

A nonresident testing technique can be achieved by compiling tsr.c with the DEBUG global variable defined. The program will have the appearance, structure, and size of its TSR version, but will function as a transient program. You test the program by running it. Instead of becoming resident, the program behaves as if the hot key had been pressed. It executes once and terminates.

Just because your program works perfectly in a transient environment is no reason to assume it will work as a TSR. A TSR is resident; each execution of it uses the same copy of code and data as the previous execution. The transient program runs a clean copy each time. If you do not initialize and restore such variables as the heap, file handles, pointers, and subscripts, a later execution of the TSR might fail. Test a single load of the transient version through several executions to be sure that global values are properly initialized and reset.

Once the program works as a nonresident program, you can relink it as a TSR and test it in the memory-resident environment. Begin with the stack and heap at high values and reduce them gradually in the manner described earlier. Get it running as a TSR without other TSRs loaded.

The final test is to see how your program fares in the company of other TSR programs and with certain ill-behaved nonresident programs. Many popular programs will not play together, so you should select those with which you want to be compatible and run tests that involve them all.

When a TSR is aimed at a specific environment, testing is simpler. You know the hardware, operating system, and associated other software that the TSR must cooperate with. You can test with confidence in that environment. Once everything is working together, you can consider the testing done. If, however, your TSR is going to be widely distributed, the possible configurations are many and undefined, and there is unlimited potential for configuration-related problems.

For example, consider the operating systems. There are eight versions of DOS: 2.0, 2.1, 2.11, 3.0, 3.1, 3.2, 3.3, and 4.0. There also is the OS/2 3.X DOS Box, which allows OS/2 users to run DOS programs. You should have copies of each of them to test your TSR (with the possible exception of the 3.X Box because it is expensive to install). Consider the BIOS. With many PCs, ATs, and clones comes a host of different BIOS ROMs. Each BIOS has several versions, further complicating matters.

A TSR might be required to work with any of the several standard video adaptor and monitor combinations. Today we have the CGA, MDA, EGA, Hercules, and VGA. Each of these has its original and its clones.

Don't forget the mice. There are many different mice, and each mouse has different versions of its software drivers. Even if your TSR does not use the mouse, the TSR and the mouse software driver could be in conflict.

Mouse drivers are not the only programs with such problems. Other device drivers, LAN packages, disk cache utilities, etc., could be incompatible with your TSR. Remember, no matter how well behaved your TSR is, the other guys might not be following the same rules.

There is a moral: A software house cannot possibly maintain the seemingly infinite number of hardware and software configurations; surely there will be a setup that fails or runs poorly when your TSR is loaded or popped up; brace yourself for the support calls.

SUMMARY

This chapter has shown you how to write an orderly and well-behaved TSR program. In Chapter 10 you will learn the techniques for using Expanded Memory in your programs. Chapter 11 discusses an advanced technique for installing multiple overlaid TSRs that execute under the control of a single TSR manager program named TSRPLUS.

CHAPTER 10

EXPANDED MEMORY

This chapter shows you how to use the Expanded Memory Manager now installed on many computers. Expanded Memory is a technique by which large amounts of extra memory are swapped in and out of the PC's address space in a paging operation. With Expanded Memory, a program can significantly increase the data memory with which it has to work. With the addition of an EM executive program, program overlays can be stored in and executed directly from Expanded Memory. This chapter shows how the EMM Application Program Interface can be called from a Turbo C program.

What you need to understand:

- Calling software interrupts
- The PC's Segmented Memory Architecture

New subjects discussed:

- The Expanded Memory Manager Applications Program Interface

THE EXPANDED MEMORY SPECIFICATION

The PC has traditionally been limited to an upper memory address of 640K. This limit reflects the 20-bit effective address of the segment:offset memory architecture, which allows an address space of one megabyte, and the location of various video memory blocks and the ROM BIOS in the top 384K.

This limit was considered to be quite generous when the PC was introduced in 1981. The traditional home and business personal computer was then limited to 64K. The first PCs had only 64K on the motherboard, and special memory add-in boards were needed to increase the memory size.

The 640K limit became a problem when the PC caught on. The first culprit was the spreadsheet. Users, given this tool, wanted it to be able to manage bigger and bigger spreadsheets. Then, as TSRs caught on, the amount of residual memory for applications began to shrink. The industry soon recognized that 640K was not enough, and three manufacturers—Lotus, Intel, and Microsoft—published a specification for using paged memory from a memory source that is outside the address space of the PC. That specification is called the LIM Expanded Memory Specification (EMS). When Expanded Memory is present in a system, the software driver that handles it is called the Expanded Memory Manager (EMM). The specification identifies the standard Applications Program Interface (API) for programs to use when calling the EMM. This standard API hides the details of the Expanded Memory (EM) implementation from the program and ensures that the program will work with all conforming Expanded Memory products.

How EMS Works

The typical EMS-conforming system is an add-in board that contains a large block of memory, usually measured in megabytes. The memory is not within the address space of the PC and must be accessed only through calls to the EMM API. Various EM implementations use various techniques for the EMM to address the memory device. Some use input-output ports. Others, designed to work only on 286 and 386 machines, use protected-mode extended memory.

The EMS specifies that a program can access EM in pages of 16K each. The EMM uses empty address space in the upper 384K of the PC. It is a rare PC that does not have at least 64K of unused address space in that region. The EMM can search for the first unused 64K block or can be told when it is run what memory address to use. Programs that use EM and that expect to run on all possible configurations must be prepared to read and use the segment address used by the EMM for pages. This address is called the "page frame" address, and its value will vary from machine to machine, depending on the video adaptor and other devices installed. Such devices as Local Area Network boards and fixed disk drive controllers use blocks of their own memory and allocate some of the available address space in the upper 384K. The video adaptors have fixed locations, but different adaptors use different address spaces.

When a program wants to use EM, it calls the EMM to allocate a number of pages. EMM assigns each such request a handle. When the program needs to access the memory, it calls EMM to map pages associated with the handle into the empty address pages used by the EMM. A program can allocate as many pages as are available, but can map only a maximum of four of them at any one time. Any four EM pages owned by the program can be mapped into the four pages of address space in any order.

Keep the above distinction clear. A program owns the many pages of EM that the EMM has allocated to it. The EMM associates the many pages with a handle. The program refers to the allocation by the handle. The program can have many handles. The limiting factor is the number of unallocated pages of EM. The program cannot see the pages it owns until it maps them into the upper 384K address space owned by the EMM. The program can see a maximum of four of its pages at a time.

When a page of EM is mapped into the page frame, the program can read and write the memory as if it were normal PC memory by using the page frame address as the segment address of the memory.

If an interrupt service routine or a TSR wants to use EM, it must preserve the current EM mapping context before remapping to its own handle. When the program is ready to return to whatever was interrupted, it must restore that mapping context. If it did not, the interrupted process, which was using its own EM when the interrupt occurred, would probably fail.

The context saving and restoring operations associate an EM context with a handle provided by the caller. This concept is not intuitive. The caller must have allocated some EM to get a handle. The caller tells the EMM to associate that handle with the current mapping context, which belongs to some other program and which has nothing to do with the caller's handle.

The EMM API is used through calls to the 0x67 interrupt with function codes in the **ah** register. If the function call is successful, the EMM returns a zero in the **ah** register. Otherwise, it returns an error code. The EMM uses the **dx** register to receive and return handles. Other values are received and returned in the **bx** register.

The Expanded Memory Manager Function Library

The EMS specifies an assembly language API. This API consists of a set of commands implemented through calls to the EMM interrupt. In this chapter, you will pull the API to a higher level, using Turbo C to interface with EMM.

Listings 10.1 and 10.2 are emm.h and emm.c, respectively. These listings have the functions that implement the EMM API for Turbo C programs. Emm.c includes a set of defined symbols for the function codes for EMM. Next are the functions that a program can call. Following the listings is a description of each of these functions.

Listing 10.1: emm.h

```
/* --------- emm.h ---------- */

/* -------- EMM prototypes ---------- */
int emm_present(void);
int emm_working(void);
int emm_pageframe(void);
int emm_pages_available(void);
int emm_allocate(int);
int emm_map(int,int,int,int);
int emm_release(int);
int emm_version(void);
int emm_savecontext(int);
int emm_restorecontext(int);
```

Listing 10.2: emm.c

```
/* ------------- emm.c -------------- */

/*
 * LIM Expanded Memory Manager Driver Functions
 */

#include <dos.h>
#include <string.h>
#include "emm.h"

#define EMM      0x67       /* EMM interrupt vector */

/* ------- EMM Function Codes ----------- */
#define TESTEMM  0x40
#define FRAME    0x41
#define PAGECT   0x42
#define ALLOCATE 0x43
#define MAPEMM   0x44
#define RELEASE  0x45
#define VERSION  0x46
#define SAVE     0x47
#define RESTORE  0x48

static int emmint(void);

static char emmsig[9];

/* ------- test for EMM installed in system -------- */
int emm_present(void)
{
    void interrupt (*emmvect)(void);
    unsigned emmseg;

    emmvect = getvect(EMM);
    emmseg = FP_SEG(emmvect);
    movedata(emmseg, 10, _DS, (unsigned) emmsig, 9);
    return (strncmp(emmsig, "EMMXXXX0", 8) == 0);
}

/* ------ test if EMM is activated -------- */
```

continued...

...from previous page

```
int emm_working(void)
{
    _AH = TESTEMM;
    return (emmint() != -1);
}

/* ------- get the EMM page frame segment address ------ */
int emm_pageframe(void)
{
    _AH = FRAME;
    if (emmint() == -1)
        return -1;
    return _BX;
}

/* ------- return number of EMM pages available --------- */
int emm_pages_available(void)
{
    _AH = PAGECT;
    if (emmint() == -1)
        return -1;
    return _BX;
}

/* ------- allocate pages of EMM to an application ------ */
int emm_allocate(int pagect)
{
    _AH = ALLOCATE;
    _BX = pagect;
    if (emmint() == -1)
        return -1;
    return _DX;
}

/* ---- map EMM pages to addressable pages in memory ----- */
int emm_map(int pagect, int first_pageno,
                int first_logical_page, int handle)
{
    while (pagect--)    {
        _AH = MAPEMM;
```

continued...

...from previous page

```
            _AL = first_pageno++;
            _BX = first_logical_page++;
            _DX = handle;
            if (emmint() == -1)
                return -1;
        }
        return 0;
}

/* ----- release the pages allocated to a handle ------ */
int emm_release(int handle)
{
    _AH = RELEASE;
    _DX = handle;
    return emmint();
}

/* ------- return the EMM version number -------- */
int emm_version(void)
{
    _AH = VERSION;
    geninterrupt(EMM);
    if (_AH != 0)
        return -1;
    return _AX;
}

/* ---- save the current mapping context ----- */
int emm_savecontext(int handle)
{
    _AH = SAVE;
    _DX = handle;
    return emmint();
}

/* ----- restore a saved mapping context ------- */
int emm_restorecontext(int handle)
{
    _AH = RESTORE;
    _DX = handle;
```

continued...

...from previous page

```
        return emmint();
    }

    /* ------ general EMM interrupt caller --------- */
    static int emmint(void)
    {
        geninterrupt(EMM);
        if (_AH != 0)
            return -1;
        return 0;
    }
```

The EMM Functions

The EMM API returns discrete error codes when you make an invalid call. The functions in this library do not. Rather, they return the -1 code if the EMM API call failed. A program is primarily concerned with whether the function worked or did not. Once you have properly established your EM environment, there is not much you can do in software to correct a subsequent error condition. The error codes are primarily for use during program debugging to tell you what you have done wrong. If you are getting an error return that you do not understand, use the Turbo debugger to look at the returns from the API into the C functions that follow. Chances are, you have done something out of order.

emm_present

This function returns a true value if the Expanded Memory Manager device driver is installed in the system. It works by comparing a string signature with the value "EMMXXXX0" to a known location in the manager. The location is determined by using the segment address in the 0x67 interrupt vector and the offset of 10. If the string matches, the EMM is assumed to be resident.

This is one of two ways that a program can test for the EMM. The other is to open a file with the name "EMMXXXX0." If the driver is present, the open will succeed. However, if there is a file on the current disk in the current subdirectory with the same name, the open will also seem to succeed even when there is no EMM installed. You will, in fact, have opened a real file. It has been suggested that the DOS function 0x44, subfunction 7 (output status) can be used to test if the handle is a file. If the function returns 0xff, the handle is not a file and must be the EMM device driver. This approach is recommended as being preferred over the first one, but some version 4.0 EMMs lock the system when the DOS 0x44 function is called with an EM handle. For this reason, **emm_present** uses the signature test described above.

None of the following functions should be called until the **emm_present** function has been called to verify the existence of the EMM device driver. Many programs take advantage of EM if it is installed and use other, perhaps slower, techniques if EM is not available.

emm_working

Even though the EMM device handler is resident, the EM might not be operational. Some EMMs provide for command line suspension of the EM feature. Others allow themselves to be loaded even when there is no EM in the system. The **emm_working** function returns a true value if EM is operational.

emm_pageframe

Remember that EM can be nearly anywhere in the upper 384K of address space. This function returns the page frame, which is the segment address of where EM pages can be accessed.

emm_pages_available

This function returns the number of EM pages that are available for allocation. As you allocate pages, the value returned by this function will decrease. As you release pages, the value will increase.

emm_allocate

This function allocates the number of pages requested by its parameter and returns a handle to the caller. All subsequent EMM API calls that are related to this allocation will refer to this handle. If you request more pages than are available, the function allocates no pages and returns -1. If your program operates in an environment with TSRs and other interrupt service routines that might be allocating EM, you will want to test for the -1 return even though the **emm_pages_available** call just said there were enough pages. A TSR could interrupt between that call and this one and steal the pages you thought would be yours. One way to prevent this theft is to surround the calls to **emm_pages_available** and **emm_allocate** with calls to the Turbo C **disable** and **enable** functions.

emm_map

This function is the one that lets you read and write the pages you have allocated. It maps logical EM pages into the physical EM space in the upper 384K of memory. You pass it the number of consecutive pages involved, the page number (0 - 3) in the page frame where the mapping is to start, the logical page number of the block of pages allocated to the handle, and the handle. The logical page number is 0 to n-1 where n is the number of pages mapped to the handle by the call to **emm_map**. When this function has successfully returned, you can access the EM pages at the page frame segment.

If, for example, you map all four physical pages and the page frame is at 0xe000, then the pages can be addressed at 0xe000:0000, 0xe000:0x4000, 0xe000:0x8000, and 0xe000:0xc000. You must use Turbo C far pointer operations to access this memory.

emm_release

This function releases pages that were allocated to the handle. The handle is returned to the EMM to be reused.

emm_version

This function returns the EMM version number as a two-byte integer where the most significant byte is the major version number and the least significant byte is the minor version number.

emm_savecontext

This function saves the current EM mapping context and associates the context with the handle passed to it. In theory, an interrupt service routine has allocated some pages to a handle and wants to use them. First it must save the current EM mapping context, and, because that operation requires a handle, the one just assigned to the interrupt service routine by the EMM is the one that the routine passes to the EMM. Now the routine can map its own (the same) handle into the physical page frame address space.

emm_restorecontext

This function restores the EM mapping context to the one associated with the handle parameter in an earlier call to **emm_savecontext**.

A Demonstration: demoemm.c

Listing 10.3 is demoemm.c, a program that calls the EMM functions to retrieve certain values and then displays them on the screen.

Listing 10.3: demoemm.c

```
/* ---------- demoemm.c ----------- */

/*
 * Demonstrate the EMM functions
 */

#include <stdio.h>
#include "emm.h"

void main(void)
{
    int em, wk, v;
    unsigned frame;
    int pages;

    em = emm_present();
    printf("\nEMM %s present.", em ? "is" : "is not");
    if (em) {
        v = emm_version();
        printf("\nEMM Version %d.%d", v >> 4, v & 15);
        wk = emm_working();
        printf("\nEMM %s working.", wk ? "is" : "is not");
    }
    if (em && wk)   {
        frame = emm_pageframe();
        pages = emm_pages_available();
        printf("\nPage Frame: %04x", frame);
        printf("\nPages Available: %d", pages);
    }
}
```

SUMMARY

In this chapter, you assembled a set of EMM API functions that your programs can call. You might wonder what use you can make of EM. Certainly, any application that needs to manipulate large matrices of data can improve its performance by using EM instead of disk files.

In Chapter 11, you will learn an unusual approach to the use of EM. Chapter 11 is about TSRPLUS, a program that manages the loading and execution of custom TSR programs in a multiprogram, overlaid environment. If EM is present in the system, TSRPLUS uses it for the overlay and swap files.

CHAPTER 11

TSRPLUS: THE TSR OVERLAY MANAGER

This chapter applies the concepts from Chapters 9 and 10 to build a special kind of TSR program—one that watches over all the other TSR programs you write and allows them to be available to pop up without occupying main memory while they are not being used. With TSRPLUS, your TSRs pop up by temporarily using the memory presently occupied by whatever program is running when the pop-up occurs. When the TSR pops down, the interrupted program is restored to memory and continues.

What you need to understand:

- Memory-Resident Programs (TSRs)
- Expanded Memory

New subjects discussed:

- TSR program management

THE PROBLEM WITH TSRs

The problem with TSRs is that they occupy memory even when they are not in use. The more TSRs you have loaded, the less memory is available for your other applications. The TSR is needed when it is needed, and you write it as a TSR because it has a function that is needed immediately. If you are on the phone with a friend and want to record her new phone number in your computer, you do not necessarily want to go to the trouble of saving your current work, terminating what you are doing, loading the phone book, updating it, and getting back to where you were. You want to pop up that old phone book and stick the new number in it without disturbing anything else. That's why TSRs were invented; however, load enough such utility programs into your computer, and you'll run out of memory to do anything else.

TSRPLUS

TSRPLUS is a program that is designed to solve the problem with TSRs. You can write a lot of TSR programs like the Personal Dialer in Chapter 9, link them with the special TSRPLUS build module, and they are ready to be integrated into the TSRPLUS environment. The programs are developed with the same guidelines as those from Chapter 9. Any program that works as a TSR with the tsr.c module from Chapter 9 can be ported without modification into the TSRPLUS environment. Following is a description of what TSRPLUS does.

TSRPLUS is itself a TSR program. When loaded by itself, it will do nothing except unload itself when you press its unload hot key (configured as Alt-U as published here). With TSRPLUS loaded, and nothing loaded above it, you load your other TSR programs one after the other—not the ones you linked with tsr.c in Chapter 9, but other versions linked with the TSRPLUS build module explained later in this chapter. Instead of becoming resident, the programs write snapshot disk files of themselves, files that TSRPLUS will recognize.

Next you unload TSRPLUS and reload it. It will see the snapshot files and register them. Everything it needs to know about the TSR is in the file—the hot key, where to load it, how big it is, and the address of its PSP. If TSRPLUS finds that Expanded Memory is installed, it copies the programs into Expanded Memory; otherwise, it remembers where the program images are on the files.

When the hot key for a registered TSR is pressed, TSRPLUS intercepts it in the manner described in Chapter 9, except that the TSRPLUS engine is able to recognize more than one hot key. TSRPLUS writes the memory required by the TSR either to Expanded Memory or to a swap disk file. Then it loads the TSR's code into that memory and executes the TSR. When the TSR returns to pop down, TSRPLUS reloads the swapped-out memory and returns to the interrupted program.

Because other non-TSRPLUS TSRs could be loaded above TSRPLUS, it is possible that some interrupt vectors point into the memory that TSRPLUS is going to swap out. For this reason, the TSRPLUS build module writes a copy of the system interrupt vectors into the snapshot file along with the image of the TSR program. When TSRPLUS swaps memory, it swaps interrupt vectors as well as code and data. This way, any interrupts that are pointing into the swapped memory will be restored to wherever they pointed when the TSR built its snapshot file.

Because of this interrupt vector swapping algorithm, you must code your TSR so that any interrupt vectors it attaches are attached after the TSR pops up. The TSR should detach those vectors before it pops down.

If you run other TSR programs that must remain resident, load them before TSRPLUS. Such programs are print spoolers and background communications programs that execute from hardware interrupts rather than from hot keys.

The TSRPLUS Software

A TSRPLUS environment consists of at least two and usually more programs. First is TSRPLUS.EXE, the TSRPLUS executive module that remains resident all the time. Next are any TSRs that you have built into the environment by linking them with the TSRPLUS build module. TSRPLUS does not use the TSR engine from Chapter 9 because it needs to respond to multiple hot keys and it needs to do so in a manner that allows the various TSRs to pop up on top of one another.

The TSRPLUS TSR Engine: tsrmult.h and tsrmult.c

TSRPLUS uses its own TSR engine, a module called tsrmult because it manages multiple hot keys and pop-ups. Listing 11.1 is tsrmult.h. This header file substitutes for tsr.h from Chapter 9 except in your TSR application program where you can use either tsr.h or tsrmult.h. The header file describes the maximum number of hot keys and, therefore, the maximum number of TSRs that TSRPLUS will manage. Because TSRPLUS uses one hot key as its unload key, the number of TSRs you can have is one less than the value assigned to MAXHOTKEYS in tsrmult.h.

The tsrmult.h header file also describes the snapshot file's header record, which contains important elements about the TSR that TSRPLUS needs to manage it. The header record has the hot key scan code and BIOS status byte key mask, the segment address where the TSR will be loaded, the length of the TSR's memory image, and an interrupt function pointer to the place to call to pop up the TSR once it is loaded into memory.

Listing 11.2 is trsmult.c, the multiple-TSR version of the TSR engine. It has a number of differences from the engine in Chapter 9, the first being an array of hot key scan codes and status masks. The program also has arrays of stack segment and pointer register save areas so that TSRs can pop up on top of one another.

The context information saved for a TSR pop-up is kept in an array of context structures with one entry for each possible pop-up, once again to allow multiple pop-ups.

The tsrmult.c program does not include the DOS 2.x measures for setting and getting the PSP address while popped up. For that reason, TSRs written with tsrmult.c will work only with DOS 3.0 and higher. If this is a problem, the **pspaddr**, **resident_psp**, and **interrupted_psp** functions from tsr.c can be moved into tsrmult.c.

The **test_hotkeys** function looks at the range of hot keys rather than at just one. It sets the **plusrunning** semaphore to keep TSRPLUS from trying to pop up before it is ready, and it maintains two other multiple-program controls. One is the **depth** variable, which indicates how many pop-ups deep TSRPLUS is managing. This variable is used throughout TSRPLUS to keep track of stack segment and pointer register saves. The other control variable is the offset to the hot key that was pressed to allow TSRPLUS to know which TSR it is managing.

The **dores** function switches context with the array of context values as subscripted by the hot key variable. When it calls **exec_popup**, it is calling a function in tsrplus.c, not the **exec_popup** function in the TSR program itself.

This is an important distinction. There is a layer of software between the TSR and the TSR engine that does not exist in the TSR environment implemented in Chapter 9. The TSR program calls the **tsr** function in the TSRPLUS build module, and the TSR program's **exec_popup** function is called from the build module. The real TSR is TSRPLUS. It calls the **tsr** function in the tsrmult.c engine, and its **exec_popup** function is called from that engine when a hot key is pressed. TSRPLUS loads the pseudo-TSR program and calls a function in its TSRPLUS build module.

The rest of tsrmult.c works very much like tsr.c in Chapter 9.

Listing 11.1: tsrmult.h

```
/* ---------- tsrmult.h ----------- */

#define MAXHOTKEYS 5          /* maximum hot keys to scan */

void tsr(void);

/* -------- application-dependent prototype --------- */
void exec_popup(int);    /* popup execution code */

struct swap_header {
    unsigned scancode;
    unsigned keymask;
    unsigned loadseg;
    unsigned length;
    unsigned psp;
    void interrupt (*startptr)(int,int far*,int far*,int far*);
};
```

Listing 11.2: tsrmult.c

```
/* --------- tsrmult.c --------- */

/*
 * A Turbo C Terminate and Stay Resident (TSR) engine
 */

#include <dos.h>
#include <stdlib.h>
#include <stdio.h>
#include <conio.h>
#include "interupt.h"
#include "tsrmult.h"

#define TRUE 1
#define FALSE 0

/* --- vectors ---- */
#define DISK    0x13
#define INT28   0x28
#define CRIT    0x24
#define CTRLC   0x23
#define CTRLBRK 0x1b

/* INITIALIZE THESE ARRAYS HERE OR AT RUNTIME BEFORE TSR */
unsigned scancode[MAXHOTKEYS];/* Keyboard (INT 9) scan codes */
unsigned keymask[MAXHOTKEYS]; /* BIOS Shift Status Byte      */

extern char signature[];     /* the TSR's signature */
extern unsigned highmemory;

/* ------ global variables for popup to set and test ------ */
int unloading;                /* TSR unload flag             */

/* ------ interrupt vector chains ------ */
static void interrupt (*oldtimer)(void);
static void interrupt (*old28)(void);
static void interrupt (*oldkb)(void);
static void interrupt (*olddisk)(void);

/* ------ ISRs for the TSR ------- */
```

continued...

...from previous page

```
static void interrupt newtimer(void);
static void interrupt new28(void);
static void interrupt newkb(void);
static void interrupt newdisk(IREGS);
static void interrupt newcrit(IREGS);
static void interrupt newbreak(void);

static unsigned sizeprogram;/* TSR's program size           */
static unsigned dosseg;     /* DOS segment address          */
static unsigned dosbusy;    /* offset to InDOS flag         */
static int diskflag;        /* Disk BIOS busy flag          */
static unsigned mcbseg;     /* address of 1st DOS mcb       */
static char far *mydta;     /* TSRPLUS's DTA                */

int plusrunning;
static int hotkey_flag;     /* Hot key pressed flag         */

static int hotkey[MAXHOTKEYS];  /* stack of hot keys      */
int tsrss[MAXHOTKEYS+1];        /* TSRPLUS's stack segment */
int tsrsp[MAXHOTKEYS+1];        /* TSRPLUS's stack pointer */
int depth = 0;                  /* popup depth             */

/* -------------- contexts for each popup ---------------- */
struct context {
    unsigned intpsp;            /* Interrupted PSP address   */
    int running;                /* TSR running indicator     */
    char far *intdta;           /* interrupted DTA           */
    unsigned intsp;             /*     "       stack pointer */
    unsigned intss;             /*     "       stack segment */
    unsigned ctrl_break;        /* Ctrl-Break setting        */
    void interrupt (*oldcrit)(void);
    void interrupt (*oldbreak)(void);
    void interrupt (*oldctrlc)(void);
} ctx [MAXHOTKEYS];

static int hkx;     /* working subscript into ctx */

/* ------- local prototypes -------- */
static void tsr_init(void);
static void resinit(void);
```

continued...

...from previous page

```
static void unload(void);
static void resterm(void);
static void dores(void);
static void resident_psp(void);
static void interrupted_psp(void);
static int resident(char *);

#define signon(s) printf("\n%s %s.", signature, s);

void tsr(void)
{
    tsr_init();
    if (resident(signature) == FALSE)   {
        /* ------ initial load of TSRPLUS program ------ */
        signon("is now available");
        /* ------ Terminate & Stay Resident ------ */
        resinit();
    }
    signon("is already resident");
}

/* ---------- initialize TSR control values ---------- */
static void tsr_init(void)
{
    unsigned es, bx;
    /* ------ get address of DOS busy flag ---- */
    _AH = 0x34;
    geninterrupt(DOS);
    dosseg = _ES;
    dosbusy = _BX;
    /* ---- get the seg addr of 1st DOS MCB ---- */
    _AH = 0x52;
    geninterrupt(DOS);
    es = _ES;
    bx = _BX;
    mcbseg = peek(es, bx-2);
    /* ----- get address of resident program's dta ----- */
    mydta = getdta();
}

```

continued...

...from previous page

```
/* -------- establish & declare residency --------- */
static void resinit(void)
{
    tsrss[0] = _SS;
    tsrsp[0] = _SP;
    oldtimer = getvect(TIMER);
    old28 = getvect(INT28);
    oldkb = getvect(KYBRD);
    olddisk = getvect(DISK);
    /* ----- attach vectors to resident program ----- */
    setvect(TIMER, newtimer);
    setvect(KYBRD, newkb);
    setvect(INT28, new28);
    setvect(DISK, newdisk);
    /* ------ compute program size ------- */
    sizeprogram = highmemory - _psp;
    /* ----- terminate and stay resident ------- */
    keep(0, sizeprogram);
}

/* ---------- break handler ------------ */
static void interrupt newbreak(void)
{
    return;
}

/* -------- critical error ISR ---------- */
static void interrupt newcrit(IREGS ir)
{
    ir.ax = 0;           /* ignore critical errors */
}

/* ------ BIOS disk functions ISR ------- */
static void interrupt newdisk(IREGS ir)
{
    diskflag++;
    (*olddisk)();
    ir.ax = _AX;         /* for the register returns */
    ir.cx = _CX;
    ir.dx = _DX;
```

continued...

...from previous page

```
    ir.fl = _FLAGS;
    --diskflag;
}

/* ------ test for the hot key ------ */
static int test_hotkeys(int ky)
{
    static unsigned biosshift;
    int hk;

    biosshift = peekb(0, 0x417);
    for (hk = 0; hk < MAXHOTKEYS; hk++) {
        if (scancode[hk] == 0 && keymask[hk] == 0)
            return FALSE;
        if (ky == scancode[hk] &&
            (biosshift & keymask[hk]) == keymask[hk]) {
            if (!ctx[hk].running && depth < MAXHOTKEYS &&
                        !plusrunning)   {
                /* ---- set hotkey indicator ---- */
                hotkey_flag = TRUE;
                hkx = hotkey[depth++] = hk;
            }
            break;
        }
    }
    return hk < MAXHOTKEYS;
}

/* ----- keyboard ISR ------ */
static void interrupt newkb(void)
{
    static int kbval;
    if (test_hotkeys(inportb(0x60)))    {
        /* --- reset the keyboard ---- */
        kbval = inportb(0x61);
        outportb(0x61, kbval | 0x80);
        outportb(0x61, kbval);
        outportb(0x20, 0x20);
    }
    else
```

continued...

...from previous page

```
        (*oldkb)();
}

/* ----- timer ISR ------- */
static void interrupt newtimer(void)
{
    (*oldtimer)();
    test_hotkeys(0);
    if (hotkey_flag && peekb(dosseg, dosbusy) == 0) {
        if (diskflag == 0)  {
            outportb(0x20, 0x20);
            hotkey_flag = 0;
            dores();
        }
    }
}

/* ----- 0x28 ISR -------- */
static void interrupt new28(void)
{
    (*old28)();
    if (hotkey_flag && peekb(dosseg, dosbusy) != 0) {
        hotkey_flag = 0;
        dores();
    }
}

/* ------ switch psp context from interrupted to TSR ----- */
static void resident_psp(void)
{
    ctx[hkx].intpsp = getpsp();
    _AH = 0x50;
    _BX = _psp;
    geninterrupt(DOS);
}

/* ---- switch psp context from TSR to interrupted ---- */
static void interrupted_psp(void)
{
    _BX = ctx[hkx].intpsp;
```

continued...

...from previous page

```
    _AH = 0x50;
    geninterrupt(DOS);
}

/* ------ execute the resident program ------- */
static void dores(void)
{
    plusrunning = TRUE;
    ctx[hkx].intsp = _SP;
    ctx[hkx].intss =  SS:
    _SP = tsrsp[depth-1];
    _SS = tsrss[depth-1];
    ctx[hkx].running = TRUE;     /* set TSR running semaphore */
    ctx[hkx].oldcrit = getvect(CRIT);/* redirect critical err */
    ctx[hkx].oldbreak = getvect(CTRLBRK);
    ctx[hkx].oldctrlc = getvect(CTRLC);
    setvect(CRIT, newcrit);
    setvect(CTRLBRK, newbreak);
    setvect(CTRLC, newbreak);
    ctx[hkx].ctrl_break = getcbrk();/* get ctrl break setting */
    setcbrk(0);                     /* turn off ctrl break    */
    ctx[hkx].intdta = getdta();     /* get interrupted dta    */
    setdta(mydta);                  /* set resident dta       */
    resident_psp();                 /* swap psps              */
    enable();
    exec_popup(hkx);         /* call the TSR C program here */
    disable();
    hkx = hotkey[depth-1];
    interrupted_psp();              /* reset interrupted psp  */
    setdta(ctx[hkx].intdta);        /* reset interrupted dta  */
    setvect(CRIT, ctx[hkx].oldcrit);/* reset critical error   */
    setvect(CTRLBRK, ctx[hkx].oldbreak);
    setvect(CTRLC, ctx[hkx].oldctrlc);
    setcbrk(ctx[hkx].ctrl_break);   /* reset ctrl break        */
    _SP = ctx[hkx].intsp;           /* reset interrupted stack */
    _SS = ctx[hkx].intss;
    if (unloading)                /* if TSR set the unload flag */
        unload();
    ctx[hkx].running = FALSE;     /* reset TSR running semaphore */
    --depth;
```

continued...

...from previous page

```
}

/* ---- test to see if the program is already resident ---- */
static int resident(char *signature)
{
    char *sg;
    unsigned df;
    unsigned blkseg, mcbs = mcbseg;

    df = _DS - _psp;
    /* ---- walk thru mcb chain & search for TSR ----- */
    while (peekb(mcbs, 0) == 0x4d)  {
        blkseg = peek(mcbs, 1);
        if (peek(blkseg, 0) == 0x20cd)  {
            /* --- this is a psp --- */
            if (blkseg == _psp)
                break;          /* if the transient copy */
            for (sg = signature; *sg; sg++)
                if (*sg != peekb(blkseg+df,(unsigned)sg))
                    break;
            if (*sg == '\0')
                /* ---- TSR is already resident --- */
                return TRUE;
        }
        mcbs += peek(mcbs, 3) + 1;
    }
    return FALSE;
}

/* --------- unload the resident program --------- */
static void unload(void)
{
    if (getvect(DISK) == (void interrupt (*)()) newdisk)
        if (getvect(KYBRD) == newkb)
            if (getvect(INT28) == new28)
                if (getvect(TIMER) == newtimer) {
                    resterm();
                    return;
                }
    /* ---- another TSR is above us, cannot unload ---- */
```

continued...

...from previous page

```
        putch(7);
}

/* ------- TSR unload function ----------- */
static void resterm(void)
{
        unsigned mcbs = mcbseg;
        /* ----- restore the interrupt vectors ----- */
        setvect(TIMER, oldtimer);
        setvect(KYBRD, oldkb);
        setvect(INT28, old28);
        setvect(DISK, olddisk);
        /* ----- obliterate the signature -------- */
        *signature = '\0';
        /* ---- walk thru mcb chain &
            release memory owned by the TSR ----- */
        while (peekb(mcbs, 0) == 0x4d)  {
            if (peek(mcbs, 1) == _psp)
                freemem(mcbs+1);
            mcbs += peek(mcbs, 3) + 1;
        }
}
```

The TSRPLUS TSR Executive Module: tsrplus.c

Listing 11.3 is tsrplus.c, the executive program that stays resident and pops up all your other TSRs. It sets its own unload hot key (Alt-U), calls the **loadtsrs** function to load any snapshot image files that might be available, and calls **tsr** in tsrmult.c to declare itself resident.

The **loadtsrs** function reads and registers any TSR snapshot files and loads the memory images into Expanded Memory if it exists. The function uses the Turbo C **findfirst** and **findnext** functions to locate all files with the extension .TSR. It uses the Turbo C **getcwd** function to build a full unambiguous path to the file name so that later pop-ups can find it no matter where the system happens to be logged on. It builds two file names, one for the .TSR file and one with an extension of .SWP. This latter file name will be used to swap out memory before the TSR is loaded. Of course, if Expanded Memory is to be used, these file names are not applicable.

The function assures that the load address for the segment is the same as the high memory location of TSRPLUS. This check assures that the snapshot was taken in the presence of the latest version of TSRPLUS with nothing else loaded above TSRPLUS.

If Expanded Memory is available, the **load_emm** function allocates the pages and loads the TSR's memory snapshot into them.

When a hot key for a registered TSR is pressed, the **exec_popup** function in TSRPLUS is called. If the hotkey is the first one in the hot key array, it is the key to unload TSRPLUS, and the **unloading** variable is set to a true value. Because TSRPLUS uses no video windows, the program sounds the audio alarm to let the user know the unload took effect.

For a TSR hot key, the program builds far pointers to the TSRPLUS stack register arrays and its own **plusrunning** semaphore. The TSR will set the semaphore and save the stack registers after it is loaded and safely running, so it will need pointers to these data variables. Then the **exec_popup** function calls **openswaps** to establish the swap files, **writeswap** to write the existing memory to its swap file, and **readtsr** to read the TSR image into memory from its snapshot file. If Expanded Memory is being used, these reads and writes use EM rather than disk files. The TSR's PSP is set from the value stored in the snapshot header record, and the TSR's startup function is called through the interrupt pointer stored in the header record.

At this point, processing picks up in the TSRBUILD module in its **start_tsr** function described later.

When the TSR returns to pop down, the TSRPLUS PSP is restored, and the **readswap** and **closeswaps** functions are called to restore the interrupted program's memory from the swap file or EM. Then TSRPLUS returns to the TSRMULT module to pop down.

The **openswaps** and **closeswaps** functions deal with EM. If EM is in use, the **emmhandle** array entry for the hot key has a handle, and **openswaps** uses this handle to save the EM mapping context and map the logical pages into the EM physical pages. When the TSR is done with EM, the **closeswaps** function restores the EM mapping context that existed before the pop-up.

There is a **writeswap**, a **readtsr**, and a **readswap** function. The **writeswap** function creates a swap disk file if EM is not being used. Then it calls **writecode** and **writevectors** and closes the disk file. If EM is not being used, the **readtsr** function opens the snapshot file associated with the hot key and seeks it past the snapshot header record. Then it calls **readvectors** followed by **readcode** and closes the disk file. The **readswap** function opens the swap file if EM is not being used and calls **readcode** followed by **readvectors** and closes the disk file.

The sequences for calling **readcode** and **readvectors** are important. When loading the TSR snapshot, you must load the interrupt vectors first. When loading the swapped memory image, you must load the image first. This is because an interrupted program might have attached some interrupt vectors. If you load the TSR code image before its vectors, an interrupt intended for the swapped-out program could land in the middle of the TSR's code. Conversely, when reloading the swapped image, if you load the vectors first, that same kind of interrupt could land in the TSR code before you get the swapped code loaded back in.

The **readcode**, **writecode**, **readvectors**, and **writevectors** functions each transfer their images between memory and either disk or EM, depending on which is being used.

Listing 11.3: tsrplus.c

```
/* ----------- tsrplus.c ------------- */

/*
 * A Multiple-TSR Overlay Executive Program
 */

#include <dir.h>
#include <dos.h>
#include <stdio.h>
#include <fcntl.h>
#include <io.h>
#include <sys/stat.h>
#include <string.h>
#include <conio.h>
#include "tsrmult.h"
#include "interupt.h"
#include "emm.h"
```

continued...

...from previous page

```

#define FALSE 0

char signature[] = "TSRPLUS";
extern unsigned _heaplen = 256;
extern unsigned _stklen  = 4096;

/* --------- hotkey arrays ------------ */
extern unsigned scancode[], keymask[];

unsigned highmemory;    /* Address of top of TSRPLUS    */
extern int unloading;   /* set to unload the TSR   */

extern int tsrss[];     /* TSRPLUS's stack segment */
extern int tsrsp[];     /* TSRPLUS's stack pointer */
extern int plusrunning;
extern int depth;

static struct ffblk ffblk;  /* for DOS directory search */

static struct swap_header swap[MAXHOTKEYS-1];
static char tsrfile[MAXHOTKEYS-1] [64];
static char swapfile[MAXHOTKEYS-1] [64];
static int emmhandle[MAXHOTKEYS-1];
static int pages[MAXHOTKEYS-1];

static int emm;                     /* indicates EMM is used */
static int keyct;                   /* hot key subscript     */
static int handle;                  /* file handle           */
static int frame;                   /* EMM frame segment     */

static union REGS rg;
static struct SREGS sr;

static void load_emm(void);
static void loadtsrs(void);
static void release_pages(void);
static void openswaps(int);
static void writeswap(int);
static void readtsr(int);
```

continued...

...from previous page

```
static void readswap(int);
static void writecode(int);
static void writevectors(int);
static void readvectors(int, int);
static void readcode(int, int);
static void readfile(unsigned, unsigned, int);
static void writefile(unsigned, unsigned, int);
static void closeswaps(int);

void main(void)
{
    highmemory = _SS + ((_SP + 256) / 16);
    segread(&sr);
    /* ------- set hot key to unload TSRPLUS ----------- */
    keymask[0] = 8;      /* ALT- */
    scancode[0] = 22;    /* U    */
    loadtsrs();
    tsr();
}

/* ------- load/reload the TSR swap files --------- */
static void loadtsrs(void)
{
    int done;

    /* ---- test for emm ----- */
    emm = (emm_present() && emm_working());
    if (emm)
        frame = emm_pageframe();
    keyct = 0;
    /* ---- scan for .TSR files and register them ---- */
    done = findfirst("*.TSR", &ffblk, 0);
    while (!done && keyct < MAXHOTKEYS-1)   {
        /* --- build full path to swap files --- */
        getcwd(tsrfile[keyct], 64);
        if (tsrfile[keyct] [strlen(tsrfile[keyct]) - 1] != '\\')
            strcat(tsrfile[keyct], "\\");
        strcat(tsrfile[keyct], ffblk.ff_name);
        strcpy(swapfile[keyct], tsrfile[keyct]);
        strcpy(swapfile[keyct]+strlen(swapfile[keyct])-3,"SWP");
```

continued...

...from previous page

```
        /* ------- open .TSR file and read header -------- */
        handle = open(ffblk.ff_name, O_RDONLY);
        read(handle, &swap[keyct], sizeof(struct swap_header));
        /*  bypass if loading other than at top of TSRPLUS  */
        if (swap[keyct].loadseg == highmemory)  {
            load_emm();
            scancode[keyct+1] = swap[keyct].scancode;
            keymask[keyct+1] = swap[keyct].keymask;
            keyct++;
        }
        close(handle);
        done = findnext(&ffblk);
    }
}

/* ------ load the TSR file into EMM swap area -------- */
static void load_emm(void)
{
    /* ---- compute EMM pages needed ---- */
    pages[keyct] = ((1024+swap[keyct].length)/16384)*2+1;
    /* ----- test for enough EMM pages available ----- */
    if (emm && pages[keyct] < 5 &&
            emm_pages_available() >= pages[keyct])  {
        /* ------ allocate the EMM pages -------- */
        emmhandle[keyct] = emm_allocate(pages[keyct]);
        emm_map(pages[keyct], 0, 0, emmhandle[keyct]);
        /* ----- read the tsrfile vectors into EMM ----- */
        readfile(frame, 0, 1024);
        /* ----- read the tsrfile code into EMM ---- */
        readfile(frame, 1024, swap[keyct].length);
    }
}

/* ---------- release pages of EMM ----------- */
static void release_pages(void)
{
    for (keyct = 0; keyct < MAXHOTKEYS-1; keyct++)  {
        scancode[keyct+1] = keymask[keyct+1] = 0;
        if (emmhandle[keyct])   {
            emm_release(emmhandle[keyct]);
```

continued...

...from previous page

```
                emmhandle[keyct] = 0;
            }
        }
}

/* -------- one of the hot keys has been pressed --------- */
void exec_popup(int hotkey)
{
    struct swap_header sw;
    int far *ss = MK_FP(_DS, (unsigned) tsrss);
    int far *sp = MK_FP(_DS, (unsigned) tsrsp);
    int far *pr = MK_FP(_DS, (unsigned) &plusrunning);

    if (hotkey < 1) {
        /* hotkey is for unload TSRPLUS */
        if (depth == 1) {
            putch(7);              /* ding! (to reinforce user) */
            release_pages();
            unloading = 1;         /* unload TSRPLUS        */
        }
        plusrunning = FALSE;
        return;
    }
    hotkey -= 1;
    sw = swap[hotkey];
    /* ----- swap TPA memory for TSR memory ------ */
    openswaps(hotkey);
    writeswap(hotkey);
    readtsr(hotkey);
    /* ----- set TSR's psp ----- */
    _AH = 0x50;
    _BX = sw.psp;
    geninterrupt(DOS);

    (*sw.startptr)(depth, ss, sp, pr);  /* execute the TSR */

    /* ----- set tsrplus's psp ----- */
    _AH = 0x50;
    _BX = _psp;
    geninterrupt(DOS);
```

continued...

...from previous page

```
    /* ------ swap the TPA memory back in -------- */
    readswap(hotkey);
    closeswaps(hotkey);
}

/* ------- set up EMM for swapping --------- */
static void openswaps(int hotkey)
{
    if (emmhandle[hotkey])  {
        emm_savecontext(emmhandle[hotkey]);
        emm_map(pages[hotkey], 0, 0, emmhandle[hotkey]);
    }
}

/* ---- restore EMM mapping context after TSR is done ---- */
static void closeswaps(int hotkey)
{
    if (emmhandle[hotkey])
        emm_restorecontext(emmhandle[hotkey]);
}

/* ---- swap out the TPA memory to make room for the TSR ---- */
static void writeswap(int hotkey)
{
    if (emmhandle[hotkey] == 0) {
        _fmode = O_BINARY;
        handle = creat(swapfile[hotkey], S_IWRITE);
    }
    writecode(hotkey);
    writevectors(hotkey);
    if (emmhandle[hotkey] == 0)
        close(handle);
}

/* ------- read the TSR in from its file or EMM ------ */
static void readtsr(int hotkey)
{
    if (emmhandle[hotkey] == 0) {
        handle = open(tsrfile[hotkey], O_RDONLY);
        lseek(handle, (long) sizeof(struct swap_header), SEEK_SET);
```

continued...

...from previous page

```
    }
    readvectors(hotkey, 0);
    readcode(hotkey, 0);
    if (emmhandle[hotkey] == 0)
        close(handle);
}

/* ----- read the swapped TPA in after the TSR is done ---- */
static void readswap(int hotkey)
{
    if (emmhandle[hotkey] == 0)
        handle = open(swapfile[hotkey], O_RDONLY);
    readcode(hotkey, 1);
    readvectors(hotkey, 1);
    if (emmhandle[hotkey] == 0)
        close(handle);
}

/* ------ write the code portion of the TPA to the swap ---- */
static void writecode(int hotkey)
{
    if (emmhandle[hotkey])
        movedata(swap[hotkey].loadseg, 0, frame,
            2048 + swap[hotkey].length, swap[hotkey].length);
    else
        writefile(swap[hotkey].loadseg, 0, swap[hotkey].length);
}

/* ---- write interrupt vectors to the swap ----- */
static void writevectors(int hotkey)
{
    if (emmhandle[hotkey])
        movedata(0, 0, frame, 1024 + swap[hotkey].length, 1024);
    else
        writefile(0, 0, 1024);
}

/* ---- read interrupt vectors from the swap ----- */
static void readvectors(int hotkey, int wh)
{
```

continued...

...from previous page

```
    if (emmhandle[hotkey])  {
        disable();
        movedata(frame, wh * (1024 + swap[hotkey].length),
                        0, 0, 1024);
        enable();
    }
    else
        readfile(0, 0, 1024);
}

/* ------ read code from the swap ------ */
static void readcode(int hotkey, int wh)
{
    if (emmhandle[hotkey])
        movedata(frame, 1024 + wh * (1024+swap[hotkey].length),
            swap[hotkey].loadseg, 0, swap[hotkey].length);
    else
        readfile(swap[hotkey].loadseg, 0, swap[hotkey].length);
}

/* ----------- read a swap file record ------------ */
static void readfile(unsigned seg, unsigned off, int len)
{
    rg.h.ah = 0x3f;
    rg.x.cx = len;
    rg.x.bx = handle;
    rg.x.dx = off;
    sr.ds = seg;
    disable();
    intdosx(&rg, &rg, &sr);
    enable();
}

/* ----------- write a swap file record ------------ */
static void writefile(unsigned seg, unsigned off, int len)
{
    rg.h.ah = 0x40;
    rg.x.cx = len;
    rg.x.bx = handle;
    rg.x.dx = off;
    sr.ds = seg;
    intdosx(&rg, &rg, &sr);
}
```

The TSRPLUS Build Module: tsrbuild.c

Listing 11.4 is tsrbuild.c. You link your TSR program with this module rather than with tsr.c from Chapter 9. Other than that, you build your TSR program by following the same guidelines you learned in Chapter 9. The tsrbuild.c file has a **tsr** function that replaces the one you called in tsr.c. It also takes care of calling your **exec_popup** function in the same manner that tsr.c did. The only difference is that setting the **unloading** variable from within your TSR has no effect. There is no point in unloading a TSRPLUS-managed TSR program because it isn't resident anyway. You can unload TSRPLUS itself with the effect that all associated TSR programs are disabled.

Begin with the **tsr** function in tsrbuild.c. Bear in mind what this function is going to do. It is going to build a snapshot file of itself and the TSR program that is linked with it. Along with that snapshot will go a header record that describes where it loads and how it runs. At the same time, the **tsr** function is going to save some information locally about itself that will be written with its memory image and that the **start_tsr** function will use when the TSR is loaded and executed by TSRPLUS.

The first things the **tsr** function saves are the values in its stack segment and pointer registers. When it pops up, its **start_tsr** function will need to switch the stack context. This is not done before the **start_tsr** function is called because the TSRPLUS **exec_popup** function passes parameters on its own stack.

The **tsr** function builds a file name from the name of its executable module as taken from the Turbo C _argv[0] element. The file name duplicates the TSR's name with an extension of .TSR, and this name will be that of the snapshot file.

The snapshot image begins with the TSR's environment block. This address is taken from the TSR's PSP at location 0x2c. The address minus one is the segment address of the DOS Memory Control Block of the environment block. The length of the record is computed from that address to the end of the stack.

The snapshot header record is written with the hot key's scan code and shift status mask, a pointer to the **start_tsr** interrupt function, the segment address of the environment block, the image length, and the address of the PSP. Following the header record is a copy of the system's interrupt vectors as they exist at the time the snapshot is taken. Finally, the TSR's program image—from the environment block to the end of the stack—is written to the snapshot file.

When the TSR is loaded by TSRPLUS and executed, everything in memory looks just as it did when the snapshot was taken. All that must be completed is the establishment of the critical CPU registers. Because **start_tsr** is an interrupt function, the code segment and data segment registers are initialized to the correct values when the function is called from TSRPLUS. The **start_tsr** function must set up the stack and clear the **plusrunning** semaphore in TSRPLUS so that other TSRs can be popped up on top of this one. TSRPLUS has passed far pointers to the **plusrunning** semaphore and its arrays of stack register save areas. These are copied into static pointers before the stack is switched to the TSR's stack. The current stack registers are written to the array kept in TSRMULT. The TSRMULT engine uses this array to know what its own stack should be when it is swapping stacks to call TSRPLUS. This complex technique allows reentrant calls through TSRMULT to TSRPLUS—sort of a stack of stacks. Don't try too hard to understand it. Be thankful it works.

The **start_psp** function sets the stack registers to the values that the **tsr** function saved before the snapshot was taken. At this point, it is safe for TSRPLUS to accept other hot keys, so **start_psp** clears the TSRPLUS **plusrunning** semaphore through the far pointer that TSRPLUS passed.

The **exec_popup** function of the TSR is now called, and the TSR does whatever the TSR is intended to do. When it returns, the **start_psp** function restores the stack from the far away array in TSRPLUS and returns to TSRPLUS to pop down. Of course, it is the responsibility of the TSR to save and restore any video and cursor contexts that it might need to disturb in order to perform its task. This convention is the same as with the TSR programs described in Chapter 9.

Listing 11.4: tsrbuild.c

```
/* ---------- tsrbuild.c --------- */

/*
 * A builder of swapped TSR programs
 */

#include <stdio.h>
#include <conio.h>
#include <process.h>
#include <fcntl.h>
#include <io.h>
```

continued...

...from previous page

```
#include <sys/stat.h>
#include <dos.h>
#include <string.h>
#include "interupt.h"
#include "tsrmult.h"

#define FALSE 0

static char tsrname[64];
static union REGS rg;
static struct SREGS sr;
static unsigned myss, mysp;

unsigned scancode, keymask;
int unloading;

static struct swap_header swap;

void interrupt start_tsr(IREGS ir, int depth, int far *tsrss,
                                int far *tsrsp, int far *plusrunning)
{
    static int dp;
    static int far *pr;
    static int far *ss;
    static int far *sp;

    dp = depth;
    pr = plusrunning;
    ss = tsrss;
    sp = tsrsp;

    *(ss + dp) = _SS;
    *(sp + dp) = _SP;

    disable();
    _SS = myss;
    _SP = mysp;
    enable();

```

continued...

...from previous page

```
    *pr = FALSE;
    exec_popup(0);

    disable();
    _SS = *(ss + dp);
    _SP = *(sp + dp);
    enable();
}

void tsr(void)
{
    int handle;
    extern int _fmode;
    long len;

    myss = _SS;
    mysp = _SP;
    mysp -= 50;
    strcpy(tsrname, *_argv);
    strcpy(tsrname+strlen(tsrname)-3, "TSR");
    swap.scancode = scancode;
    swap.keymask = keymask;
    swap.startptr = MK_FP(_CS, (unsigned) start_tsr);
    /*  get the address of the program's environment block */
    swap.loadseg = peek(_psp, 0x2c) - 1;
    /* --- compute the program's length and address --- */
    len = ((long) (myss - swap.loadseg) * 16) + mysp;
    if (len > 65536L)   {
        cprintf("\r\n%s is too big (%ld)", *_argv, len);
        exit(1);
    }
    swap.length = (unsigned) len;
    swap.psp = _psp;
    /* ----- write the swap file header record ------- */
    _fmode = O_BINARY;
    handle = creat(tsrname, S_IWRITE);
    write(handle, &swap, sizeof swap);
    /* ------- write the interrupt vectors -------- */
    segread(&sr);
    rg.h.ah = 0x40;
```

continued...

...from previous page

```
        rg.x.cx = 1024;
        rg.x.bx = handle;
        rg.x.dx = 0;
        sr.ds = 0;
        intdosx(&rg, &rg, &sr);
        /* --------- write the program code record -------- */
        segread(&sr);
        rg.h.ah = 0x40;
        rg.x.cx = swap.length;
        rg.x.bx = handle;
        rg.x.dx = 0;
        sr.ds = swap.loadseg;
        intdosx(&rg, &rg, &sr);
        /* ------- done --------- */
        close(handle);
}
```

TSRPLUS Example TSR Programs

Having built the TSRPLUS executive program, it is only proper that you should build some TSR programs to use it. The first and most obvious choice would be to build the Personal Dialer program from Chapter 9 into the TSRPLUS environment.

The TSRPLUS Dialer: buildial.exe

There is no source code to be shown with this example. You have seen it all. The dialer.c program links as well with the TSRPLUS environment as it does with the TSR engine in Chapter 9. The difference is that it is now a nonresident pop-up utility. The buildial.exe file described in Appendix C and built with the Turbo C makefile in Appendix B is the Personal Dialer program in a TSRPLUS environment.

The Personal Notepad: tinynote.c

Listing 11.5 is tinynote.c, a Personal Notepad that is included here, not because it is a great program, but because it demonstrates the multi-pop-up capabilities of TSRPLUS. You could link it with the Chapter 9 TSR engine, and it would be a conventional TSR. Link it with the TSRPLUS build module, tsrbuild.c, and it is a TSRPLUS pop-up program. The tinynote.exe file built with the makefile in Appendix B is the TSRPLUS version of the program.

Tinynote.c is not a full-featured notepad program. Its purpose is to demonstrate TSRPLUS. It saves the cursor context and opens a file named tinynote.dat. The contents of that file are read into an array of text lines. A window is opened and the array is displayed in the window with a series of **cputs** calls. If you press F1, you get a little help window. If you press F2, the window is cleared. F3 clears the line where the cursor rests. When you press the Esc key, the array is written back to the file, the file is closed, the window is closed, the cursor is restored, and the program returns to pop down.

Listing 11.5: tinynote.c

```
/* --------- tinynote.c ----------- */

/*
 * A tiny TSR notepad
 */

#include <stdio.h>
#include <conio.h>
#include <mem.h>
#include <string.h>
#include <dir.h>
#include <ctype.h>
#include "cursor.h"
#include "window.h"
#include "keys.h"
#include "tsr.h"

char signature[] = "Personal Notepad";
```

continued...

...from previous page

```
extern unsigned _heaplen = 3072;
extern unsigned _stklen  = 1024;

/* --------- hotkey arrays ------------ */
extern unsigned scancode[], keymask[];

#define LINES 10
#define WIDTH 78

char notepad[LINES][WIDTH+1];
static void clearpad(void);
static void clearline(int);
static void tinyhelp(void);
static int readline(int);
static int poppedup;
static char filename[65];

void main(void)
{
    clearpad();
    *scancode = 52;      /* set Ctrl-period as the hot key */
    *keymask = 4;
    getcwd(filename, 64);
    if (filename[strlen(filename) - 1] != '\\')
        strcat(filename, "\\");
    strcat(filename, "tinynote.dat");
    tsr();               /* set up dialer as a TSR */
}

/* -------- this code is executed upon popup -------- */
void exec_popup(void)
{
    int line, ch = 0;
    FILE *fp;

    savecursor();
    normalcursor();
    if ((fp = fopen(filename, "rb")) != NULL)    {
        fread(notepad, sizeof notepad, 1, fp);
        fclose(fp);
```

continued...

...from previous page

```
    }
    open_window(1,10,80,10+LINES+2,BLACK,YELLOW,2,0);
    for (line = 0; line < LINES; line++)    {
        gotoxy(1,line+1);
        cputs(notepad[line]);
    }
    line = poppedup = 1;
    while(ch != ESC)    {
        gotoxy(1,line);
        ch = readline(line);
        switch (ch) {
            case F1:    tinyhelp();
                        break;
            case F2:    clearpad();
            case F3:    clearline(line-1);
                        break;
            case ESC:   break;
            default:    break;
        }
    }
    close_window();
    fp = fopen(filename, "wb");
    fwrite(notepad, sizeof notepad, 1, fp);
    fclose(fp);
    restorecursor();
}

static void clearpad(void)
{
    int line;
    for (line = 0; line < LINES; line++)
        clearline(line);
}

static void clearline(int line)
{
    if (poppedup)
        gotoxy(1,line+1);
    setmem(notepad[line], WIDTH, ' ');
    notepad[line] [WIDTH] = '\0';
```

continued...

...from previous page

```
    if (poppedup)
        cputs(notepad[line]);
}

static void tinyhelp(void)
{
    hidecursor();
    open_window(25, 17, 60, 22, WHITE, GREEN, 1, 1);
    cprintf(" F2 = Clear screen\r\n");
    cprintf(" F3 = Clear line\r\n");
    cprintf(" Esc = Quit\r\n");
    cprintf("  (Any key to Exit HELP");
    getkey();
    close_window();
    unhidecursor();
}

/* ------- read a line from the keyboard ------------ */
static int readline(int line)
{
    int done = FALSE;
    int x = 1, c = 0;

    while (TRUE)    {
        gotoxy(x, line);
        c = c ? c : getkey();
        switch (c)  {
            case HOME:  line = 1;
                        break;
            case UP:    if (line > 1)
                            --line;
                        break;
            case END:   line = LINES;
                        break;
            case FWD:   if (x < WIDTH)  {
                            x++;
                            break;
                        }
            case '\r':  x = 1;
                        c = 0;
```

continued...

...from previous page

```
                case DN:    if (line < LINES)
                                line++;
                            break;
                case BS:    if (x > 1)
                                --x;
                            break;
                case '\b':  if (x > 1)
                                --x;
                case DEL:   movmem(notepad[line-1]+x,
                                    notepad[line-1]+x-1,WIDTH-x);
                            gotoxy(1, line);
                            notepad[line-1][WIDTH-1] = ' ';
                            cputs(notepad[line-1]);
                            break;
                default:    if (c == F1 || c == F2 ||
                                    c == F3 || c == ESC)    {
                                done = TRUE;
                                break;
                            }
                            if (!isprint(c))    {
                                putch(BELL);
                                break;
                            }
                            notepad[line-1][x-1] = (char) c;
                            putch(c);
                            if (x < WIDTH)
                                x++;
                            else
                                c = '\r';
                            break;
        }
        if (done)
            break;
        if (c != '\r')
            c = 0;
    }
    return c;
}
```

Executing TSRPLUS

To set up the TSRPLUS environment, you need to understand the relationship between the TSRPLUS memory-resident executive program and the TSR-like snapshot images that it processes.

TSRPLUS expects the snapshots to begin at the memory location where TSRPLUS ends. To make this happen, you load TSRPLUS into memory and then execute the TSR-like programs one at a time. Each one will load immediately following TSRPLUS, will write its snapshot, and will exit, not staying resident. Before this procedure, it is a safe measure to delete all .TSR files so that no residual ones confuse TSRPLUS. To set up the two example programs included in this book, enter the following commands at the console:

```
c>del *.tsr
c>tsrplus
c>buildial
c>tinynote
```

Now press Alt-U to unload TSRPLUS and reload it with the following command:

```
c>tsrplus
```

This second load is necessary because TSRPLUS attempts to register TSRs only when TSRPLUS is first loaded. The first time you loaded it, there were no TSRs, but you needed TSRPLUS in memory so that the TSR-like programs would load into and write their images from the correct location.

Now you can press Alt-Period to run the Personal Dialer and Ctrl-Period to run the tiny notepad, and you can run them on top of one another in any sequence.

From then on, you need only to run TSRPLUS to enable all the TSR-like programs. Be sure, however, to always run it from the same DOS environment with respect to other resident programs and device drivers so that its top memory location matches the load addresses of the TSR-like programs.

SUMMARY

This brings to a close the grab bag of programs that will allow you to extend the Turbo C Professional package and your use of it. In Chapter 12, you will explore the Turbo Debugger and learn how to use it in effectively debugging your programs.

CHAPTER 12

THE TURBO DEBUGGER

This chapter discusses the Turbo Debugger. Consistent with the theme of *Extending Turbo C Professional*, these discussions address themselves to unusual ways to use the Turbo Debugger, ways not covered in the *User's Guide*.

Debugging is a personal, private endeavor. Everyone goes about it in his or her own way. But no matter how you debug computer programs, you will find that the practice is a lot easier and a lot more fun with the Turbo Debugger. Many programmers bypass the Turbo C Integrated Development Environment Debugger altogether, preferring to use the command-line compiler and debug with the Turbo Debugger.

The tips and techniques presented in this chapter will enable you to get much more out of the Turbo Debugger.

What you need to understand:

- A touch of assembly language
- Interrupts

New subjects discussed:

- Debugging in general
- The NMI interrupt
- Debugging TSRs

DEBUGGING

Debugging C programs used to be a matter of inserting **printf** calls in places where programs were suspected of going awry. With the source-level debuggers now available with most C compilers, that old technique is out of style, although many programmers still use it for a quick-and-dirty look at where the program is going and what it is doing.

The latest and best of the source-level debuggers is the Turbo Debugger. It was built to leave the others in the dust, and that it has done. It is one of the most powerful tools a C programmer can use.

Testing vs. Debugging

Consider the difference between testing and debugging. Testing is when you or the users of your program determine if the program is functionally correct, that it satisfies its functional requirements, that it does what it is supposed to do. Testing, of course, reveals bugs. Sometimes, use of the program after testing reveals bugs. Debugging is the process of finding and correcting some bug that was either observed during testing or that showed up later, after the program was in use.

To test, you do not need a debugger. Perhaps you need a data base, some data entry values, and an understanding of the anticipated results. Certainly, you need a test plan. When the test delivers the wrong answers, then you must debug.

Sometimes what is mistaken for debugging is really a matter of correcting the programmer's understanding of what the algorithms should be. ("No, debits are on the left, not the right.") Other times the solution modifies the problem, and the user wants more features. ("Well, you can make it do that, but I always thought it would do. . . .") While these changes seem to be bug repair, they are really modifications and do not warrant a debugger. They seem to be bug-related to the user, because the program is not performing the way the user expects it to. Real bugs exist, however, when the program does not perform the way the programmer expects it to. The former is a misunderstanding; the latter a bug.

Real bugs, too, are the ones that you cannot see by looking at the code. When a bug is hiding in the depths of the system, you usually need a debugger. There is no better debugger for the PC than the Turbo Debugger, and you can use it to find almost anything, but first you must be prepared.

Preparing to Debug the Program

Before you embark on a Turbo Debugging session, there are some steps you should take to prepare yourself and your program.

- **Read up.** First, read the *Turbo Debugger User's Guide.* It is a well-written manual with many examples and a decent tutorial. This chapter does not attempt to replace the *User's Guide.* Learn all the features of the debugger.

- **Write good code.** Next, write a good program. That's right, the most important component in a successful debugging session is a well-written program. There are many good texts on this subject, and it certainly deserves a book of its own. There are also as many opinions about what constitutes good programs as there are programmers to write them.

  Think of it this way. An old maxim says that the solution to a problem should resemble the problem. In program design, that wisdom can be translated to say that the architecture of a program should resemble the functions of the application the program supports. The user views the system from the perspective of his or her job: the functional requirements supported by the system. If the user reports that the system has a problem in a certain functional area, the programmer must relate that report to some place in the software to look for the problem. If the software looks enough like the application, the search is easier.

  Below that, the program itself should be written to facilitate debugging. If the program decomposes to small functions, each with a discrete purpose, and each functionally separate, protected, and hidden from the rest of the program, the program will be easier to debug. This "black box" approach to programming is not a new idea. It has long been promoted as a method that contributes to program understanding and maintenance. It is also a healthy way to write a program that you might need to debug—that is to say, almost any program.

  Therefore, proper debugging begins with good program and system design.

- **Make the code debugger-conforming.** The software must be compiled and linked to include the things the debugger needs. Compile programs from the command line with the tcc -v option. If you are compiling and linking separately, use the tlink /v option.

  If you build your programs from the Turbo C Integrated Development Environment, set the debugging options on by typing Alt-O, C, C, O to navigate down to the "Obj debug information" menu selection. In the Debug menu, set Source debugging on.

- **Plan ahead.** Organize your debugging with an approach in mind. Have a plan. Get the data base together. Make sure the hardware can handle the program and the debugger.

- **Duplicate the bug.** Establish a procedure where you can consistently duplicate the bug. No bug is harder to find than the one that cannot be reliably and consistently duplicated. You need to know and understand the steps necessary to make the bug happen.

  If the bug-replication procedure involves starting with some data records that get modified on the way to the bug, set up a baseline of those records in a safe place. As you move among iterations of the debugging sessions, you will need to re-establish the baseline of data records each time you start over. Build a batch file that does that.

  Make sure that you have the hardware and software that reproduces the bug. You might be working on a problem that only occurs in the company of a very specific configuration. This is particularly possible when debugging TSRs.

- **Test to see what you broke.** Often a bug fix creates another bug. After you have fixed one, run a complete system test to see what new bugs hatched in the process.

- **Eliminate the riff-raff.** Attempt to reduce the system's expression of the error to the smallest possible configuration. Use the least number of data records required to make the bug happen. Start from a point that uses the least number of steps to get to the bug. Try to eliminate all extraneous programs from the procedure. The fewer components involved in the search, the fewer suspects you have to interrogate.

Debugging the Program

This discussion will not tell you how to debug a program. In fact, every bug is different, every bug is debugged differently, and every programmer will debug it differently. Instead, this section is a list of very general guidelines for conducting a debugging session.

- **Keep a one-track mind.** While the debug session is underway, maintain a constant objective and approach. Do not hop-scotch around among different things to try and different things to do. You'll just confuse yourself. Do not move to a different tack until you are ready to abandon the present one, at least for the moment.

- **Too many chiefs, too many Indians.** Run off the kibitzers. Testing can be done with a cast of thousands, but debugging is a solo activity. Everyone has a different approach, and everyone is thinking in a different direction. If you allow yourself to be distracted by the well-intentioned helpers, you will be constantly diverting your attention to deal with their observations, some of which may be valid, but all of which will be, for the present at least, out of tempo with your thoughts.

  This advice should be applied to the managers, too, who will be hanging around to see when the bug is going to get found and fixed. Often they think it necessary to do something, to manage something, to contribute to (and ultimately take credit for) the solution. Usually, they just get in the way.

When You Can't Find the Bug

Every now and then there will be a bug so elusive that not even Turbo Debugger will find it. Then you must tackle it from another angle. Here are some things to try.

- **Call for help.** When you can't find the bug after a reasonable amount of time, ask someone to help, explain the situation, and then get out of that person's way for all of the reasons discussed in the previous section. A fresh look is called for.

- **Talk it through.** Sit another programmer next to you at the computer and talk through the bug, the things you are trying, and the results you are getting. Sometimes, the act of your explaining it to another programmer will explain it to you. Other times, the other person will see something you have been missing.

- **Get some sleep.** Turn off the computer, go home, and get some sleep. It will come to you tomorrow.

The next section discusses Turbo Debugger (hereinafter called TD). First you are going to learn about and maybe build some hardware. Don't get scared and run off; you'll be glad you stuck around.

UNLOCKING A LOCKED-UP COMPUTER

There are bugs that will lock up your computer tighter than a harp string. If you want to create a program with such a bug, code the following:

```
main()
{
    while (1)
        ;
}
```

If you run that program without TD, there is no way out other than to reboot with Ctrl-Alt-Del (the three-fingered salute) or reach for the power switch. Ctrl-Break does not work because DOS does not check for Ctrl-Break until some program makes a DOS call, and this program is not making any DOS calls at the moment. A cold boot is your only way out, and your work will be lost.

Now, of course, you would not write such a program on purpose, but suppose you had one that did a lot of in-memory operations, no DOS calls, and failed to break out of the **while** loop. This situation sounds more like the kind of bugs you get from time to time. The little stub program above just clears out all the extra stuff to reveal the bug's bare bones.

The Turbo Debugger helps. If you run that program with TD, Ctrl-Break does break you out of the dead **while** loop because TD is watching the keyboard and is smart enough to break out of a looping program. The only way, however, that even TD can know you pressed the Ctrl-Break key is if interrupts are enabled. Suppose you had the following bug in your program:

```
main()
{
    disable();
    while (1)
        ;
}
```

Neither Ctrl-Break nor Ctrl-Alt-Del will break out of this program. It takes an interrupt to get any keystroke—including Ctrl-Alt-Del—into the computer, and the **disable** function call disables interrupts. TD by itself would not be able to break out because it cannot see that Ctrl-Break has been pressed. You must turn off the computer and turn it back on, losing everything in memory. Or, if your computer has a reset button, you can press that, also losing everything. Now wouldn't you like to be able to break into this bug, save everything in memory, and get on with the debugging?

The Non-Maskable Interrupt

The 8088, 80286, and their relatives all have an interrupt that has not been discussed yet. It is the Non-Maskable Interrupt (NMI), and when it is asserted, the address in interrupt vector 2 is called. The NMI is a hardware interrupt and it has the highest priority of all the interrupts. It is asserted when the signal on the NMI pin of the processor chip goes from 0 to +5 volts. Software cannot disable the NMI. When the signal level changes, the code pointed to by interrupt vector 2 is going to be executed, no matter what else is going on and regardless of the condition of the CPU's interrupt enable/disable flag.

The purpose of the NMI is to handle high-priority interrupts, ones that can't wait for anything else. The hardware memory system asserts the NMI when it senses a parity error. Usually, interrupt vector 2 points to an interrupt service routine in BIOS that displays a memory parity error message.

The NMI signal is available on the system bus so that devices can assert it if they need to. The bus signal is the opposite polarity of the one on the CPU, meaning that there is inverter logic between the bus signal and the CPU pin. An inverter circuit changes an "off" to an "on" and vice versa. So any device that wants to assert NMI simply grounds the NMI bus signal, thus setting it to zero volts. The inverter changes the zero to a one, sends the one to the CPU's NMI pin, and an INT 2 takes place. Of course, the device must have the address of its interrupt service routine in interrupt vector 2, or the computer will think a memory parity error has occurred.

The NMI BUS signal is on pin A1 of the system bus. The system BUS is brought out to the world of expansion cards through the expansion slots. If you look at a card in a slot, pin A1 is on the side of the board that has the integrated circuits. It is the right-most pin on the edge connector (if the card has a conductor strip for pin A1—many do not) and in the expansion slots. If, while the computer was running, you were to hold the bare end of a wire against pin A1 of an expansion slot and touch the other end to the frame of the computer, you would cause an NMI to occur.

Turbo Debugger and the NMI

When you run TDINST to install TD, it asks you if you want TD to watch the NMI. If you answer yes, TD will attach interrupt vector 2. You certainly do want TD to attach NMI. It's your way out of most of those bugs that otherwise hopelessly lock the computer.

The Turbo Debugger Breakout Switch

Do you have an automatic garage door opener that also has a push button on the garage wall? If so, you already have a Turbo Debugger Breakout Switch. Perhaps you do not, or perhaps someone at your house would not agree to your taking part of the garage door opener system for your computer. In that case, you will have to build one. And it is easy.

Figure 12.1 is a picture of the Turbo Debugger Breakout Switch built from parts that you can buy at Radio Shack. The total cost is less than $10. What the switch does is momentarily ground the NMI BUS signal so that the NMI is asserted.

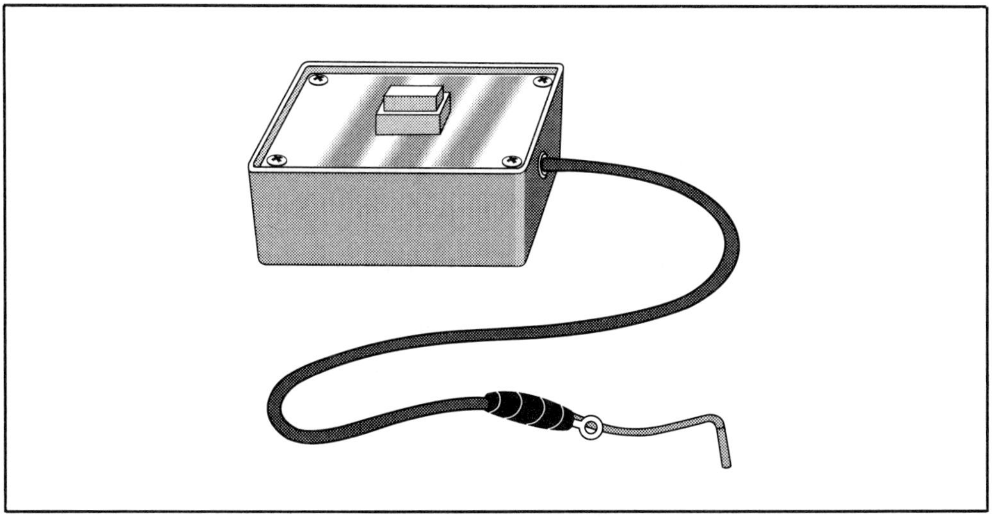

Figure 12.1 Turbo Debugger breakout switch

The home-grown device shown in Figure 12.1 has a normally open single-pole-single-throw momentary push-button switch (Radio Shack catalog number 275-1566, $1.99). It is mounted in a plastic experimenter box (RS Cat. No. 270-231, $1.69). This box lets the switch sit stably on the desk. The cable is made from common telephone wire and is threaded through a hole in the box with a vinyl grommet (RS assortment of 31: Cat. No. 64-3025, $1.19). A knot is tied in the cable inside the box to keep any tension from pulling it loose from the switch terminals. Only two of the four telephone cable lines are needed. Two of the wires are soldered to the two terminals on the switch. The other ends of those wires are to be connected inside your computer. One of the wires has a solderless ring tongue (RS assortment of 24: Cat. No. 64-3030, $1.19) connected to it. The other wire is soldered to a short length of insulated heavier gauge rigid single-strand wire. The two ends are taped together just ahead of the ring tongue so that about 3 1/2 inches of the single-strand wire extends beyond the joining. This extension has about 3/4 inches of exposed wire. Here is how you install the switch.

Remove the power cable from your computer and open the case. Thread the two ends of the cable into the case through the back. There are a number of places you can do that. Each computer is different. Try not to install it in a way that will crimp the cable when you replace the case.

Locate pin A1 on the extension card that is the easiest to reach. Usually, this will be on the disk controller card, the card to your right as you face the computer. Pin A1 is the rear-most pin on the right (component) side of the expansion card. Remove the retaining screw that holds the expansion card in place. Connect the solderless ring tongue to the computer's chassis by inserting the retaining screw into the tongue and replacing the screw.

With a flashlight to guide you, push the exposed wire end of the other connector down into the A1 pin of the expansion slot where the card is inserted. This is why you need rigid wire. You will need to bend the wire into an L shape to make it easy to insert. The wire will slide firmly into place, completing the connection.

Replace the case and the power cord. Power up the computer. If, when you do so, you get an immediate parity error, the switch or its wiring has a short circuit. Take everything apart and check it out.

If the computer powers up properly, wait for the DOS prompt and press the switch. If you get a parity error, the switch is properly installed.

nmi.c: For When TD Is Not Running

What if you bump the switch when TD is not running? Different PC clones will behave differently, but all of them will think you have a memory parity error. To avoid that problem, Listing 12.1 is nmi.c, a small TSR that attaches the NMI vector and sounds a horn when the NMI occurs. Then it returns to whatever was happening when you bumped the switch. You should have this program resident whenever the TD Breakout Switch is installed.

If you start to hear horns blowing when you are not pressing the button, maybe you are getting real memory parity errors. Reboot to remove the NMI program from memory before you take any other steps.

Listing 12.1: nmi.c

```
/* ---------- nmi.c --------------- */
/*
 * A small TSR to capture the NMI interrupt
 */
#include <dos.h>
#define NMI 2

static void interrupt newnmi(void)
{
    enable();
    sound(440);
    delay(750);
    nosound();
}
void main(void)
{
    setvect(NMI, newnmi);
    delay(0);
    keep(0, 200);
}
```

TDNMI.COM

Some PC and AT clones turn off the NMI hardware after the first time the interrupt occurs. Every time you press the TD Breakout Switch without TD running but with NMI installed, you should hear the horn. If it blows only the first time you press the button and never again, perhaps you have one of those clones. You need TDNMI.COM to deal with this problem.

The Turbo Debugger package includes the program called TDNMI.COM. This program is a small TSR that turns NMI back on once every half second. Install it, and you should now get the horn blown every time you press the button.

Breaking Any Loop

Your programs are not the only ones that go into loops. Every now and then a computer locks up. Some commercial software packages, when used along with some others, will lock your system with varying degrees of certainty. The TD Breakout Switch can't save your work for you, but it can keep you from having to turn the power off. Press Ctrl-Alt-Del and then press the TD Breakout Switch, and your computer should reboot itself. If you are a very clever programmer, you might make a TSR program that responds to the NMI and saves all of memory to a snapshot file that you could root around in later and find the work you lost. But that's another project.

What the TD Breakout Switch Will Not Break Out of

If you have a bug that has destroyed memory in such a way that the NMI vector or the memory image of TD is trashed, then the switch is not going to help. To deal with these extreme disasters, you need a hardware debugger such as the Periscope I or Periscope III from The Periscope Company in Atlanta, GA.

Using the TD Breakout Switch with TD

With the TD Breakout Switch installed as described above, when you run the Turbo Debugger and get into a loop that will not break, press the switch. Now try it out.

Listing 12.2 is demotdbs.c, a program that you can use to demonstrate the switch.

Listing 12.2: demotdbs.c

```
/* ---------- demotdbs.c ---------- */

/*
 * A program to demonstrate the Turbo Debugger Breakout Switch
 */

#include <stdio.h>
#include <dos.h>

void main(void)
{
    printf("\nI am about to expire.");
    printf("\nAaargh!");
    disable();
    while (1)
        ;
    printf("\n(Whew!) Alive again!");
}
```

To run the demonstration, install the switch and NMI.EXE. Compile the program to use the debugger like this:

```
c>tcc -v demotdbs
```

Run the program with the debugger like this:

```
c>td demotdbs
```

You will see the screen shown in Figure 12.2. The program is ready to go.

```
 File   View   Run   Breakpoints   Data   Window   Options                 READY
Module: DEMOTDBS  File: demotdbs.c (modified) 10                              1
 /* ---------- demotdbs.c ---------- */

 /*
  * A program to demonstrate the Turbo Debugger Breakout Switch
  */

 #include <stdio.h>
 #include <dos.h>

► void main(void)
 {
     printf("\nI am about to expire.");
     printf("\nAaargh!");
     disable();
     while (1)
         ;
     printf("\n(Whew!) Alive again!");
 }
Watches                                                                       2

F2-Bkpt F3-Close F4-Here F5-Zoom F6-Next F7-Trace F8-Step F9-Run F10-Menu
```

Figure 12.2 Initial screen display for demotdbs.c

Press F9 to run the program. The screen shown in Figure 12.3 is displayed, and the computer is locked. Do not press Ctrl-Alt-Del. If you do, the system will reboot when you press the TD Breakout Switch, which is not what you want. You want to break into the deadlock and continue debugging.

```
C>td demotdbs
Turbo Debugger  Version 1.0  Copyright (c) 1988 Borland International

I am about to expire.
Aaargh!
```

Figure 12.3 Locked computer program

Press the TD Breakout Switch. TD will take over, and you will see the screen shown in Figure 12.4. Notice the little window that tells you that the NMI occurred. Press the Esc key.

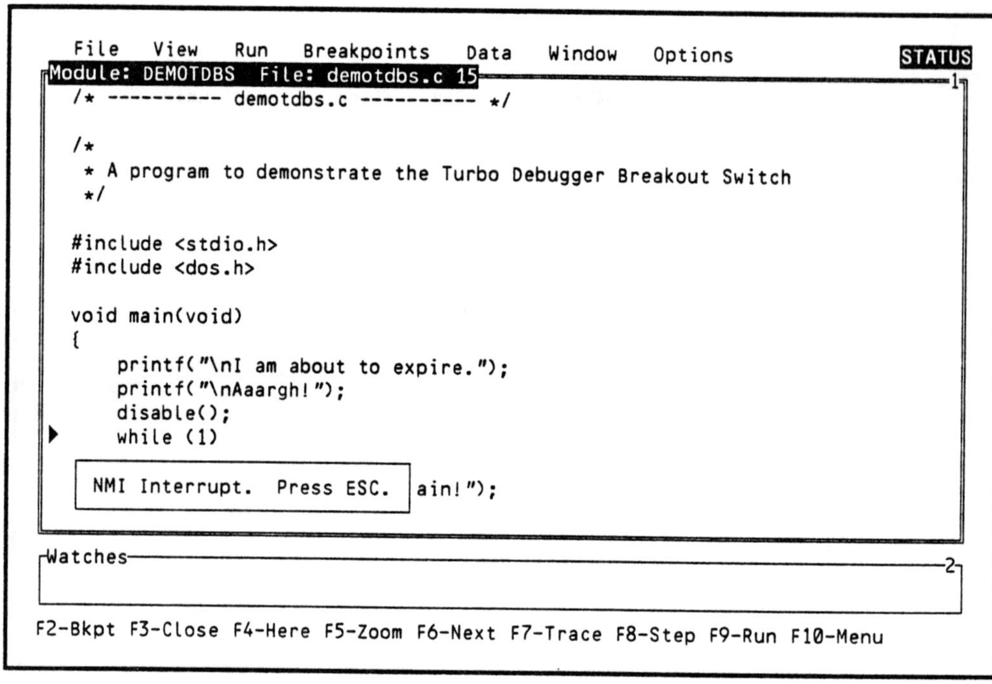

Figure 12.4 *TD screen displaying NMI has occurred*

You are looking at the C source code, and that is not going to get you out of the loop. You need to change the program's Instruction Pointer (IP) register to get past the dead loop, and to do that, you need to be looking at the assembly language. Press Alt-V, and you will see the screen shown in Figure 12.5.

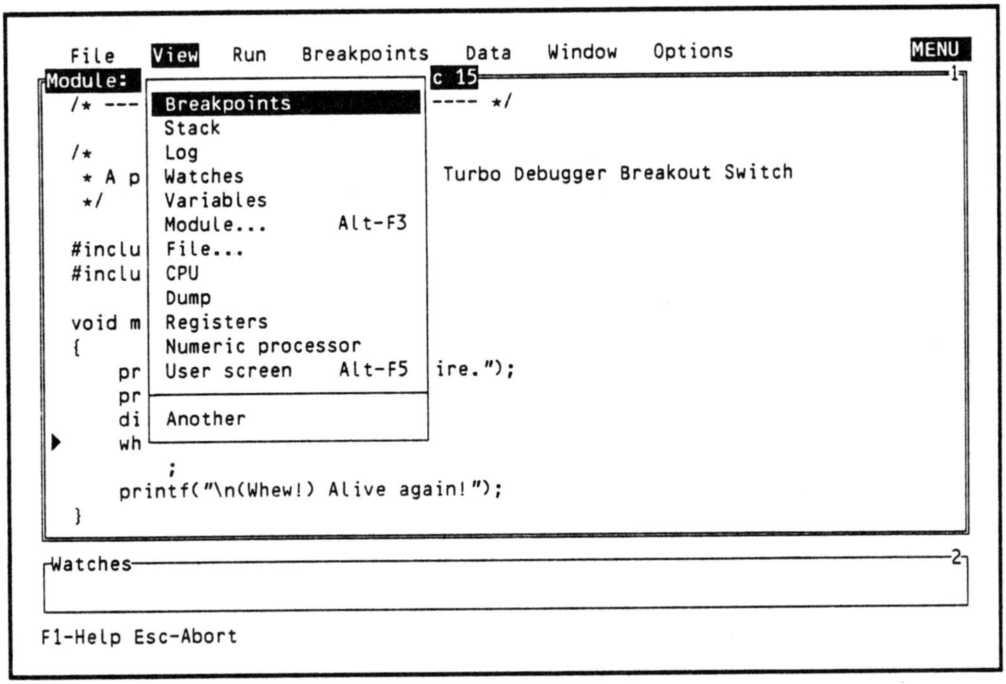

Figure 12.5 View menu

Press "C" to say you want to view the CPU, and you will see the screen shown in Figure 12.6. The window that popped up shows the compiled assembly language, the registers, and other information.

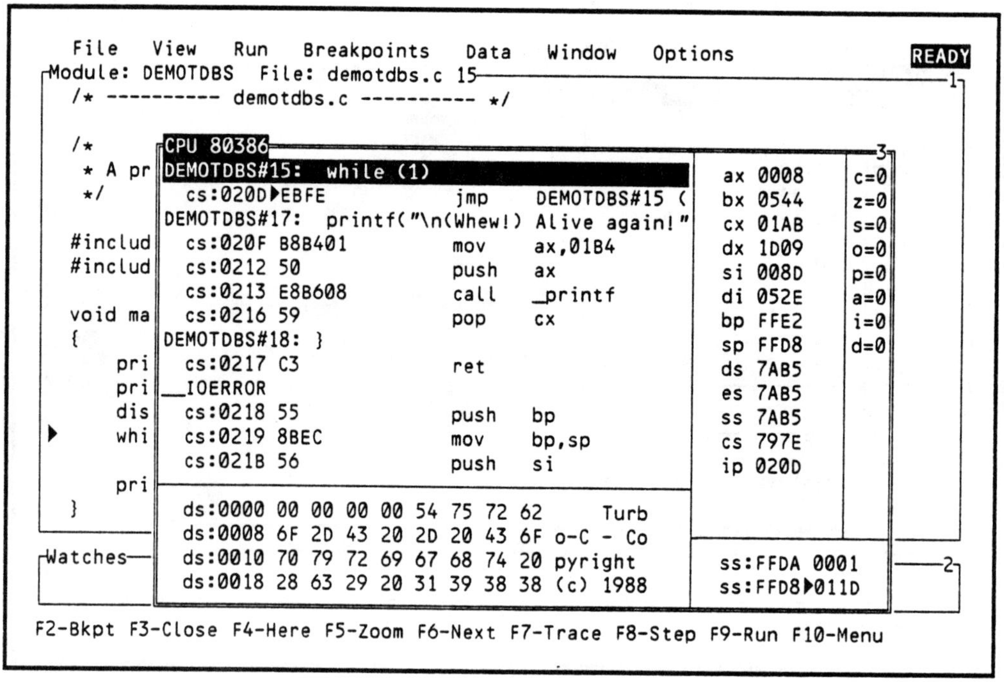

Figure 12.6 *CPU window*

You would really like to see more of the assembly language, so press F5 to zoom the window. The screen shown in Figure 12.7 is displayed. Look closely at the small triangle on the first assembly language statement. That is the IP cursor, and it shows the instruction about to be executed. Its address is 020d (hex) offset from the code segment register. If you look over at the registers, you will see that the IP register has that same value. Look at the instruction. It is a jump to itself. With interrupts disabled, there is no way you could get out of that jump without using the NMI.

```
  File   View   Run   Breakpoints   Data   Window   Options                          READY
CPU 80386                                                                              3
DEMOTDBS#15:  while (1)                                        ax 0008      c=0
  cs:020D▶EBFE            jmp     DEMOTDBS#15 (020D) ↓         bx 0544      z=0
DEMOTDBS#17:  printf("\n(Whew!) Alive again!");                cx 01AB      s=0
  cs:020F B8B401          mov     ax,01B4                      dx 3DA8      o=0
  cs:0212 50              push    ax                           si 008D      p=0
  cs:0213 E8B608          call    _printf                      di 052E      a=0
  cs:0216 59              pop     cx                           bp FFE2      i=0
DEMOTDBS#18: }                                                 sp FFD8      d=0
  cs:0217 C3              ret                                  ds 7AB5
__IOERROR                                                      es 7AB5
  cs:0218 55              push    bp                           ss 7AB5
  cs:0219 8BEC            mov     bp,sp                        cs 797E
  cs:021B 56              push    si                           ip 020D
  cs:021C 8B7604          mov     si,[bp+04]
  cs:021F 0BF6            or      si,si

  ds:0000 00 00 00 00 54 75 72 62     Turb                     ss:FFDA 0001
  ds:0008 6F 2D 43 20 2D 20 43 6F o-C - Co                     ss:FFD8▶011D
  ds:0010 70 79 72 69 67 68 74 20 pyright                      ss:FFD6 7002
  ds:0018 28 63 29 20 31 39 38 38 (c) 1988                     ss:FFD4 797E
  ds:0020 20 42 6F 72 6C 61 6E 64  Borland                     ss:FFD2 020D

F2-Bkpt F3-Close F4-Here F5-Zoom F6-Next F7-Trace F8-Step F9-Run F10-Menu
```

Figure 12.7   Zoomed view of assembly language

To get the program running outside of that loop, you can use the Run menu (Alt-R) to restart the program, or you can change the IP. Do that now. Use the Tab key to move the cursor to the register window. Use the Down Arrow key to move the cursor down to the IP register. Press Alt-F10 to pop up the Register Pane Local Menu, and press "C" to say you want to change the register. You can see that if you get past that jump, the program will execute the next C statement, which is a call to **printf**. Type the address of the first instruction, 0x020f as shown in Figure 12.8.

You must use the C notation for a hexadecimal address because that is the format expected by TD when it is debugging a C program.

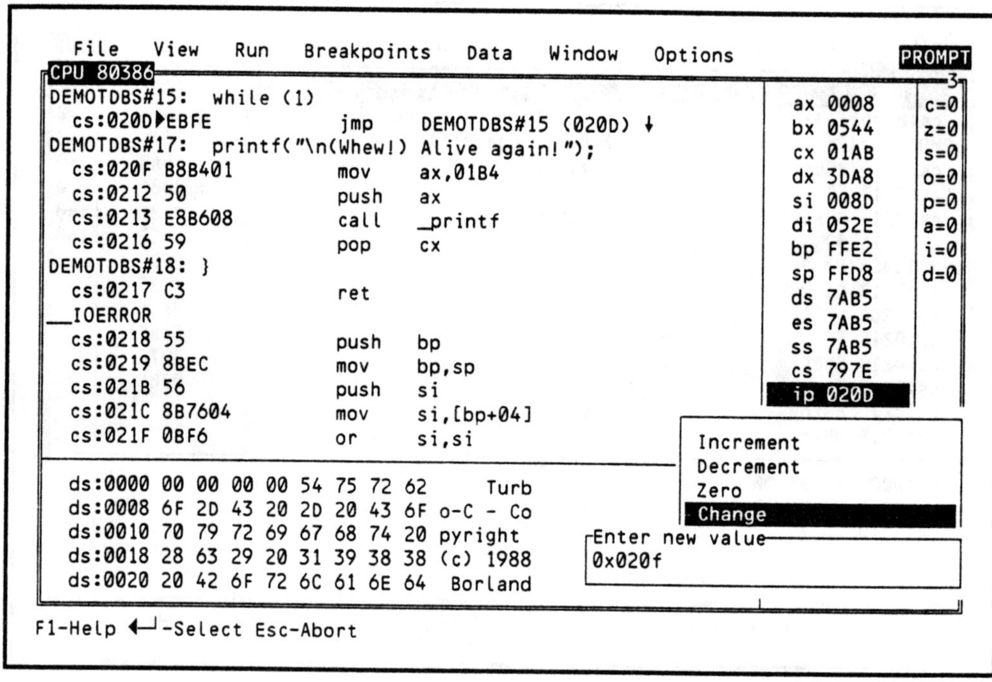

Figure 12.8 *Address entered to bypass loop*

Press Enter after typing the address and see that the IP pointer moves to the next instruction as shown in 12.9.

```
  File   View   Run   Breakpoints   Data   Window   Options                          READY
CPU 80386                                                                          3
DEMOTDBS#15:  while (1)                                         ax 0008         c=0
  cs:020D EBFE           jmp    DEMOTDBS#15 (020D)              bx 0544         z=0
DEMOTDBS#17:  printf("\n(Whew!) Alive again!");                 cx 01AB         s=0
  cs:020F▶B8B401         mov    ax,01B4                         dx 3DA8         o=0
  cs:0212 50             push   ax                              si 008D         p=0
  cs:0213 E8B608         call   _printf                         di 052E         a=0
  cs:0216 59             pop    cx                              bp FFE2         i=0
DEMOTDBS#18: }                                                  sp FFD8         d=0
  cs:0217 C3             ret                                    ds 7AB5
__IOERROR                                                       es 7AB5
  cs:0218 55             push   bp                              ss 7AB5
  cs:0219 8BEC           mov    bp,sp                           cs 797E
  cs:021B 56             push   si                              ip 020F
  cs:021C 8B7604         mov    si,[bp+04]
  cs:021F 0BF6           or     si,si

  ds:0000 00 00 00 00 54 75 72 62      Turb                     ss:FFDA 0001
  ds:0008 6F 2D 43 20 2D 20 43 6F o-C - Co                      ss:FFD8▶011D
  ds:0010 70 79 72 69 67 68 74 20 pyright                       ss:FFD6 7002
  ds:0018 28 63 29 20 31 39 38 38 (c) 1988                      ss:FFD4 797E
  ds:0020 20 42 6F 72 6C 61 6E 64  Borland                      ss:FFD2 020D

F2-Bkpt F3-Close F4-Here F5-Zoom F6-Next F7-Trace F8-Step F9-Run F10-Menu
```

Figure 12.9 *IP pointer moves to next instruction*

You do not need the CPU display anymore, so you can press F3 to close its window. The screen in Figure 12.10 shows that the C statement cursor has moved to the **printf** statement, and you are out of the deadlock with everything preserved.

```
  File   View   Run   Breakpoints   Data   Window   Options                READY
 Module: DEMOTDBS  File: demotdbs.c 15 ------------------------------------------1
  /* ---------- demotdbs.c ---------- */

  /*
   * A program to demonstrate the Turbo Debugger Breakout Switch
   */

  #include <stdio.h>
  #include <dos.h>

  void main(void)
  {
      printf("\nI am about to expire.");
      printf("\nAaargh!");
      disable();
      while (1)
          ;
▶     printf("\n(Whew!) Alive again!");
  }
 Watches----------------------------------------------------------------------2

 F2-Bkpt F3-Close F4-Here F5-Zoom F6-Next F7-Trace F8-Step F9-Run F10-Menu
```

Figure 12.10 Cursor moved to printf statement and program resumed

Press F9 now to continue running the program. Figure 12.11 shows that the program terminates normally. Press the Esc key.

```
  File   View   Run   Breakpoints   Data   Window   Options                STATUS
 Module: DEMOTDBS  File: demotdbs.c 15                                          1
  /* ---------- demotdbs.c ---------- */

  /*
   * A program to demonstrate the Turbo Debugger Breakout Switch
   */

  #include <stdio.h>
  #include <dos.h>

  void main(void)
  {
      printf("\nI am about to expire.");
      printf("\nAaargh!");
      disable();
      while (1)
   Terminated, exit code 21.  Press ESC.

 Watches                                                                        2

 F2-Bkpt F3-Close F4-Here F5-Zoom F6-Next F7-Trace F8-Step F9-Run F10-Menu
```

Figure 12.11 Program terminates normally

To see your completed output screen, press Alt-F5. The screen shown in Figure 12.12 shows you that the program did in fact execute the statement following the dead loop. Press any key to return to TD and Alt-X to return to DOS. Your debugging session is done.

```
C>td demotdbs
Turbo Debugger  Version 1.0  Copyright (c) 1988 Borland International

I am about to expire.
Aaargh!
(Whew!) Alive again!
```

Figure 12.12 Completed output screen

DEBUGGING A TSR PROGRAM

Chapter 9 shows you how to write a TSR program. You were advised there to do your testing and debugging with the program initially configured as a normal, nonresident program, and that advice is correct. There are, however, some TSRs that cannot be debugged that way, and there are bugs in other TSRs that will not show up that way. Sometimes, you need to get close to the metal and debug your TSR in its native environment as a memory-resident program.

The Turbo Debugger is not particularly adept at debugging TSRs. Some highly skilled technical folks will tell you that it cannot be done at all. That, however, is not completely true. What TD will not do is let you step through your Turbo C TSR at the source code level the way it does for nonresident programs. But the mechanism for getting into the TSR is there, and the information to allow you to read your program is available to you through TD. All it takes is some imagination to make it work for you.

You need several files available to let you debug a TSR with TD. The first of these are built by the tcc compiler and the Turbo Assembler. You need a link map and a listing of the assembly code compiled by the Turbo C compiler. It is helpful to have a source code listing with line numbers after the fashion of the listings in this book. In the absence of such listings, you can observe the source files with a text editor that tells you what line the cursor is on.

You need one other file that relates the compiled assembly language to the C source code. To get that file, you will use a utility program provided in this chapter and described here.

tsrdebug.c

Listing 12.3 is tsrdebug.c, a utility program that reads the compiled assembly language file and the original C source program and builds a file that you can use to relate the instructions being executed in TD with your C TSR program. Remember that TD cannot give you source level debugging of a TSR because it finds the debug information when a program is loaded, and the TSR is memory-resident. Tsrdebug.c partially solves that problem for you. To understand how it and TSR debugging with TD work, step through the exercise following the program listing.

Listing 12.3: tsrdebug.c

```
/* -------------- tsrdebug.c --------------- */

/*
 * A program to merge Turbo C source code
 * with the tcc -S .ASM output
 */

#include <stdio.h>
#include <string.h>
#include <process.h>
#include <stdlib.h>
#include <ctype.h>

#define bypass_white(cp) while(*cp==' '||*cp=='\t')cp++
static unsigned atox(char *);
```

continued...

...from previous page

```

void main(int argc, char *argv[])
{
    FILE *fp1, *fp2, *fp3;
    char fname[64];
    int c_lineno = 0;
    int asm_lineno;
    unsigned mnoff = 0;
    char line[200];
    char *cp;

    if (argc > 1)   {
        strcpy(fname, argv[1]);
        strcat(fname, ".c");
        if ((fp2 = fopen(fname, "rt")) == NULL) {
            printf("\nCannot find %s", fname);
            exit(1);
        }
        strcpy(fname + (strlen(fname) - 1), "lst");
        if ((fp1 = fopen(fname, "rt")) == NULL) {
            printf("\nCannot find %s", fname);
            exit(1);
        }
        strcpy(fname + (strlen(fname) - 3), "dbg");
        if ((fp3 = fopen(fname, "wt")) == NULL) {
            printf("\nCannot open %s", fname);
            exit(1);
        }
        /* --- offset to main function on command line --- */
        if (argc > 2)
            mnoff = atox(argv[2]);
        /* ------- flush the first three lines ------ */
        fgets(line, 200, fp1);
        fgets(line, 200, fp1);
        fgets(line, 200, fp1);
        while (fgets(line, 200, fp1) != NULL)   {
            /* ------- flush page header lines -------- */
            if (*line == '\f')  {
                fgets(line, 200, fp1);
                fgets(line, 200, fp1);
```

continued...

...from previous page

```
                fgets(line, 200, fp1);
            }
            /* --- look for debug statements ---- */
            if ((cp = strstr(line, "?debug")) == NULL)  {
                /* -- copy all non-debug .LST statements -- */
                if (isdigit(line[8]))   {
                    sprintf(line+8, "%04x", atox(line+8)+mnoff);
                    line[12] = ' ';
                }
                fprintf(fp3, "  %-22.22s%s", line+8, line+37);
                continue;
            }
            /* ------- debug statement --------- */
            cp += 6;
            bypass_white(cp);
            /* --- look for line number debug statement --- */
            if (*cp++ == 'L')   {
                /* --- line number statement --- */
                bypass_white(cp);
                asm_lineno = atoi(cp);
                /* --- pass .C file to the matching line --- */
                while (!feof(fp2) && c_lineno < asm_lineno) {
                    if (fgets(line, 200, fp2) == NULL)
                        break;
                    c_lineno++;
                }
                if (!feof(fp2)) {
                    /* in case L is out of order */
                    if (c_lineno == asm_lineno)
                        cp = line;
                    else
                        cp = "";
                    bypass_white(cp);
                    /* ---- merge the C code ---- */
                    fprintf(fp3, "%s#%3d: %s",
                        argv[1], asm_lineno, cp);
                }
            }
        }
        fclose(fp1);
```

continued...

...from previous page

```
        fclose(fp2);
        fclose(fp3);
    }
}

/* -------- convert ascii from hex to decimal --------- */
static unsigned atox(char *cp)
{
    unsigned val = 0;

    while (*cp && (isdigit(*cp) || isalpha(*cp)))   {
        val = val << 4;
        if (isalpha(*cp))
            val += toupper(*cp) - 'A' + 10;
        else
            val += *cp - '0';
        cp++;
    }
    return val;
}
```

Build the tsrdebug.exe program with the tcc command-line compiler like this:

```
c>tcc tsrdebug
```

Exercise: Debug the Personal Dialer

As an exercise, you will use the memory-resident Personal Dialer program from Chapter 9 to show TSR debugging with TD. For this exercise, you will debug the program by setting a breakpoint at its **text_search** function, the function that is called when the user presses F3 to search the dialer data base for a name match.

The first step is to build the executable copy of dialer.exe. You can use the makefile in Appendix B to do that. Be sure you include debugging information in the program if you do not use the makefile as published.

You need the compiled assembly language of any source module you are going to debug this way. And you need a link map. Type the following command at the command line:

```
c>tcc -v -S -M dialer
```

This will generate the DIALER.ASM and DIALER.MAP files. Now you need the assembler listing file from the compiled assembly language. Run the following command:

```
c>tasm dialer,nul,dialer
```

This generates the DIALER.LST file. At this time, you need to know the code offset address of the **main** function in the DIALER.EXE program. The DIALER.MAP file will tell you that. Use your editor to read it and find the entry for the **main** function. You will see a line that looks like this:

```
0000:01FA        _MAIN
```

The 01FA value is the address you want. It will be used by the tsrdebug program to adjust the offset address of the code. Remember it for the moment. The value you see might not be what is shown here. The value can vary depending on how the program is linked. Also, you use the **main** function because that is the first one in the source module where **text_search** is located. For debugging other functions, you will use the code offset address of the first function in the source module where your targeted function is located.

Now you need to build the file that merges the DIALER.LST file and the DIALER.C files. Run this command:

```
c>tsrdebug dialer 01fa
```

The 01fa parameter is the same as the code offset address you got from the previous DIALER.MAP file. This command builds the DIALER.DBG file. You can look at it with your editor if you like. It consists of the assembled source code with the associated C language statements merged in at the appropriate places. Its format resembles that of the Turbo Debugger's display of a C program's CPU instructions.

You are ready to begin your test. First, load the dialer with the following command:

```
c>dialer
```

Now, believe it or not, you need a nonresident program to run with the debugger. Write this simple program and call it test.c:

```
#include <bios.h>
#include <stdio.h>
void main(void)
{
    printf("\nAny key ...");
    bioskey(0);
}
```

Compile the program this way:

```
c>tcc test
```

Keep the program around for all your TSR debugging sessions. Run it with the Turbo Debugger like this:

```
c>td test
```

You will see the screen shown in 12.13. This is the usual TD C language debug session.

```
  File   View   Run   Breakpoints   Data   Window   Options                READY
┌Module: TEST  File: test.c 4═══════════════════════════════════════════════1┐
  #include <bios.h>
  #include <stdio.h>

▶ void main(void)
  {
      printf("\nAny key ...");
      bioskey(0);
  }

┌Watches─────────────────────────────────────────────────────────────────────2┐

F2-Bkpt F3-Close F4-Here F5-Zoom F6-Next F7-Trace F8-Step F9-Run F10-Menu
```

Figure 12.13 TD C language debug session screen

The test program is of little interest here other than as a way to get TD going. You need to set a breakpoint in the resident dialer program. To do that, you need to know where its code segment is located. Because the dialer program is attached to some interrupt vectors, you can get the address of its code segment from one of them. Press Alt-V to open the View menu; press "D" to open the Dump Window; and press Alt-F10 to open the Dump Window's Data Pane Local Menu. You will see the screen shown in Figure 12.14.

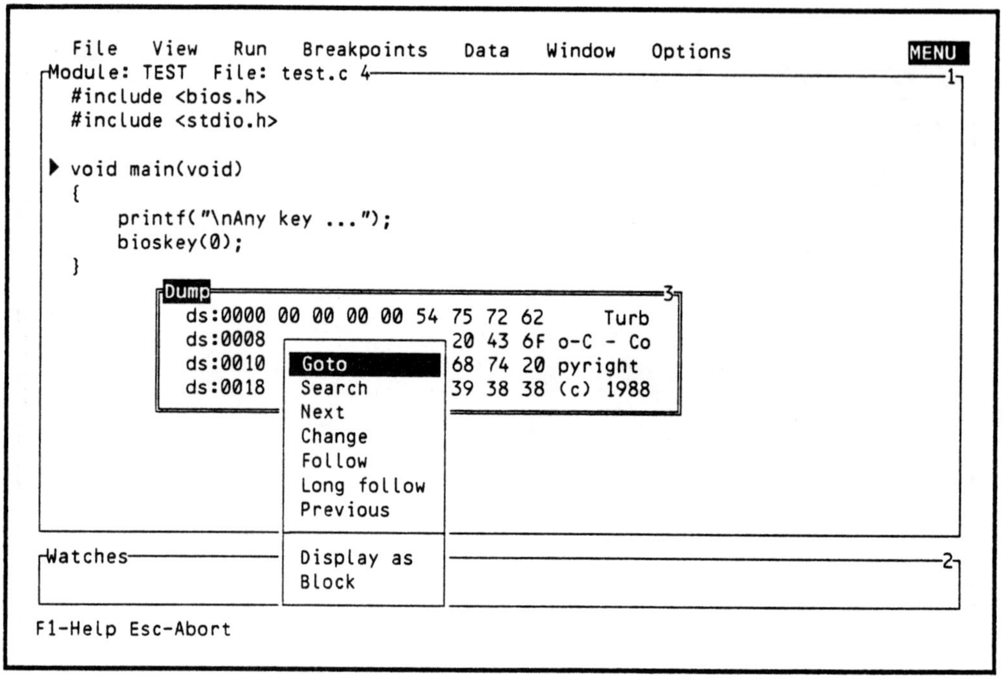

Figure 12.14 Data Pane Local menu

Press the Enter key or "G" to activate the Goto command. You want to look at an interrupt vector that the dialer program has attached. You know that interrupt 8, the timer interrupt, is one of the interrupt vectors. Interrupt vectors begin in memory location 0:0, and each one uses 4 bytes. So the address of interrupt vector 8 is 32 or 0x20. Type 0:0x20, and you will see the screen shown in Figure 12.15.

```
  File   View   Run   Breakpoints   Data   Window   Options                PROMPT
┌Module: TEST  File: test.c 4─────────────────────────────────────────────────1┐
│ #include <bios.h>
│ #include <stdio.h>
│
▶ void main(void)
│ {
│     printf("\nAny key ...");
│     bioskey(0);
│ }
│       ┌Dump═══════════════════════════════════════════════════3┐
│       │ ds:0000 00 00 00 00 54 75 72 62      Turb
│       │ ds:0008 ┌──────────┐20 43 6F o-C - Co
│       │ ds:0010 │ Goto     │68 74 20 pyright
│       │ ds:0018 │┌Enter address to position to──┐
│       └─────────││0:0x20                        │
│                 │└──────────────────────────────┘
│                 │ Follow   │
│                 │ Long follow
│                 │ Previous │
└─────────────────├──────────┤────────────────────────────────────────────────┘
┌Watches──────────│ Display as ─────────────────────────────────────────────2┐
│                 │ Block    │                                              │
└─────────────────└──────────┘──────────────────────────────────────────────┘
F1-Help ←┘-Select Esc-Abort
```

Figure 12.15 Address entered for interrupt vector 8

Press the Enter key to change the Dump Window's display to start at the address of interrupt vector 8. You will see the screen shown in Figure 12.16.

```
  File   View   Run   Breakpoints   Data   Window   Options                READY
┌Module: TEST  File: test.c 4─────────────────────────────────────────────────1┐
  #include <bios.h>
  #include <stdio.h>

  void main(void)
  {
      printf("\nAny key ...");
      bioskey(0);
  }
            ┌Dump──────────────────────────────────────3┐
            │0000:0020 0D 0E 70 41 5B 02 EA 5B   pA[  [ │
            │0000:0028 19 02 1C 15 A1 77 A1 28 ↓    w ( │
            │0000:0030 29 03 1C 15 B1 03 1C 15 )   ▒    │
            │0000:0038 39 04 1C 15 56 07 70 00 9   V p  │
            └───────────────────────────────────────────┘

┌Watches────────────────────────────────────────────────────────────────────2┐
└───────────────────────────────────────────────────────────────────────────┘
F2-Bkpt F3-Close F4-Here F5-Zoom F6-Next F7-Trace F8-Step F9-Run F10-Menu
```

Figure 12.16 Dump Window display starts at address for interrupt vector 8

Interrupt vectors are far pointers, and they appear backwards when you read them from a dump. The four bytes at 0:0x20 are 0D 0E 70 41 and are read as the address 0x4170:0x0E0D. The first word in this representation is the code segment address where the vector points. From this display, you know that the dialer program's code segment address is 0x4170.

Once again, you will see different numbers, depending on what other programs are ahead of your dialer program in memory. Many things alter the starting segment of a TSR. Among them are other TSRs, the DOS version, the size of the environment block, device drivers, and the value of your FILES= statement in the CONFIG.SYS file.

As an aside, suppose you are debugging a memory-resident program that has no interrupt vectors attached. Or suppose your debug environment involves several TSRs, and the object TSR's interrupt vectors are all attached and chained by TSRs that were loaded later. How do you find the code segment address? One very simple way is to insert the following statement into your startup code before the program calls the Turbo C **keep** function to declare itself resident.

```
printf("\nMy code segment is %04x",_CS);
```

When the program loads, it will tell you its code segment, and you can write it down to remember it later when you are debugging.

With the address of the code segment, you now need the address of the **text_search** function so you can set a breakpoint.

Next, you need to look at the DIALER.DBG file. But, you say, DIALER.DBG is a text file, and you are in the middle of TD. How do you get to the link map? One way is to have installed your favorite editor into TD. But you don't really need to do that. TD has the File Window, which lets you look at text files. Press Alt-V for the View menu. and "F" for the File Window. Type "dialer.dbg" to view the file you built with the tsrdebug program. You need to look at this file along with the code that is being debugged. So press the Scroll Lock key and use the Arrow and Shift-Arrow keys to resize and position the File Window in the bottom half of the screen. Use Alt-F10, "S" to find the **text_search** function, searching past the references to it in the code. You will see the screen shown in Figure 12.17. Notice the line number. If you refer to the Listing 9.3 in Chapter 9, you will see that the line numbers are the same.

```
  File   View   Run   Breakpoints   Data   Window   Options                READY
┌Module: TEST  File: test.c 4──────────────────────────────────────────────1┐
  #include <bios.h>
  #include <stdio.h>

  void main(void)
  {
      printf("\nAny key ...");
      bioskey(0);
  }

┌File dialer.dbg 598───────────────────────────────────────────────────────4┐
    051b                    dial_phone      endp
  dialer#229: static void text_search(void)
    051b                    text_search     proc    near
    051b  56                        push    si
  dialer#231: int dcode = 0;
    051c  33 F6                     xor     si,si
  dialer#232: clear_template(template, prompts);
    051e  B8 0014r                  mov     ax,offset DGROUP:prompts
    0521  50                        push    ax
    0522  B8 005Ar                  mov     ax,offset DGROUP:template

F2-Bkpt F3-Close F4-Here F5-Zoom F6-Next F7-Trace F8-Step F9-Run F10-Menu
```

Figure 12.17 *text_search function found*

Now you need to set a breakpoint. You already know from your look at interrupt vector 8 that the segment address is 0x4170. The offset is given in the DIALER.DBG file as the address of the instruction where you want to break. Just past the entry for line 229 is the address 0x051b associated with the **proc** statement for **text_search**. That is the offset address for the breakpoint. Press Alt-B for the Breakpoint menu and A for the At command. Type 0x4170:0x051b as shown in Figure 12.18.

```
   File   View   Run   Breakpoints   Data   Window   Options                PROMPT
┌Module: TEST  File: t┌──────────────────────────┐──────────────────────────1┐
│  #include <bios.h>   │ Toggle                F2 │                           │
│  #include <stdio.h>  │ At...             Alt-F2 │                           │
│                      ┌Enter code address for breakpoint┐                   │
│  void main(void)     │0x4170:0x051b                    │                   │
│  {                   └─────────────────────────────────┘                   │
│      printf("\nAny k └──────────────────────────┘                          │
│      bioskey(0);                                                           │
│  }                                                                         │
│                                                                            │
┌File dialer.dbg 598─────────────────────────────────────────────────────────4┐
│    051b                    dial_phone      endp                             │
│  dialer#229: static void text_search(void)                                  │
│    051b                    text_search     proc     near                    │
│    051b  56                        push    si                               │
│  dialer#231: int dcode = 0;                                                 │
│    051c  33 F6                     xor     si,si                            │
│  dialer#232: clear_template(template, prompts);                             │
│    051e  B8 0014r                  mov     ax,offset DGROUP:prompts         │
│    0521  50                        push    ax                               │
│    0522  B8 005Ar                  mov     ax,offset DGROUP:template        │
└─────────────────────────────────────────────────────────────────────────────┘
F1-Help ←┘-Select Esc-Abort
```

Figure 12.18 Code address entered for breakpoint

Press the Enter key to set the breakpoint. Now you need to look at the dialer's actual code, the code that corresponds to the File Window in the bottom half of the screen. Press Alt-V for the View Menu, "C" to view the CPU, Alt-F10 for the CPU Pane Local Menu, "G" for the Goto command, and enter 0x4170:0x051b for the address to go to. You will see the screen shown in Figure 12.19.

```
   File   View   Run   Breakpoints   Data   Window   Options                 READY
┌Module: TEST  File: test.c 4──────────────────────────────────────────────────1┐
   #include <bios.h>
   #include <stdio.h>
             ┌CPU 80386──────────────────────────────────────────────────────3┐
   void ma  │4170:051B 56            push   si       │ ax 0000   │c=0│
   {        │4170:051C 33F6          xor    si,si    │ bx 051C   │z=1│
        pri │4170:051E B8A801        mov    ax,01A8  │ cx 0012   │s=0│
        bio │4170:0521 50            push   ax       │ dx 5A11   │o=0│
   }        │4170:0522 B8EE01        mov    ax,01EE  │ si 008D   │p=1│
            │4170:0525 50            push   ax       │ di 0506   │a=0│
            │4170:0526 E8180E        call   1341     │ bp FFE6   │i=1│
┌File dial  │4170:0529 59            pop    cx       │ sp FFDC   │d=0│──4┐
     051b   │4170:052A 59            pop    cx       │ ds 8083   │   │
   dialer#  │4170:052B B8CD02        mov    ax,02CD  │ es 8083   │   │
     051b   │4170:052E 50            push   ax       │ ss 8083   │   │
     051b   │4170:052F E8BF01        call   06F1     │ cs 7F49   │   │
   dialer#  │4170:0532 59            pop    cx       │ ip 01FA   │   │
     051c   │─────────────────────────────────────────│           │   │
   dialer#  │ ds:0000 00 00 00 00 54 75 72 62     Turb│           │   │
     051e   │ ds:0008 6F 2D 43 20 2D 20 43 6F o-C - Co│───────────────│
     0521   │ ds:0010 70 79 72 69 67 68 74 20 pyright │ ss:FFDE 0001  │
     0522   │ ds:0018 28 63 29 20 31 39 38 38 (c) 1988│ ss:FFDC 011D  │
 F2-Bkpt F3-Close F4-Here F5-Zoom F6-Next F7-Trace F8-Step F9-Run F10-Menu
```

Figure 12.19 Dialer's actual code

The CPU Window covers too much of the DIALER.DBG file, and yet is too narrow for you to see everything. Press F5 to zoom the window. Press Scroll Lock and use the Arrow and Shift-Arrow keys to resize and reposition the window in the top half of the screen. You will see the screen shown in Figure 12.20.

```
  File   View   Run   Breakpoints   Data   Window   Options                 READY
 CPU 80386
 4170:051B 56                push   si                          ax 0000    c=0
 4170:051C 33F6              xor    si,si                       bx 051C    z=1
 4170:051E B8A801            mov    ax,01A8                     cx 0012    s=0
 4170:0521 50                push   ax                          dx 5A11    o=0
 4170:0522 B8EE01            mov    ax,01EE                     si 008D    p=1
 4170:0525 50                push   ax                          di 0506    a=0

   ds:0000 00 00 00 00 54 75 72 62     Turb                     ss:FFDE 0001
   ds:0008 6F 2D 43 20 2D 20 43 6F o-C - Co                     ss:FFDC 011D

 File dialer.dbg 598                                                        4
     051b                    dial_phone     endp
   dialer#229: static void text_search(void)
     051b                    text_search    proc    near
     051b  56                        push    si
   dialer#231: int dcode = 0;
     051c  33 F6                     xor     si,si
   dialer#232: clear_template(template, prompts);
     051e  B8 0014r                  mov     ax,offset DGROUP:prompts
     0521  50                        push    ax
     0522  B8 005Ar                  mov     ax,offset DGROUP:template

 F2-Bkpt F3-Close F4-Here F5-Zoom F6-Next F7-Trace F8-Step F9-Run F10-Menu
```

Figure 12.20 Code window zoomed and resized

Now you are ready to debug the Personal Dialer TSR. What TD is actually running, however, is the little TEST.EXE program you built a few steps back; however, the breakpoint is in the TSR. You will run the TEST program, pop up the TSR, and get your breakpoint that way. Press F9 to start the execution of the TEST program. You will see the screen shown in Figure 12.21.

```
C>td test
Turbo Debugger  Version 1.0  Copyright (c) 1988 Borland International

Any key ...
```

Figure 12.21 Initial screen for TEST program

Press the Personal Dialer's hot key (Alt-Period). The Personal Dialer will pop up, and you will see the screen shown in Figure 12.22.

```
C>td test
Turbo Debugger  Version 1.0  Copyright (c) 1988 Borland International

Any
                          PERSONAL DIALER

         Name       Malachi Constant
         Address    Rumfoord Estate

         City       Newport                       State RI
         Zip              Phone

        Ins=Add,F2=Dial,F3=Sch,F4=Chg,Del=Delete,Esc=Quit,F10=Unload
```

Figure 12.22 Personal Dialer pop-up program

To get to the breakpoint at the **text_search** function, press the Personal Dialer's Search function key, F3. The breakpoint will occur, TD will take over, and you will see the screen shown in Figure 12.23.

```
 File  View  Run  Breakpoints  Data  Window  Options                     READY
[CPU 80386]==========================================================3=====
  cs:051B>56           push  si                           ax 0001  c=0
  cs:051C 33F6         xor   si,si                        bx 0002  z=0
  cs:051E B8A801       mov   ax,01A8                      cx 0005  s=0
  cs:0521 50           push  ax                           dx 0452  o=0
  cs:0522 B8EE01       mov   ax,01EE                      si 00BD  p=0
  cs:0525 50           push  ax                           di 0020  a=1

8083:0000 00 00 00 00 54 75 72 62     Turb                ss:1A20 008D
8083:0008 6F 2D 43 20 2D 20 43 6F o-C - Co                ss:1A1E 036C

File dialer.dbg 598-----------------------------------------------------4-
   051b                  dial_phone      endp
  dialer#229: static void text_search(void)
   051b                  text_search     proc    near
   051b  56                      push    si
  dialer#231: int dcode = 0;
   051c  33 F6                   xor     si,si
  dialer#232: clear_template(template, prompts);
   051e  B8 0014r                mov     ax,offset DGROUP:prompts
   0521  50                      push    ax
   0522  B8 005Ar                mov     ax,offset DGROUP:template

F2-Bkpt F3-Close F4-Here F5-Zoom F6-Next F7-Trace F8-Step F9-Run F10-Menu
```

Figure 12.23 Breakpoint of text_search function reached

Now you can begin debugging inside the TSR. The top half of the screen shows the machine instructions as they are executing. The bottom half is the display of the DIALER.DBG file. As you move from instruction to instruction, use the file to relate the machine instructions being executed to the C language statements in the original source file. You will debug this program as if it were an assembly language program, but you will have the guidance of the C code to tell you where you are and what you are doing. As the program jumps and calls among the other functions, use the File Window's Search command to locate the associated code segment offset address. To observe the behavior of data variables, observe from the File Window how they are referenced. Use the CPU window to get absolute addresses. Some local variables are kept in the SI and DI registers. Others are offsets from the BP register in the Turbo C stack frame. External and static variables are offsets from the DGROUP segment, which is pointed to by the data segment register.

When your exploration of the TSR is complete, you can reset all breakpoints and press F9 to finish the session. The Personal Dialer will return in its text search operation. Press Esc to leave the text search operation and press Esc again to pop down. This puts you back into the TEST program, which is still waiting for you to press any key. Press something and you are back in TD with the Terminated message. Press Esc and Alt-X and you are back at the DOS prompt.

SUMMARY

With the conclusion of this exercise comes the end of the chapter and the end of the book. The three appendices provide reference tools to help you use all the methods and programs you have explored. But this is only the beginning. There are many more ways that you can extend Turbo C Professional to enhance your use of it and to write better, more interesting programs. Perhaps this book has kick-started your imagination. Perhaps your exploration of these tips, tricks, and techniques will get the old creative juices surging, and you will find newer and better ways to use these tools and to invent your own. If just a little bit of that happens, then this book has done its job and filled a need.

APPENDIX A

REFERENCE GUIDE

This appendix is a reference guide to the functions and macros that are described in this book. It contains a list of the functions by category, a list of all global #defines that you might modify to change the configuration of the software, and a reference guide description of all functions and macros. The descriptions are in alphabetic sequence for easy reference. Each description includes the C source listing and line number where the function appears, the header file that contains the #define or prototype, and the chapter where the function is discussed. The index to the book provides page number references for each function and macro.

GLOBAL SYMBOLS

Following are the global symbols that appear in the source code that you would alter to modify the behavior of the programs that you build. They are organized by the source files in which they appear.

pmom.h (Chapter 3)

```
#define MAXARGS 10
```

This symbol defines the maximum number of arguments a root module can pass to an overlay module.

window.h (Chapter 4)

```
#define MAX_WINDOWS 10
```

This symbol defines the maximum number of concurrent open windows.

handles.c (Chapter 5)

```
#define MAXFILES 30
```

This symbol defines the maximum concurrent open files for a program that is extending the DOS limit of 20. The value in this global includes the five handles initially opened by DOS for STDIN, STDOUT, STDERR, STDAUX, and STDPRN.

typematc.c (Chapter 5)

```
#define DELAY 0
#define REPEAT 0
```

These symbols define the typematic rate being programmed for the AT keyboard.

The DELAY symbol defines the period of time that the keyboard waits after a key press before repeating. The values can be 0 through 3 for 250, 500, 750, and 1000 milliseconds.

The REPEAT symbol defines the key repeat rate in characters per second. The values can be from 0 through 31 to set repeat rates of from 30 characters per second to 2 characters per second.

fastkeys.c (chapter 5)

```
#define TICKS 6
```

This symbol defines the number of clock ticks that the fastkeys typematic accelerator program waits before it starts repeating the key being held down. This is the PC/XT equivalent of the DELAY global in typematc.c, except that the unit of measurement here is 18ths of a second.

menu.h (Chapter 6)

```
#define MENUBG BLUE
#define MENUFG WHITE
#define SELECTBG WHITE
#define SELECTFG BLACK
#define DISABLEFG LIGHTGRAY
```

These are the colors for window menus. MENUBG and MENUFG define the menu display itself. SELECTFG and SELECTBG define the selector cursor bar. DISABLEFG defines the foreground color of a menu item that is disabled (not available to be selected).

The color values are taken from the Turbo C conio.h file.

entry.h (Chapter 7)

```
#define ENTRYFG WHITE
#define ENTRYBG BLUE
#define FIELDFG BLACK
#define FIELDBG WHITE
```

These are the colors for window data entry templates. ENTRYFG and ENTRYBG define the window display for data entry templates. FIELDFG and FIELDBG describe the color of the fields when they are selected for data entry.

The color values are taken from the Turbo C conio.h file.

serial.h (Chapter 8)

```
#define SERIALBUFFERSIZE 1024
#define SAFETYLEVEL (SERIALBUFFERSIZE/4)
#define THRESHOLD (SAFETYLEVEL*3)
```

These symbols define the serial input buffer. SERIALBUFFERSIZE is the size of the buffer. SAFETYLEVEL is the level of buffer fill at which the system will send the XOFF character to the sending program. THRESHOLD is the level at which the system will send the XON character to the sender.

serial.c (Chapter 8)

```
int SERIALPORT  = 1;    /* COM1 or COM2                      */
int PARITY      = 0;    /* 0 = none, 1 = odd, 2 = even       */
int STOPBITS    = 1;    /* 1 or 2                            */
int WORDLEN     = 8;    /* 7 or 8                            */
int BAUD        = 2400; /* 110,150,300,600,1200,2400         */
```

These variables define the communications port and their operating parameters. They are variables rather than symbols because they are as likely to be changed while a program is running as they are when you compile the program.

modem.c (Chapter 8)

```
char DIAL[] = "ATDT";
```

This string is the modem's dialing command. As shown, it uses touch-tone dialing. For rotary pulse dialing, it must contain "ATDP" instead.

tsr.c (Chapter 9)

```
unsigned scancode;   /* Keyboard (INT 9) scan code */
unsigned keymask;    /* BIOS Shift Status Byte     */
```

These are the scan code and BIOS shift key status mask for the hot key of a TSR. Following are tables that define the valid values for these variables.

KEYBOARD SCAN CODES

Function Keys		ASCII Keys								Numeric Keypad	
Key	**Code**	**Key**	**Code**	**Key**	**Code**	**Key**	**Code**	**Key**	**Code**	**Key**	**Code**
F1	59	‘	41	Tab	15	A	30	Z	44	Esc	1
F2	60	1	2	Q	16	S	31	X	45	Home	71
F3	61	2	3	W	17	D	32	C	46	Up	72
F4	62	3	4	E	18	F	33	V	47	PgUp	73
F5	63	4	5	R	19	G	34	B	48	PrtSc	55
F6	64	5	6	T	20	H	35	N	49	<-	75
F7	65	6	7	Y	21	J	36	M	50	5	76
F8	66	7	8	U	22	K	37	,	51	->	77
F9	67	8	9	I	23	L	38	.	52	Minus	74
F10	68	9	10	O	24	;	39	/	53	End	79
		0	11	P	25	'	40			Down	80
		-	12	[	26					PgDn	81
		=	13	]	27					Ins	82
		\	43	Enter	28					Del	83
		<-	14							Plus	78

BIOS SHIFT KEY STATUS MASK

Key	Value
Ins	128
Caps Lock	64
Num Lock	32
Scroll Lock	16
Alt	8
Ctrl	4
Left Shift	2
Right Shift	1

The Ins, Caps Lock, Num Lock, and Scroll Lock bits are toggles. When the key is pressed, the value of the corresponding bit flips. The others are momentary values — the bit is on only as long as the key is held down. The only use you should make of the first four is to make sure Num Lock is off if the hot key is going to be the 5 on the numeric keypad (scan code 76).

tsrmult.h (Chapter 11)

```
#define MAXHOTKEYS 5
```

This symbol defines the maximum number of hot keys that tsrmult.c will watch for. When used with TSRPLUS, the value minus one is the maximum number of TSR-like programs supported in the TSRPLUS environment.

FUNCTIONS AND MACROS BY CATEGORY

KEYBOARD and SCREEN

autotype
block_cursor
cgets
clear_biosbuff
default_cursor
getkey
hidecursor
normalcursor
repeat_rate
restorecursor
savecursor
stuffkey
unhidecursor

VIDEO WINDOWS

clear_option
clear_template
close_window
data_entry
disable_selection
enabled
enable_selection
error_message
executive
field_tally
notice
open_window
set_option
test_option
yesno

COMMUNICATIONS

answer_modem
call_remote
clear_serial_queue
hangup
initializemodem
initserialport
input_char_ready
readserial
release_modem
restore_serialint
writeserial

EXPANDED MEMORY

emm_allocate
emm_map
emm_pageframe
emm_pages_available
emm_present
emm_release
emm_restorecontext
emm_savecontext
emm_version
emm_working

TIMERS

intercept_timer
restore_timer
set_timer
timed_out

OVERLAYS

ENTER
EXIT
getarg
load_overlay
RETURN

TSR PROGRAMS

tsr

FILES

findpath
init_handles
return_handles

THE EXTENDING TURBO C PROFESSIONAL LIBRARY REFERENCE

The following pages contain the library function reference guide to all the functions and macros in this book. Each function and macro appears alphabetically and follows this format:

function or macro name

Function: ANSI prototype

Parameters: Descriptions of the parameters passed to the function.

Returns: A description of the value returned from the function.

Description: A brief statement of the purpose for the function or macro.

Source File: The name, listing number, and line number of the source file where the function is declared.

Prototype in:
-or-
#defined in: The name of the header (.H) file.

Discussed in: Chapter <*chapter number*>

answer_modem

Function: void answer_modem(void)

Parameters: none

Returns: nothing

Description: This function prepares the modem to automatically answer incoming calls.

Source File: MODEM.C (Listing 8.4, Line 54)

Prototype in: MODEM.H

Discussed in: Chapter 8

autotype

Function: void autotype(char *s)

Parameters: pointer to the string to automatically type

Returns: nothing

Description: This function sets up a string for automatic typing.

Source File: AUTOTYPE.C (Listing 5.8, Line 24)

Prototype in: KEYS.H

Discussed in: Chapter 5

block_cursor

Function: void block_cursor(void)

Parameters: none

Returns: nothing

Description: This function turns the cursor into a non-blinking block.

Source File: CURSOR.C (Listing 5.12, Line 95)

Prototype in: CURSOR.H

Discussed in: Chapter 5

call_remote

Function: void call_remote(char *phoneno)

Parameters: pointer to the string telephone number

Returns: nothing

Description: This function uses the modem to call the phone number passed in the parameter.

Source File: MODEM.C (Listing 8.4, Line 45)

Prototype in: MODEM.H

Discussed in: Chapter 8

cgets

Function: char *cgets(char *s)

Parameters: pointer to the string into which characters are read

Returns: pointer to the first data character

Description: This function replaces the Turbo C **cgets** function. It is functionally identical but, unlike the Turbo C version, this one works within the boundaries of the window system.

Source File: CGETS.C (Listing 5.5, Line 14)

Prototype in: KEYS.H

Discussed in: Chapter 5

clear_biosbuff

Function: void clear_biosbuff(void)

Parameters: none

Returns: nothing

Description: This function clears the BIOS keyboard read-ahead buffer, flushing any typed but as yet unread keystrokes.

Source File: BIOSBUFF.C (Listing 5.1, Line 28)

Prototype in: KEYS.H

Discussed in: Chapter 5

clear_option

Macro: clear_option(MENU *mn, int h, int v)

Parameters: MENU pointer
horizontal menu bar selection number
vertical pop-down menu selection number

Returns: nothing

Description: This macro turns off a pop-down menu selection that is defined as a toggled option.

Source File: ----------

#defined in: MENU.H

Discussed in: Chapter 6

clear_serial_queue

Function: void clear_serial_queue(void)

Parameters: none

Returns: nothing

Description: This function clears all characters out of the serial input buffer.

Source File: SERIAL.C (Listing 8.2, Line 84)

Prototype in: SERIAL.H

Discussed in: Chapter 8

clear_template

Function: void clear_template(FIELD *fld, PROMPT *pt)

Parameters: pointer to the FIELD array for the template
pointer to the PROMPT array for the template

Returns: nothing

Description: This function clears the data collection buffers for a data entry template to all null-terminated space strings and displays a blank template in the current window.

Source File: ENTRY.C (Listing 7.2, Line 41)

Prototype in: ENTRY.H

Discussed in: Chapter 7

close_window

Function: void close_window(void)

Parameters: none

Returns: nothing

Description: This function closes the current video window, restoring the video display to whatever was there when the window was opened.

Source File: WINDOW.C (Listing 4.2, Line 116)

Prototype in: WINDOW.H

Discussed in: Chapter 4

data_entry

Function: int data_entry(FIELD *fld, PROMPT *pt)

Parameters: pointer to the FIELD array for the template
pointer to the PROMPT array for the template

Returns: the keystroke that terminated data entry

Description: This function begins user data entry into a window data entry template.

Source File: ENTRY.C (Listing 7.2, Line 78)

Prototype in: ENTRY.H

Discussed in: Chapter 7

default_cursor

Function: void default_cursor(void)

Parameters: none

Returns: nothing

Description: This function returns to the cursor configuration that existed before the most recent call to **block_cursor**.

Source File: CURSOR.C (Listing 5.12, Line 105)

Prototype in: CURSOR.H

Discussed in: Chapter 5

disable_selection

Macro: disable_selection(MENU *mn, int h, int v)

Parameters: pointer to the MENU array
horizontal menu bar selection number
vertical pop-down menu selection number

Returns: nothing

Description: This function disables a pop-down menu selection. The selection is displayed in the color selected by the global symbol DISABLEFG, and the menu selector cursor bar skips over the selection until **enable_selection** is called for the same menu item.

Source File: ---------

#defined in: MENU.H

Discussed in: Chapter 6

emm_allocate

Function: int emm_allocate(int pagect)

Parameters: number of EM pages to allocate

Returns: handle of the EM allocation or -1 if error

Description: This function allocates the selected number of Expanded Memory pages to the calling program, associating the allocation with a handle.

Source File: EMM.C (Listing 10.2, Line 78)

Prototype in: EMM.H

Discussed in: Chapter 10

emm_map

Function: int emm_map(int pages, pageno, log_pageno, handle)

Parameters: number of allocated pages to map
first physical page number (0 to 3)
first logical page number (0 to pages allocated-1)
EM handle assigned to allocation

Returns: 0 if OK, -1 if error

Description: This function maps pages from an allocated block of Expanded Memory into the physical EM page frame.

Source File: EMM.C (Listing 10.2, Line 88)

Prototype in: EMM.H

Discussed in: Chapter 10

emm_pageframe

Function: int emm_pageframe(void)

Parameters: none

Returns: EM page frame segment address or -1 if error

Description: This function returns the segment address of the EM physical page frame.

Source File: EMM.C (Listing 10.2, Line 60)

Prototype in: EMM.H

Discussed in: Chapter 10

emm_pages_available

Function: int emm_pages_available(void)

Parameters: none

Returns: number of available pages

Description: This function returns the number of Expanded Pages pages available for allocation.

Source File: EMM.C (Listing 10.2, Line 69)

Prototype in: EMM.H

Discussed in: Chapter 10

emm_present

Function: int emm_present(void)

Parameters: none

Returns: true if EMM is installed, false if not

Description: This function tells if the Expanded Memory Manager is installed.

Source File: EMM.C (Listing 10.2, Line 41)

Prototype in: EMM.H

Discussed in: Chapter 10

emm_release

Function: int emm_release(int handle)

Parameters: EM handle

Returns: 0 if OK, -1 if error

Description: This function releases the pages allocated to an Expanded Memory handle.

Source File: EMM.C (Listing 10.2, Line 103)

Prototype in: EMM.H

Discussed in: Chapter 10

emm_restorecontext

Function: int emm_restorecontext(int handle)

Parameters: EM handle

Returns: 0 if OK, -1 if error

Description: This function restores the Expanded Memory mapping context that was associated with a handle by a call to **emm_savecontext**.

Source File: EMM.C (Listing 10.2, Line 129)

Prototype in: EMM.H

Discussed in: Chapter 10

emm_savecontext

Function: int emm_savecontext(int handle)

Parameters: EM handle

Returns: 0 if OK, -1 if error

Description: This function saves the current Expanded Memory mapping context and associates it with the handle that is passed. A later call to **emm_restorecontext** will restore this context.

Source File: EMM.C (Listing 10.2, Line 121)

Prototype in: EMM.H

Discussed in: Chapter 10

emm_version

Function: int emm_version(void)

Parameters: none

Returns: EM version number or -1 if error

Description: This function returns the current Expanded Memory Manager version number in a two-byte integer. The most significant byte is the major version number. The least significant byte is the minor version number. Version 3.2 is returned as 0x32. Version 4.0 is returned as 0x40.

Source File: EMM.C (Listing 10.2, Line 111)

Prototype in: EMM.H

Discussed in: Chapter 10

emm_working

Function: int emm_working(void)

Parameters: none

Returns: true if EM is operating, false if not

Description: This function tells if Expanded Memory is operating. The Expanded Memory Manager must be resident for this function to be used.

Source File: EMM.C (Listing 10.2, Line 53)

Prototype in: EMM.H

Discussed in: Chapter 10

enabled

Macro: enabled(MENU *mn, int h, int v)

Parameters: pointer to the MENU array
horizontal menu bar selection number
vertical pop-down menu selection number

Returns: true if the selection is enabled, false if not

Description: This function returns true if the pop-down menu selection is enabled.

Source File: ---------

#defined in: MENU.H

Discussed in: Chapter 6

enable_selection

Macro: enable_selection(MENU *mn, int h, int v)

Parameters: pointer to the MENU array
horizontal menu bar selection number
vertical pop-down menu selection number

Returns: nothing

Description: This function enables a disabled pop-down menu selection. The selection is displayed with the MENUFG color, and the selector bar is allowed to stop on the selection.

Source File: ---------

#defined in: MENU.H

Discussed in: Chapter 6

ENTER

Macro: ENTER

Parameters: none

Returns: nothing

Description: This macro is used in a global function that is resident in a root module and that is called from an overlay module. This macro must be the first code executed by the global function after the parameters on the stack are moved to static copies by the function. The ENTER macro switches the context from the overlay program to the root program.

Source File: ---------

#defined in: PMOM.H

Discussed in: Chapter 3

error_message

Function: void error_message(char *ermsg)

Parameters: pointer to the string error message

Returns: nothing

Description: This function posts an error message in a small window on the screen. It sounds the audible alarm and prompts the user to press any key to erase the error window and proceed.

Source File: WINDOW.C (Listing 4.2, Line 141)

Prototype in: WINDOW.H

Discussed in: Chapter 4

executive

Function: void executive(MENU *mn)

Parameters: pointer to the MENU array

Returns: nothing

Description: This function causes the execution of the menu structure defined in the MENU array. The menu bar pops up, and all program execution is driven from the menus until the user presses the Esc key while all pop-down menus disappear from the screen and the horizontal menu bar is displayed.

Source File: MENU.C (Listing 6.2, Line 24)

Prototype in: MENU.H

Discussed in: Chapter 6

EXIT

Macro: EXIT

Parameters: ------

Returns: ------

Description: This macro is the exit point from a global function in a root module that was called from an overlay module. It may be followed by the RETURN macro, but nothing else should follow it.

Source File: ------

#defined in: PMOM.H

Discussed in: Chapter 3

field_tally

Function: void field_tally(FIELD *fld, PROMPT *pt)

Parameters: pointer to the FIELD array
pointer to the PROMPT array

Returns: nothing

Description: This function redisplays all the data collection buffers for a data entry template in the window.

Source File: ENTRY.C (Listing 7.2, Line 24)

Prototype in: ENTRY.H

Discussed in: Chapter 7

findpath

Function: char *findpath(char *fname)

Parameters: pointer to a file name string

Returns: pointer to a path or NULL

Description: This function finds the unambiguous path to a specified file name by first checking the logged in subdirectory, then tracing the DOS PATH, and finally looking in the subdirectory where the executing program was run from.

Source File: FINDPATH.C (Listing 5.15, Line 16)

Prototype in: ----------

Discussed in: Chapter 5

getarg

Function: void far *getarg(int argv_number)

Parameters: command line argument number

Returns: a void far pointer

Description: This function converts a command-line argument string into a far pointer. The string is assumed to have the ASCII format "ssss:oooo" representing a segment, offset far address.

Source File: PMOM.C (Listing 3.2, Line 62)

Prototype in: PMOM.H

Discussed in: Chapter 3

getkey

Function: int getkey(void)

Parameters: none

Returns: the next key pressed

Description: This function reads the keyboard and calls interrupt 0x28 while it waits for a keystroke. This call allows TSRs to pop up in the case where the caller to **getkey** is itself a TSR that popped up as a result of a call to the interrupt 0x28.

The **getkey** function converts a function key sequence into a single unique character value conforming to the definitions in keys.h.

Source File: KEYBOARD.C (Listing 5.3, Line 10)

Prototype in: KEYS.H

Discussed in: Chapter 5

hangup

Function: void hangup(void)

Parameters: none

Returns: nothing

Description: This function hangs the phone up when a modem connection has been made.

Source File: MODEM.C (Listing 8.4, Line 61)

Prototype in: MODEM.H

Discussed in: Chapter 8

hidecursor

Function: void hidecursor(void)

Parameters: none

Returns: nothing

Description: This function hides the cursor so that **cprintf** calls and others that display windows and menus use an invisible cursor.

Source File: CURSOR.C (Listing 5.12, Line 73)

Prototype in: CURSOR.H

Discussed in: Chapter 5

initializemodem

Function: void initializemodem(void)

Parameters: none

Returns: nothing

Description: This function initializes the modem.

Source File: MODEM.C (Listing 8.4, Line 25)

Prototype in: MODEM.H

Discussed in: Chapter 8

initserialport

Function: void initserialport(void)

Parameters: none

Returns: nothing

Description: This function initializes the serial port.

Source File: SERIAL.C (Listing 8.2, Line 48)

Prototype in: SERIAL.H

Discussed in: Chapter 8

init_handles

Function: void init_handles(void)

Parameters: none

Returns: nothing

Description: This function establishes the extended handle capability for programs that need more than the default of 20 open files.

Source File: HANDLES.C (Listing 5.16, Line 44)

Prototype in: -------

Discussed in: Chapter 5

input_char_ready

Macro: input_char_ready()

Parameters: none

Returns: true if a serial input character is ready, false if not

Description: This macro tells if a character has been read into the serial input buffer.

Source File: ---------

#defined in: SERIAL.H

Discussed in: Chapter 8

intercept_timer

Function: void intercept_timer(void (*fn)(void))

Parameters: pointer to function to call upon time-out

Returns: nothing

Description: This function intercepts the timer interrupt vector and sets up a caller's function to be called when a programmed timer value times out.

Source File: TIMER.C (Listing 2.2, Line 14)

Prototype in: TIMER.H

Discussed in: Chapter 2

load_overlay

Function: int load_overlay(char *overlayname, ...)

Parameters: name of overlay module
far pointer to argument 1, 2, . . . n

Returns: DOS return code from overlay module

Description: This function is called from a root module to load an overlay module.

Source File: PMOM.C (Listing 3.2, Line 26)

Prototype in: PMOM.H

Discussed in: Chapter 3

normalcursor

Function: void normalcursor(void)

Parameters: none

Returns: nothing

Description: This function programs a normal, DOS-default cursor.

Source File: CURSOR.C (Listing 5.12, Line 63)

Prototype in: CURSOR.H

Discussed in: Chapter 5

notice

Function: void notice(char *note)

Parameters: pointer to screen notice

Returns: nothing

Description: This function posts a notice in a small video window. The window includes a prompt for the user to press any key to erase the notice window and proceed.

Source File: WINDOW.C (Listing 4.2, Line 147)

Prototype in: WINDOW.H

Discussed in: Chapter 4

open_window

Function: void open_window(left,top,right,bottom, foreg,backg,frame,shadow)

Parameters: left coordinate of window (1-80)
top coordinate of window (1-25)
right coordinate of window (1-80)
bottom coordinate of window (1-25)
foreground color
background color
0 = no frame, 1 = single-line frame, 2 = double
0 = no shadow, 1 = transparent, 2 = opaque

Returns: nothing

Description: This function opens a window and displays it. All subsequent conio.h functions will be directed into this window as if it were a virtual terminal.

Source File: WINDOW.C (Listing 4.2, Line 26)

Prototype in: WINDOW.H

Discussed in: Chapter 4

readserial

Function: int readserial(void)

Parameters: none

Returns: next serial input character

Description: This function reads the next available serial character from the serial input buffer. If no character is in the buffer, the function waits until the serial input interrupt service routine puts one there or a 60-second timeout occurs. If a timeout occurs, a zero byte is returned. The caller can test for the timeout with the **timed_out** macro.

Source File: SERIAL.C (Listing 8.2, Line 117)

Prototype in: SERIAL.H

Discussed in: Chapter 8

release_modem

Function: void release_modem(void)

Parameters: none

Returns: nothing

Description: This function resets the modem and the serial port.

Source File: MODEM.C (Listing 8.4, Line 35)

Prototype in: MODEM.H

Discussed in: Chapter 8

repeat_rate

Function: void repeat_rate(int n)

Parameters: milliseconds between autotyped characters

Returns: nothing

Description: This function sets the number of milliseconds of delay between automatically typed characters.

Source File: AUTOTYPE.C (Listing 5.8, Line 35)

Prototype in: KEYS.H

Discussed in: Chapter 5

restorecursor

Function: void restorecursor(void)

Parameters: none

Returns: nothing

Description: This function restores the cursor configuration to the setting it had at the time of the most recent call to the function **savecursor**.

Source File: CURSOR.C (Listing 5.12, Line 49)

Prototype in: CURSOR.H

Discussed in: Chapter 5

restore_serialint

Function: void restore_serialint(void)

Parameters: none

Returns: nothing

Description: This function restores the serial input interrupt vector.

Source File: SERIAL.C (Listing 8.2, Line 77)

Prototype in: SERIAL.H

Discussed in: Chapter 8

restore_timer

Function: void restore_timer()

Parameters: none

Returns: nothing

Description: This function restores the system timer interrupt vector.

Source File: TIMER.C (Listing 2.2, Line 24)

Prototype in: TIMER.H

Discussed in: Chapter 2

RETURN

Macro: RETURN(r)

Parameters: int,long,pointer returned to overlay from root function

Returns: nothing

Description: This macro is used at the end of a global function in a root module to return a value to the overlay module that called the global function. If used, this macro is the last executed statement in the global function.

Source File: ---------

#defined in: PMOM.H

Discussed in: Chapter 3

return_handles

Function: void return_handles(void)

Parameters: none

Returns: nothing

Description: This function turns off the handle extension logic for versions of DOS prior to 3.3. The function is necessary so that the intercepted DOS interrupt vector gets restored.

Source File: HANDLES.C (Listing 5.16, Line 61)

Prototype in: --------

Discussed in: Chapter 5

savecursor

Function: void savecursor(void)

Parameters: none

Returns: nothing

Description: This function saves the current cursor configuration. The saved configuration can be restored by a call to the function **restorecursor**.

Source File: CURSOR.C (Listing 5.12, Line 39)

Prototype in: CURSOR.H

Discussed in: Chapter 5

set_option

Macro: set_option(MENU *mn, int h, int v)

Parameters: pointer to MENU array
horizontal menu bar selection number
vertical pop-down menu selection number

Returns: nothing

Description: This macro sets a toggled menu selection to its on condition.

Source File: ---------

#defined in: MENU.H

Discussed in: Chapter 6

set_timer

Macro: set_timer(secs)

Parameters: number of seconds for timer to run

Returns: nothing

Description: This macro starts a timer running. The timer condition can be tested with the **timed_out** macro.

Source File: ---------

#defined in: TIMER.H

Discussed in: Chapter 2

stuffkey

Function: void stuffkey(int k)

Parameters: keystroke to stuff into the BIOS buffer

Returns: nothing

Description: This function inserts a keystroke into the BIOS read-ahead buffer so that a later keyboard read will read the character as though the user had pressed the key. Function keys and key combinations are encoded in the keystroke parameter with the values defined in keys.h.

Source File: BIOSBUFF.C (Listing 5.1, Line 14)

Prototype in: KEYS.H

Discussed in: Chapter 5

test_option

Macro: test_option(MENU *mn, int h, int v)

Parameters: pointer to MENU array
horizontal menu bar selection number
vertical pop-down menu selection number

Returns: true if the menu option is on, false if not

Description: This macro tests to see if a toggle menu selection is on or off.

Source File: ----------

#defined in: MENU.H

Discussed in: Chapter 6

timed_out

Macro: timed_out()

Parameters: none

Returns: true if the timer count has expired, false if not

Description: This macro tests to see if a timer that is running because of a call to the **set_timer** macro has expired.

Source File: ----------

#defined in: TIMER.H

Discussed in: Chapter 2

tsr

Function: void tsr(void)

Parameters: none

Returns: nothing

Description: Programs that are to become memory-resident utility pop-ups call this function to declare themselves resident or to register themselves with the TSRPLUS environment.

Source File: TSR.C (Listing 9.2, Line 77)

Prototype in: TSR.H, TSRMULT.H

Discussed in: Chapters 9 and 11

unhidecursor

Function: void unhidecursor(void)

Parameters: none

Returns: nothing

Description: This function makes the invisible cursor visible.

Source File: CURSOR.C (Listing 5.12, Line 84)

Prototype in: CURSOR.H

Discussed in: Chapter 5

writeserial

Function: int writeserial(int c)

Parameters: character to send to serial port

Returns: true if character sent, false if timed out

Description: This function writes a character to the serial port.

Source File: SERIAL.C (Listing 8.2, Line 134)

Prototype in: SERIAL.H

Discussed in: Chapter 8

yesno

Function: int yesno(char *ques)

Parameters: pointer to string question

Returns: true if affirmative answer, false if negative

Description: This function displays a question in a small window and prompts the user to answer "y" or "n." After the answer, the window is erased, and the result is returned to the caller.

Source File: WINDOW.C (Listing 4.2, Line 153)

Prototype in: WINDOW.H

Discussed in: Chapter 4

APPENDIX B

THE MAKEFILE

This appendix contains the makefile for all the software in this book. If you have purchased the companion diskette or keyed in the listings, you can use this makefile to build the example executable programs.

Listing B.1 (listed at the end of this appendix) is the makefile. The makefile operates under a few assumptions. First it assumes that you have installed the Turbo C compiler and the Turbo Assembler exactly as recommended by the installation procedures for each package. The compiler is assumed to be in the \tc subdirectory for the current drive. The compiler's include files are assumed to be in the \tc\include subdirectory, and the compiler's library files are assumed to be in the \tc\lib subdirectory. If these assumptions are incorrect, you must change the makefile's STARTUP and LIBS macros at the beginning of the file to reflect where you have installed the software. The most common variation from this convention will occur when the compiler and assembler are on different drives from the source code.

The makefile assumes that the DOS path will lead to the compiler and assembler. The conventional path would be as follows,

```
PATH=\tc;\tasm
```

along with paths to your other software.

The makefile assumes that you want to compile with debugging information included. To remove the debugging information, comment out the LINKDEBUG and COMPILEDEBUG macros at the beginning of the makefile.

The makefile uses the MODEL macro to specify the memory model.

BUILDING THE SOFTWARE

To build all the software, copy all the source code and the makefile into a subdirectory where the software will be built. Type the following command at the command line:

```
C>make
```

This will compile all modules, build the XTCPRO.LIB library, and link all the executable files.

If you want to make a single executable file without building all the others, type the file name after the "make" command. For example, to build only the DIALER program, enter this command:

```
C>make dialer.exe
```

This convention is handy when you are modifying one of the program modules that are kept in the XTCPRO.LIB file. The procedure prevents the make process from making all the unrelated executable modules. The makefile relinks most programs after the library file changes.

Listing B.1 (makefile)

```
# -------------------------------------------------------
#   A makefile to build the software in
#   Extending Turbo C Professional
#   April, 1989
# -------------------------------------------------------

# -------------------------------------------------------
#   Macros to establish the memory model, debug, and libraries
# -------------------------------------------------------

MODEL        = s
STARTUP      = \tc\lib\c0s
LIBS         = xtcpro \tc\lib\cs
LINKDEBUG    = /m /v
COMPILEDEBUG = -y

# -------------------------------------------------------
#   An implicit rule to build .EXE files
# -------------------------------------------------------

.obj.exe:
    tlink $(LINKDEBUG) $(STARTUP) $*, $*,,$(LIBS)

# -------------------------------------------------------
#   An implicit rule to build .OBJ files
# -------------------------------------------------------
```

continued...

...from previous page

```

.c.obj:
    tcc $(COMPILEDEBUG) -c -m$(MODEL) $*

# ------------------------------------------------------------
#  The first target that causes everything to be built
# ------------------------------------------------------------

all :   pseudo.exe                  \
        scrnsave.exe                \
        root.exe                    \
        overlay.exe                 \
        demowind.exe                \
        newkeys.exe                 \
        typematc.exe                \
        fastkeys.exe                \
        demoauto.exe                \
        driver.exe                  \
        demoblck.exe                \
        demopath.exe                \
        tune.exe                    \
        handles.exe                 \
        demomenu.exe                \
        demoentr.exe                \
        sender.exe                  \
        receiver.exe                \
        xsend.exe                   \
        xrecv.exe                   \
        dialer.exe                  \
        demoemm.exe                 \
        buildial.exe                \
        tsrplus.exe                 \
        tinynote.exe

# ------------------------------------------------------------
#  XTCPRO.LIB
# ------------------------------------------------------------

xtcpro.lib :  timer.obj                 \
              pmom.obj                  \
```

continued...

...from previous page

```
                    window.obj              \
                    autotype.obj            \
                    biosbuff.obj            \
                    cgets.obj               \
                    keyboard.obj            \
                    cursor.obj              \
                    menu.obj                \
                    entry.obj               \
                    modem.obj               \
                    serial.obj              \
                    tsr.obj                 \
                    emm.obj
        del xtcpro.lib
        tlib xtcpro @xtcpro.bld

#  -----------------------------------------------------------
#  Chapter 1
#  -----------------------------------------------------------

pseudo.exe    : pseudo.obj xtcpro.lib

pseudo.obj    : pseudo.c

#  -----------------------------------------------------------
#  Chapter 2
#  -----------------------------------------------------------

scrnsave.exe : scrnsave.obj xtcpro.lib

scrnsave.obj : scrnsave.c interupt.h timer.h

timer.obj     : timer.c timer.h interupt.h

#  -----------------------------------------------------------
#  Chapter 3
#  -----------------------------------------------------------

root.exe      : root.obj xtcpro.lib

overlay.exe   : overlay.obj xtcpro.lib
```

continued...

...from previous page

```

root.obj     : root.c pmom.h interupt.h

overlay.obj  : overlay.c pmom.h

pmom.obj     : pmom.c pmom.h interupt.h

#  -----------------------------------------------------------
#  Chapter 4
#  -----------------------------------------------------------

demowind.exe : demowind.obj xtcpro.lib

demowind.obj : demowind.c window.h

window.obj   : window.c window.h keys.h

#  -----------------------------------------------------------
#  Chapter 5
#  -----------------------------------------------------------

newkeys.exe  : newkeys.obj xtcpro.lib

typematc.exe : typematc.obj xtcpro.lib

fastkeys.exe : fastkeys.obj xtcpro.lib

demoauto.exe : demoauto.obj xtcpro.lib

driver.exe   : driver.obj xtcpro.lib

demoblck.exe : demoblck.obj xtcpro.lib

demopath.exe : demopath.obj xtcpro.lib

tune.exe     : tune.c
    tcc tune

handles.exe  : handles.obj xtcpro.lib

```

continued...

...from previous page

```
biosbuff.obj : biosbuff.c keys.h

keyboard.obj : keyboard.c keys.h

newkeys.obj  : newkeys.c interupt.h keys.h

cgets.obj    : cgets.c keys.h

typematc.obj : typematc.c

fastkeys.obj : fastkeys.c interupt.h keys.h

autotype.obj : autotype.c interupt.h keys.h

demoauto.obj : demoauto.c keys.h

driver.obj   : driver.c keys.h

cursor.obj   : cursor.c cursor.h interupt.h

demoblck.obj : demoblck.c cursor.h window.h keys.h

demopath.obj : findpath.c
    tcc -DDEMOPATH -y -c -v -odemopath findpath

findpath.obj : findpath.c

handles.obj  : handles.c interupt.h

# ---------------------------------------------------------------
#  Chapter 6
# ---------------------------------------------------------------

demomenu.exe : demomenu.obj xtcpro.lib

menu.obj     : menu.c menu.h window.h keys.h cursor.h

demomenu.obj : demomenu.c cursor.h window.h menu.h

```

continued...

...from previous page

```
# ---------------------------------------------------------------
#  Chapter 7
# ---------------------------------------------------------------

demoentr.exe : demoentr.obj xtcpro.lib

demoentr.obj : demoentr.c window.h cursor.h entry.h keys.h

entry.obj    : entry.c window.h entry.h keys.h cursor.h

# ---------------------------------------------------------------
#  Chapter 8
# ---------------------------------------------------------------

sender.exe   : sender.obj xtcpro.lib

receiver.exe : receiver.obj xtcpro.lib

xsend.exe    : xsend.obj xtcpro.lib

xrecv.exe    : xrecv.obj xtcpro.lib

serial.obj   : serial.c serial.h timer.h

modem.obj    : modem.c modem.h timer.h

sender.obj   : sender.c serial.h modem.h keys.h

receiver.obj : receiver.c serial.h modem.h keys.h

xrecv.obj    : xrecv.c serial.h modem.h keys.h timer.h

xsend.obj    : xsend.c serial.h modem.h keys.h timer.h

# ---------------------------------------------------------------
#  Chapter 9
# ---------------------------------------------------------------

dialer.exe   : dialer.obj xtcpro.lib

```

continued...

...from previous page

```
dialer.obj    : dialer.c window.h cursor.h entry.h keys.h tsr.h

tsr.obj       : tsr.c interupt.h tsr.h

#  -----------------------------------------------------------
#  Chapter 10
#  -----------------------------------------------------------

demoemm.exe   : demoemm.obj xtcpro.lib

demoemm.obj   : demoemm.c emm.h

emm.obj       : emm.c emm.h

#  -----------------------------------------------------------
#  Chapter 11
#  -----------------------------------------------------------

buildial.exe : dialer.obj tsrbuild.obj xtcpro.lib
    tlink $(LINKDEBUG) $(STARTUP) dialer tsrbuild,$*,,$(LIBS)

tsrplus.exe  : tsrplus.obj tsrmult.obj xtcpro.lib
    tlink $(LINKDEBUG) $(STARTUP) $* tsrmult, $*,,$(LIBS)

tinynote.exe : tinynote.obj tsrbuild.obj xtcpro.lib
    tlink $(LINKDEBUG) $(STARTUP) $* tsrbuild, $*,,$(LIBS)

tinynote.obj : tinynote.c cursor.h window.h keys.h tsr.h

tsrmult.obj  : tsrmult.c interupt.h tsrmult.h

tsrbuild.obj : tsrbuild.c tsrmult.h interupt.h

tsrplus.obj  : tsrplus.c tsrmult.h interupt.h emm.h
```

Listing B.2 (xtcpro.bld)

```
+pmom.obj      &
+autotype.obj &
+emm.obj       &
+modem.obj     &
+serial.obj   &
+tsr.obj       &
+timer.obj     &
+entry.obj     &
+menu.obj      &
+biosbuff.obj &
+window.obj    &
+cgets.obj     &
+keyboard.obj &
+cursor.obj
```

APPENDIX C

THE EXAMPLE PROGRAMS

This book contains many example programs that illustrate the use of the library functions and techniques. You can build the example programs from the source files in this book by using the makefile in Appendix B. This appendix describes each of the programs.

The descriptions in this appendix are organized by book chapter and include operating instructions. The operating instructions include command-line entries that assume you are running from the C: drive. Where you see this format,

```
c>command
```

you type the words represented by "command" and not the C> prompt.

If you are reading this appendix before you read the book, you are likely to be unimpressed with the functionality of these programs. They are not turnkey programs that you will rush to install and use. The Personal Dialer is the only one that has real use other than to demonstrate the expanded uses of Turbo C that are presented in the chapters that precede this appendix. And that is the purpose of these programs.

CHAPTER 1—TURBO C: THE UNIQUE FEATURES

pseudo.exe

This program is an example of the use of the Turbo C register pseudovariables. It calls two functions—one that returns an integer and one that returns a long integer—and displays the values returned by the functions. The functions do not use the C language **return** statement; rather, they put their values into Turbo C register pseudovariables in a manner consistent with the way C returns values from functions.

Operating Instructions

At the command line, enter

```
c>pseudo
```

The console will display the following:

```
the int is: 1234
the long is 654321
```

CHAPTER 2—INTERRUPTS

scrnsave.exe

This program illustrates attached interrupt vectors. It is a screen saver utility program.

Operating Instructions

At the command line, enter

```
C>scrnsave <timeout-count>
```

The timeout count is optional. If you omit it, the timeout will be 60 seconds.

As long as you keep typing, nothing unusual happens. If you abstain from typing for the timeout period, the screen goes blank. When you type again, the screen is displayed.

CHAPTER 3—OVERLAYS

root.exe

This is a program that demonstrates overlaid programs with Turbo C. It is an example of a root module that calls an overlay module (overlay.exe, described next).

Operating Instructions

At the command line, enter

```
C>root
```

You will see the display shown in Figure C.1.

```
C>root

==============================================
[1] Begin processing in the root
    Load and execute Overlay
==============================================
[2]   Overlay is executing
      The structure data argument contains:
        --original data--
        --CRISPY DATA--
      Overlay calls Root function with 3
==============================================
[3]     Root global function running
        inside = 4444
        Overlay passed 3 to root
        Root function returns 4
==============================================
[4]   Root returns to Overlay
      Overlay is exiting with return code 5
==============================================
[5] Continue in the root
    Overlay changed P2 to: --Changed Data--
    Exit from the root
==============================================
C>
```

Figure C.1 Initial display screen for root.exe

overlay.exe

This program is the overlay module that is called by root.exe described earlier. It is executed from within root.exe and contributes to the results shown for root.exe.

CHAPTER 4—VIDEO WINDOWS

demowind.exe

This program is an example of video windows.

Operating Instructions

At the command line, enter

```
c>demowind
```

You will see the three windows shown in Figure C.2. Type some string values into the top window. When you have seen enough of that, press Enter, type "end," and press Enter. The program will erase the window. Read the next window down and press Enter. Do that again.

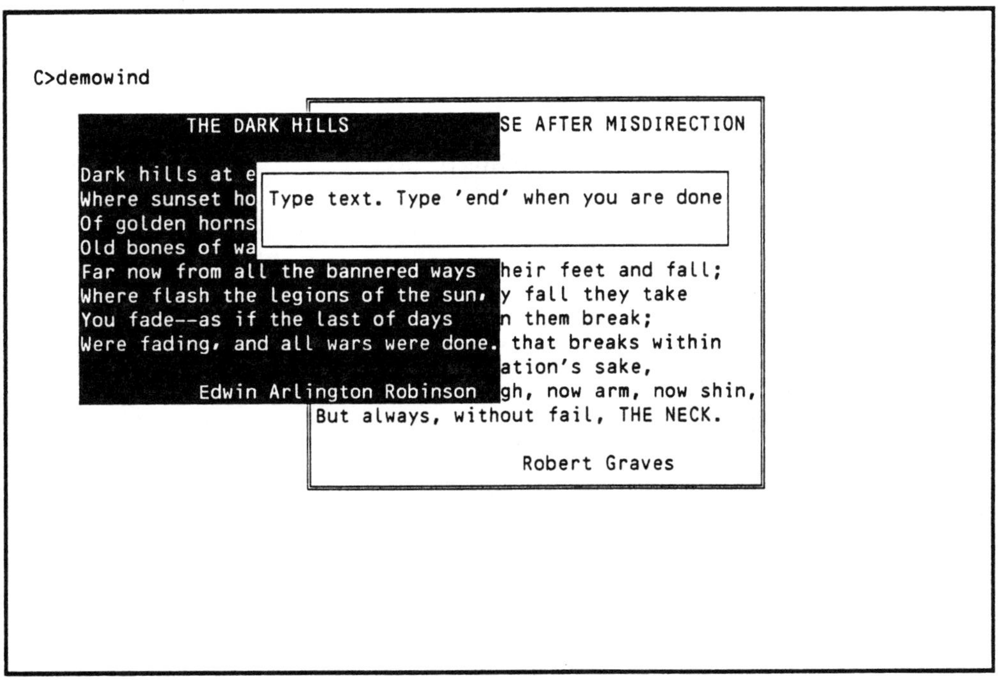

Figure C.2 *Three windows from demowind.exe*

CHAPTER 5—PROGRAMMING TRICKS WITH TURBO C, MS-DOS, AND THE PC

newkeys.exe

This program illustrates the expansion of the keyboard to deliver values for the keystroke combinations that BIOS leaves out (Ctrl-Up Arrow, for example).

Operating Instructions

At the command line, enter

```
C>newkeys
```

Now begin pressing keys. For each key you press, you will see a display of the value returned by the **getkey** function. For example, if you type the "a" key, you will see the following display:

```
    getkey returns 97 (a)
```

If you type Ctrl-Up Arrow, you will see this display:

```
    getkey returns 141 (.)
```

The character in parentheses is the ASCII display character returned by the key. For nondisplayable ASCII characters such as the 141 for Ctrl-Up arrow, the program displays a period.

When you are done looking at the key values, press the Esc key to terminate the program's execution.

typematc.exe

This program reprograms the AT and extended keyboards to a rate of 30 characters per second.

Operating Instructions

At the command line, enter

```
C>typematc
```

You must reboot your computer to return to the default 10 cps. A good exercise would be to rewrite typematc.c to accept the desired rate on the command line.

fastkeys.exe

This program is a memory-resident program that effectively speeds the key repeat rate of the PC and XT keyboards to a rate specified on the command line.

Operating Instructions

At the command line, enter

```
C>fastkeys <optional parameter>
```

You can specify a command-line parameter that controls the speed somewhat. The default parameter is 1, and it delivers a typematic rate of about 26 characters per second, close to the 30 cps (characters per second) maximum of the programmable AT keyboard. Higher parameters give faster rates. Anything higher than 3 becomes too fast for most users to control, but you can experiment with this parameter.

demoauto.exe

This program demonstrates automatic typing by allowing you to define one simple keyboard macro.

Operating Instructions

At the command line, enter

```
C>demoauto
```

You will see this prompt:

```
    Press a key to use for a macro ...
```

Press any key. This will be the macro hot key. You will then see this prompt:

```
    Enter the macro string ...
```

Type a string of characters. Finish it by pressing the Enter key. You will see this prompt:

```
    Now type some text (Esc when done) ...
```

Begin typing. Every now and then, press the hot key and see the macro string automatically typed for you. After a while, press Esc to terminate the program's execution.

driver.exe

This program shows how you can set up some automatic typing, execute another program, and have the keys you programmed typed into the other program.

Operating Instructions

At the command line, enter

```
c>driver
```

The driver program sets up some text to type and calls the demowind program described earlier. You will see the same window shown in Figure C.2, except that the program will slowly type the phrase, "I will type for you." Then it will execute the Enter key, type out "end," and execute three more Enter keys to finish the program.

demoblck.exe

This program demonstrates the unblinking block cursor.

Operating Instructions

At the command line, enter

```
c>demoblck
```

You will see the window shown in Figure C.3. As you type into the window, you will see that the cursor is a solid, steady reverse-video block. When you are done typing, press Esc.

Figure C.3 Initial screen for demoblck.exe

demopath.exe

This program demonstrates the ability to find the unambiguous path to a file that is located either in the current subdirectory, in the DOS path, or in the subdirectory where the demopath program is run from.

Operating Instructions

At the command line, enter

```
c>demopath <filename>
```

Where <filename> is the name of the file your program would want to locate. The program will display the following:

```
The path is <drive:path>
```

or

```
The path is nowhere to be found
```

tune.exe

This program demonstrates sound and music from the PC's speaker.

Operating Instructions

At the command line, enter

```
c>tune
```

Sit back, relax, and listen.

handles.exe

This program demonstrates the ability to have more than 20 files open in a Turbo C program.

Operating Instructions

At the command line, enter

```
C>handles
```

You will see the following messages:

```
Handle for testfile.000 is 5
Handle for testfile.001 is 6
Handle for testfile.002 is 7
Handle for testfile.003 is 8
Handle for testfile.004 is 9
Handle for testfile.005 is 10
Handle for testfile.006 is 11
Handle for testfile.007 is 12
Handle for testfile.008 is 13
Handle for testfile.009 is 14
Handle for testfile.000 is 15
Handle for testfile.011 is 16
Handle for testfile.012 is 17
Handle for testfile.013 is 18
Handle for testfile.014 is 19
Handle for testfile.015 is 20
Handle for testfile.016 is 21
Handle for testfile.017 is 22
Handle for testfile.018 is 23
Handle for testfile.019 is 24
Handle for testfile.020 is 25
Handle for testfile.021 is 26
Handle for testfile.022 is 27
Handle for testfile.023 is 28
Handle for testfile.024 is 29
```

You can use the DIR command to see that 25 files were created and the TYPE command to see the contents of any of them (use the DEL command to get rid of them).

CHAPTER 6—WINDOW MENUS

demomenu.exe

This program demonstrates how you would incorporate the menu bar and pop-down menus into your programs.

Operating Instructions

At the command line, enter

```
c>demomenu
```

You will see the display shown in Figure C.4. Each pop-down menu selection can be executed by pressing its first letter or by using the arrow keys to move the cursor bar to the selection and pressing Enter. When you execute a selection, a small window opens to identify its operation. You press any key to close the window and return to the menu. Note that the Save selection on the File menu is dimmer and has an asterisk to its right. This means that the selection is disabled. Use the New selection on the same menu to enable it and the Open selection to disable it. That might not seem to make sense. It is only an example.

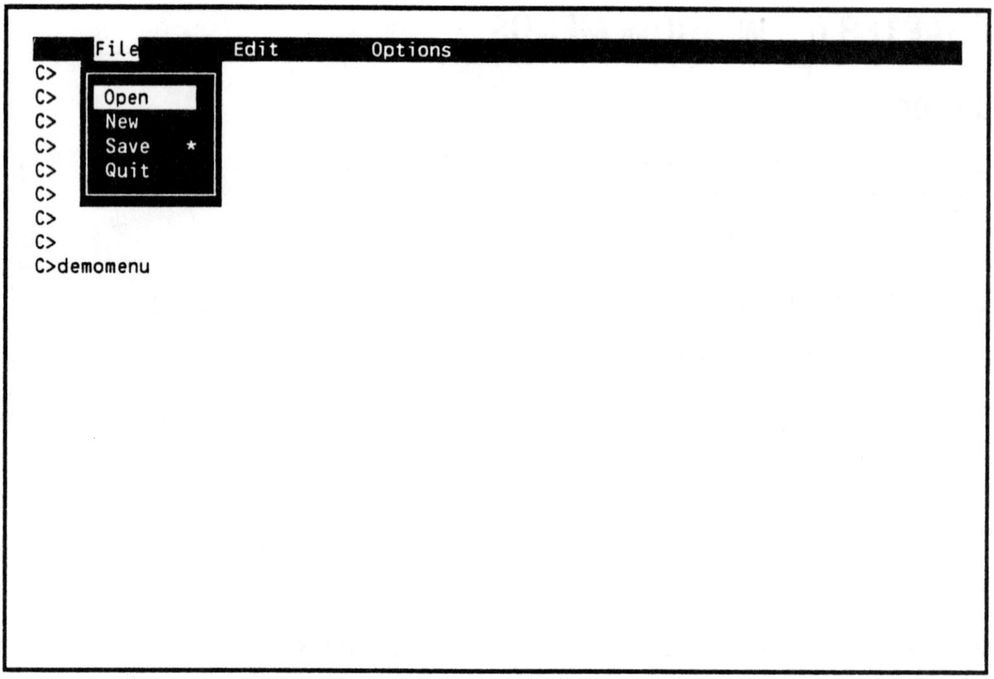

Figure C.4 *Initial screen for demomenu.exe*

CHAPTER 7—WINDOW DATA ENTRY TEMPLATES

demoentr.exe

This program demonstrates window data entry templates.

Operating Instructions

At the command line, enter

```
c>demoentr
```

You will see the display shown in Figure C.5. Type values into the data entry fields. Move from field to field with the Enter, Tab, and Arrow keys. When you are done, press Esc or any function key.

```
C>demoentr

              --- NAME AND ADDRESS RECORDS ---

        Name
        Address

        City                                        State
        Zip             Phone
```

Figure C.5 Initial screen for demoentr.exe

CHAPTER 8—SERIAL COMMUNICATIONS AND THE MODEM

sender.exe

This program demonstrates two-way conversations between programs equipped with modems and serial ports. The program works with the receiver.exe program (described next) running in another computer. You can also use sender.exe as a terminal program to call bulletin boards and on-line services.

Operating Instructions

At the command line, enter

```
C>sender <phone number>
```

where <phone number> is the number of the other computer. The phone will be dialed, and the other end will answer if all goes well. When you see the CONNECT message generated by your modem, you and the user on the other side can type messages to one another. Use the Esc key to terminate the connection.

receiver.exe

This program is the other end of the sender.exe phone call. It answers the phone and allows you to type messages to the caller.

Operating Instructions

At the command line, enter

```
C>receiver
```

and wait for the call to come in. When you see the CONNECT message generated by your modem, you and the user on the other side can type messages to one another. Use the Esc key to terminate the connection.

xsend.exe

This program transmits a file to the xrecv program described next. The XMODEM file transfer protocol is used.

Operating Instructions

At the command line, enter

```
C>xsend <filename> <phone number>
```

where <filename> is the name of the file to be transmitted and <phone number> is the number of the remote computer. The phone will be dialed, and you will see the following prompts:

```
Press 's' after CONNECT to send
Press Esc any time to abort
```

When the xrecv program answers, you will see the CONNECT message. Press the "s" key. As the file is being transmitted, this message will be displayed,

```
Block n
```

where "n" is the block number just transmitted. If an error occurs, you will see this message,

```
n tries
```

where "n" is the number of retries for the block in error. After 12 unsuccessful retries, you will see this message:

```
Transfer Aborted
```

If the file is successfully transferred, you will see this message:

```
Transfer Completed
```

xrecv.exe

This program receives a file from the xsend program just described. The XMODEM file transfer protocol is used.

Operating Instructions

At the command line enter

```
C>xrecv <filename>
```

where <filename> is the name of the file to be received. The phone will be answered, and you will see the following prompts:

```
Press 'r' after CONNECT to receive
Press Esc any time to abort
```

When the xsend program calls and the xrecv program answers, you will see the CONNECT message. Press the "r" key. As the file is being transmitted, this message will be displayed,

```
Block n
```

where "n" is the block number just transmitted. If an error occurs, you will see this message,

```
n tries
```

where "n" is the number of retries for the block in error. After 12 unsuccessful retries, you will see this message:

```
Transfer Aborted
```

If the file is successfully transferred, you will see this message:

```
Transfer Completed
```

CHAPTER 9—MEMORY-RESIDENT PROGRAMS

dialer.exe

This program is a memory-resident Personal Dialer program.

Operating Instructions

At the command line, enter

```
C>dialer
```

The program will become resident. At any time, press Alt-Period, the Personal Dialer hot key. You will see the display shown in Figure C.6.

```
C>

                         PERSONAL DIALER

    Name
    Address

    City                                    State
    Zip             Phone

   Ins=Add,F2=Dial,F3=Sch,F4=Chg,Del=Delete,Esc=Quit,F10=Unload
```

Figure C.6 Initial screen for dialer.exe

Following are descriptions of how you use function and command keys to manipulate and move around the program:

- **Adding Records.** To add records to your Personal Dialer data base, press the Ins key. Enter data values just as you did with the demoentr.exe program that demonstrated data entry templates. When a template is correct, press F2 to record the new record in the data base. To discard a new entry, press Esc.

- **Moving Through the Data Base.** Once you have inserted a number of records in the data base, you can move from record to record by pressing the Home, End, PgUp, and PgDn keys.

- **Searching for Names.** You can find a name in the data base by Pressing F3. The template will be cleared, the cursor will move to the name field, and the bottom of the window will say "Enter search string." Type in any part of a name and press Enter. The program will search for and stop on the first record that has a match anywhere in the name field for the string you entered. If that is not the record you want, press F3 again followed by Enter to search to the next matching record. If no records match the string, the program will display a small window that says, "String not found." Press any key to erase the window.

- **Changing Records.** To change the record that is in the template, press F4. Use the same procedure for data entry that you used for inserting a record.

- **Deleting Records.** To delete a record, press the Del key. You will see a small window that says "Delete this name? (Y/N). . . ." Press "y" to delete it and "n" to reject the deletion.

- **Dialing a Number.** To dial a number, press F2. First you will see a little window that says, "Dialing. . . ." Then a little window will tell you to "Pick up phone and press any key. . . ." Do that and complete your call.

- **Unloading the Personal Dialer.** Press F10 to unload the Personal Dialer. You will see a small window that displays the prompt, "Unload Personal Dialer? (Y/N). . . ." If no other TSR programs are above it, the program will unload itself from memory.

CHAPTER 10—EXPANDED MEMORY

demoemm.exe

This program demonstrates the Expanded Memory Manager Applications Program Interface.

Operating Instructions

At the command line, enter

```
c>demoemm
```

If the Expanded Memory Manager is installed, you will see a series of messages similar to the following:

```
EMM is present.
EMM Version 4.0
EMM is working.
Page Frame: e000
Pages Available: 192
```

If the Expanded Memory Manager is installed but not operating, you will see this series of messages:

```
EMM is present.
EMM Version 4.0
EMM is not working.
```

If the Expanded Memory Manager is not installed, you will see this message:

```
EMM is not present.
```

This program has hidden usefulness beyond its function as an illustration of the EMM API. You can use it while you are testing to see the effect of your programs on the EMM.

CHAPTER 11—TSRPLUS: THE TSR OVERLAY MANAGER

tsrplus.exe

This program is the TSRPLUS multiple-TSR executive program.

Operating Instructions

At the command line, enter

```
c>tsrplus
```

If TSR-like programs have already been registered, you may now pop them up. Otherwise, you must register them in the manner described next for buildial.exe and tinynote.exe.

Press Alt-U to unload the tsrplus.exe program from memory.

buildial.exe

This is a version of the Personal Dialer described earlier that works in the TSRPLUS environment.

Operating Instructions

With the tsrplus.exe just executed and nothing else loaded above it, at the command line, enter

```
c>buildial
```

This procedure registers the Personal Dialer with TSRPLUS. To incorporate that registration into TSRPLUS, unload the tsrplus.exe program by pressing Alt-U and rerun it as described earlier.

The TSRPLUS Personal Dialer pops up from the Alt-Period hot key and is operated exactly as is its dialer.exe version, which is described earlier.

tinynote.exe

This program is a tiny notepad pop-up that runs in the TSRPLUS environment.

Operating Instructions

With the tsrplus.exe just executed and nothing else loaded above it, at the command line, enter

```
c>tinynote
```

This procedure registers the Tiny Notepad with TSRPLUS. To incorporate that registration into TSRPLUS, unload the tsrplus.exe program by pressing Alt-U, and rerun it as described earlier.

The TSRPLUS Tiny Notepad pops up from the Ctrl-Period hot key. It displays the notepad window shown in Figure C.7. Use the Enter, Home, End, Up Arrow, and Down Arrow keys to move the cursor around the screen. Press F1 for a help window. Type wherever you want to change a line. Use F2 to clear the screen, F3 to clear a line, and Esc to pop down from the notepad.

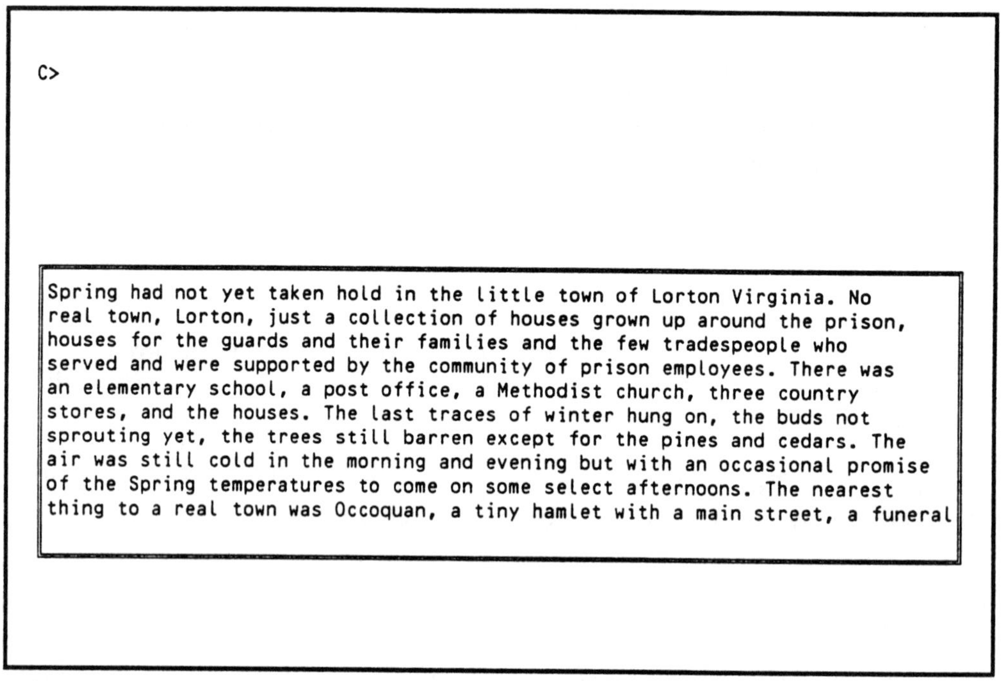

Figure C.7 Notepad window for Tiny Notepad

BIBLIOGRAPHY

Angermeyer, Jaeger, Bapna, Barkakati, Dhesikan, Dixon, Dumke, Fleig, and Goldman. *MS-DOS Developer's Guide, Second Edition*. Indianapolis: Howard W. Sams & Company, 1989.

Campbell, Joe. *C Programmer's Guide to Serial Communications*. Indianapolis: Howard W. Sams & Company, 1987.

Duncan, Ray. *Advanced MS-DOS*. Redmond, WA: Microsoft Press, 1986.

Gofton, Peter W. *Mastering Serial Communications*. Alameda, CA: SYBEX, 1986.

Kernighan, Brian and Dennis Ritchie. *The C Programming Language, Second Edition*. Englewood Cliffs, NJ: Prentice Hall, 1988.

Norton, Peter. *Programmer's Guide to the IBM PC*. Redmond, WA: Microsoft Press, 1985.

Porter, Kent. *Stretching Turbo C*. New York: Brady Books, 1989.

Rector, Russell and George Alexy. *The 8086 Book*. Berkeley, CA: Osborne/McGraw-Hill, 1980.

Stevens, Al. *Turbo C Memory-Resident Utilities, Screen I/O, & Programming Techniques*. Portland, OR: MIS:Press, 1987.

Wilton, Richard. *Programmer's Guide to PC & PS/2 Video Systems*. Redmond, WA: Microsoft Press, 1987.

Young, Michael J. *Performance Programming Under MS-DOS*. Alameda, CA: SYBEX, 1987.

INDEX

E

G

M

N

O

P

R

S

T

W

X

Y

ORDER FORM

PROGRAM LISTINGS ON DISKETTE

This diskette contains the complete program listings for all programs and applications contained in this book. By using this diskette, you will eliminate time spent typing in pages of program code.

you did not buy this ook with diskette, use is form to order now:

Only: **$25.00**

MANAGEMENT INFORMATION SOURCE, INC.
P.O. Box 5277 • Portland, OR 97208-5277
(503) 282-5215

NAME(Please print or type) ______________________

Address ______________________

CITY ______________ STATE ______ ZIP ______

Call free
1-800-MANUALS

❑ *Extending Turbo C Professional disk only $25.00*
Please add $2.00 for shipping and handling. (Foreign $6.00)

Check one:

❑ *VISA* ❑ *MasterCard* ❑ *American Express*

❑ *Check enclosed $_________*

ACCT. ______________________

EXP. DATE ______________________

SIGNATURE ______________________

MIS: PRESS

M A N A G E M E N T I N F O R M A T I O N S O U R C E , I N C .